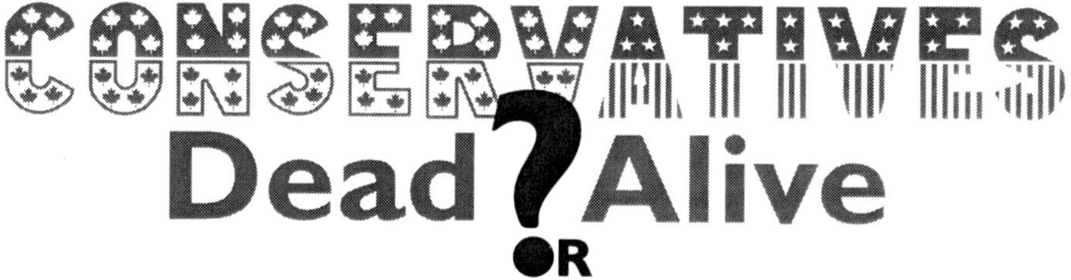

Marcel G. Latouche

CONSERVATIVES: Dead or Alive?

Published by
Freedom Press Canada Inc.

Freedom Press
12-111 Fourth Ave., Suite 185
St. Catharines, ON L2S 3P5
Printed in the United States of America

Cover Design: Design Asylum
Book Design: David Bolton

ISBN: 978-1-927684-14-6

James

As a liberal you are more fiscally conservative than so-called conservatives on Council

CONSERVATIVES:
Dead or Alive?

Marcel Latouche
Dec 2014

Marcel G. Latouche

SUMMARY

The eighties were the golden age of conservatism. With leaders like Ronald Reagan, Margaret Thatcher and Brian Mulroney in power in their respective countries, it was a time when the values and principles of conservatism were at their apogee.

After a significant downturn under the weak leadership of then President Jimmy Carter, we saw an up-turn in free trade and economic growth. America came back as a proud country after the Iran debacle. Communism was being challenged and was on its death bed. We saw the fall of apartheid, and South Africa was finally moving towards a true democracy. During George H. W Bush tenure as president we witnessed unprecedented events; as The Soviet Union lost its hold, the Cold War ended and the Berlin Wall fell

Upon Bill Clinton's arrival things changed rapidly as America became increasingly progressive in its policies. The left had been growing in stature in the free world, despite the 8 years of George W. Bush. President Obama's promise of 'hope and change' brought more leftist policies which gradually morphed into socialism.

The U.S and Canada shared border, close geographical and cultural proximity has a major effect on our political landscape. In the US and Canada you have a celebrity cultural norm backing leftist candidates via social media. The electoral process has turned into something of a media circus. Canada needs to keep close tabs on its media to ensure unbiased reporting that influences election results. The US media has significant influence on how Canadians think and vote.

The twice elected Obama certainly gave hope to the left, but we rarely see a true evaluation of his policies by the Canadian media. Since generally we have been a more 'progressive' nation, any perceived Obama success emboldens Canada's left. It is important to expose his blunders, to show how socialist/liberal ideas and policies not only fail but also endanger the security and economic liberty of us all.

"Conservatives: Dead or Alive?" analyses the differing positions and paradigms facing both the left and the right today. We tackle how both the left vs the right ideology ideas attempt to remedy the major issues, including education, healthcare, climate change, national divides, immigration, and cultural/social values facing the next generation and generations to come.

Some very important elections will be faced by both Canada and the US in the coming 2014, 2015 and 2016 years. Like all previous elections they will have consequences of its past to bear. In the U.S the failed policies of Obama may give rise the Republicans. In Canada despite a Canadian Conservative government for the past eight years, we are not guaranteed the progressives have disappeared.

This book is meant to be provocative, to elicit a discussion about the values of conservatism vs liberalism. Today's small 'c' conservatives seem to have disappeared as progressivism has made large inroads, especially in Canada. Too often we are seeing many conservatives fighting among each other in their search for power. These actions have known and well documented reactions, contributing to the erosion of conservative values and principles. In order for conservatism to survive this book will act as a sounding to conservatives everywhere, as a call to put social issues on the back burner, and concentrate on true conservative principles in order to survive and flourish in the future.

For

Judy, Guy, Claire and Collette

CONTENTS

PREFACE

As a young boy living on the tiny island of Mauritius, I grew up in a middle-class family who had always been involved in politics in one way or another. With many professionals in the family, we were economically secure and enjoyed the trappings of a comfortable life. Very early in my life I was exposed to the workings of stock market investments and the need for frugality and conservative financial management; I was always encouraged to look after myself and others who were less fortunate. My family had a culture of helping those in need and they instilled in me the duty to do the same.

I was educated in a private school, where I was exposed to the rigorous beliefs of the Catholic Church and the special culture of the order of Jesus. During that time I was also involved in school organizations and was a Head Boy. As a result of both my family and my teachers' influence, I grew up as a conservative. At eighteen, as part of my civic training, I started to get involved in politics, both as a party volunteer and as a Deputy Returning Officer when elections were held.

In 1968, when Mauritius sought its independence from Great Britain, I became involved in the political campaign which was in favour of an Association with Great Britain but against outright independence. When Mauritius was granted independence, I decided to go to England to pursue my education. I had little idea before leaving home that I would get involved in politics upon my arrival.

A student revolution had begun in 1968 at the Sorbonne in Paris and eventually made its way to England and other European countries. The protest was about the war in Vietnam and incorporated multiple issues, i.e student rights, capitalism and the bureaucratic elite. Notable student activists of the time were Daniel Cohn-Bendit in France and Tariq Ali in Great Britain. Both activists are currently still involved on the left of the political spectrum. Not so remarkably and far less famous stood yours truly, taking the 'right side' of things by debating fellow students during those heady days of the leftist uprising. I was labelled 'the first black fascist' by some members of the student union.

Once my studies in Economics and Accounting were completed I stayed in Britain where I worked for ten years. I had a successful career as an accountant in Banking, Publishing and Consulting. However the policies of the Labour Government took a toll on my economic wellbeing. Those were the days when the United Kingdom started its descent to being the 'sick man of Europe'. The Labour government put into place punitive income tax laws, essentially the equivalent of Barak Obama's attack on the so-called "1%". Reflecting on my chartered accountant diary of 1978 helps me recall with precision, the income tax rates applicable at that time: 'Top rate 98% (unearned income), 83% (earnings)'. Ironically, as the result of a promotion where I was provided a car, my take home pay shrank. I decided it was time for me to leave Britain. I became part of the first wave of young people who left the U.K for richer economic prospects.

In 1978 I immigrated to Canada making Calgary my home ever since. The fact that I had left the socialist regime of England for the socialist Canadian environment of Pierre Trudeau left me rather disconcerted. In addition to Trudeau's policies of high taxes, the National Energy Program simultaneously gutted the national and Albertan economies. These policies became a central point for the East/West resentment that still exists today. Coupled with the United States' economic situation under an inept President Carter, the world economy stagnated, high interest rates, and terrible foreign policies, culminating in the Iranian hostage crisis where Americans were held captive in Tehran. Fortunately, however, both the United Kingdom and the United States recovered under conservative leaders: Margaret Thatcher and Ronald Reagan.

I worked for 17 years at the City of Calgary and witnessed first-hand, the ineptitude of public sector employees. I went back to my graduate education roots and finished a Master's in Business Administration at the Manchester Business School – my thesis was entitled 'Change in the Public Sector'. When I found out that such desperately needed change was not readily achievable, I switched careers to consulting; finally, in semi-retirement, I chose to give back through lecturing in Economics, and Public Sector Finance.

As a '*laissez-faire*' conservative, I also got involved more directly in politics by advising local politicians on municipal and public sector financial matters. I got involved in electoral campaigns of 'common sense' conservatives. I founded the Institute for Public Sector Accountability to promote transparency in the public sector. I enjoy the sparring that occurs during political campaigns, however, the defeat of my friend Ric McIver in the 2010 Calgary municipal election was a real eye opener, as was the defeat of Mitt Romney in the 2012 Presidential election. The policies of the two eventual winners, Naheed Nenshi as Mayor of Calgary and Barack Obama for his second term, have been the catalysts for me to write this book. The social engineering of Calgary and the mismanagement of the United States' economic and foreign affairs policies provide the platform for this examination of socialist dogmas against conservative values.

Living in Canada, I cannot ignore the fact that many of our policies are affected by what happens in the United States. I therefore draw comparisons between events and policies in the two countries to elicit a debate about the rights of conservatism and the wrongs of liberalism/socialism.

INTRODUCTION

A WALK ON THE RIGHT SIDE

Since 2007 the world economy has been in a free fall with little recovery. During that time we have seen the complete economic collapse of many European countries, and still in 2014 we barely see signs of recovery.

To be frank, there are a variety factors which have contributed to the financial demise of many industrialised countries. Bankers and financial executives have been blamed, but in the final analysis much of this turmoil can be attributed to political ideology in one way or another.

The rise of socialist policies, often adopted by many European countries has resulted in an entitlement generation which haunts our civilization in the present and will continue to do so in the future. The refusal to come to grips with massive deficits, and the growing amount of government debt has taken its toll on countries including Greece, Spain, Italy and Portugal, among others. Furthermore, France and England have had their credit ratings downgraded.

The United States, the bastion of the free market economy, has not fared well. Policies based on the redistribution of wealth and the establishment of more government regulations are not helping. The constant use of Keynesian economic theories to get out of the difficulties has not produced any significant result. In fact, the unemployment rate is still hovering around 7%. If the number of able people who have dropped out of the race to find a job is included, the real unemployment rate would be closer to 13%. The most significant statistic is the huge number of unemployed young people, the same demographic which voted in droves for President Obama in 2008. Armed with a second mandate, President Obama has continued to push for more regulations and socialist policies to redistribute wealth. The media have supported him in every way possible. Nevertheless, his signature policy of Affordable Care is gradually unravelling and has the potential to hurt his legacy – this in addition to his dismal foreign policy.

During these difficult times, Canada has fared better than most of the G7 countries. However, a heavy reliance on trade with its neighbour to the south does not bode well for the immediate future. If Canada does not significantly expand its trading markets, and continues to conduct close to 85% of its trade with the United States, the sluggish economic recovery of that country may prove to be a real problem in coming years.

To exacerbate the Canadian situation, the constant opposition to the development of the Oil Sands of Alberta by environmentalists is likely to compound this state of affairs. The climate change or global warming rhetoric of environmentalists has the potential to pose more pitfalls to the country than its issues in the arenas of international trade and energy exploration.

While this book is concerned with a Canadian perspective, one cannot ignore the influence of the politics of the United States. The close proximity and shared media between the two countries have a definite impact on how Canadians think. Bombarded by American television, print media and radio programs, one cannot ignore the effects of cultural influence on political decisions. The manner in which Canadian media reports events from the States and how it sources its information from major American media outlets drastically shapes the minds of Canadians.

The values of the younger generation are shaped by what happens in the United States despite the fact that the vast majority of these young people do not even read newspapers or listen to the news. The bulk of their information comes through social media over the Internet. The information superhighway is, of course, liable to proffer misreported events as fact and may even present conspiracy theories and political agendas as ideas based in sound empirical observations and critical analyses.

This book discusses the role of conservative ideology on our lives, based primarily on my previous columns and published articles. It looks at the recent political events in Canada, the United States as well as internationally. In a world where conservative values are constantly under attack by the mainstream media, it is important to look at the different ideologies at play in today's political arena.

This book is not an indictment of any political ideology; it is merely an attempt to achieve a more accurate view of how political ideologies have been interpreted and used to shape our lives in both the past and today. Using examples of recent electoral results and their consequences, I try to explain why the next generation may be in for a rude awakening.

Globally speaking, conservatives have been passive in their response to a bombardment of criticisms by their opponents. Often labelled as 'extreme', they have allowed their principles to be vilified. The debate about conservative values and principles has been generally one sided. While a small minority of conservatives may harbour extreme views, the majority does not deserve the 'extreme right-wing' labeling. Most 'common sense' conservatives are more concerned with fiscal rather than social conservative values.

This book is about how conservative and left-leaning policies impact our lives. I contrast how conservative and liberal ideologies affect some of the more important issues of this historical time period: the economy, healthcare, the environment, education, foreign policy, human rights and freedom of speech. More importantly, this book will provide the reader with an insider's view on how conservatives tend to self-destruct and allow liberals to upstage them.

In today's world, many citizens do not truly understand the difference between the values of the right and leftist ideologies. They often vote based on what they hear through media sound bites, not what they actually know. Given the many examples of failed socialist policies, why is it that conservatives cannot gain more ground in the political arena?

Ultimately, we are forced to ask the question: Are conservatives dead or alive?

CHAPTER 1

WHAT'S IN A NAME?

The terms 'far-right' and 'far-left' have been used by political opponents to belittle each other. The problem is that in most cases, either description does not really fit the opponent's point of view. For example, a typical Republican or conservative policy is not necessarily far-right, while a Democrat or liberal policy is equally not automatically a far-left policy.

In many instances, the description of an opponent's position is not clearly understood by the public at large. By labelling an opponent as extreme, the other side gets to create doubt in the minds of the electorate and unfairly distort the facts. How political events and facts are reported have a great bearing on how the public makes decisions. As Andrew Heywood explained:

> *"People do not see the world as it is, but only as they expect it to be; in other words, they see it through a veil of ingrained beliefs, opinions and assumptions."*[1]

To this effect, it would be wise to spend some time explaining the origins and ideology associated with the more common political philosophies and existing political parties. Communism is excluded, because today there are very few countries that espouse this form of ideology. The Soviet Union has collapsed and even China, arguably, has moved away from it as it opens its doors to world trade and a freer market economy.

On the other hand, as more young Americans become disillusioned by the politics of the past decade, libertarianism is making inroads in mainstream American politics. With Senator Rand Paul considering a run at the Presidency in 2016, it would be deficient not to spend time discussing this ideology.

In this chapter we will look at the more common political ideologies which dominate our lives. At the very least, we shall attempt to define these ideologies in order to understand the need for rethinking why we support one political party or another. With a clearer understanding of what a party actually stands for, we will be able to remove the masks politicians wear and recognize what they want us to believe as opposed to what these parties' goals and motives really are.

Liberalism

Liberal ideology has been shaped over many years from the classical liberalism of the early nineteenth century to modern liberalism of the twentieth century. The development of liberal ideology has been influenced by thinkers like Jean Jacques Rousseau (1712–1778), Immanuel Kant (1724–1804) and Adam Smith (1723–1790) who were part of the Enlightenment project. The movement represented the aspirations of the middle class which rejected the absolute power of the monarchy and aristocracy.

Liberalism is in many ways based on the philosophies of liberty and the equality of the individual. Liberals believe that merit, ability and the willingness to work hard should be rewarded. Although democracy as expressed through the ballot box may constrain power, it should always be done within a constitutional framework; liberals, however, do not believe that individuals are entitled to absolute freedom.

> *"During the twentieth century liberal parties and liberal governments have usually championed the cause of social welfare."*[2]

Society, as viewed by liberals, is a collection of individuals who promote harmony and equilibrium. On the economic front, classical liberals favoured *laissez-faire* capitalism, but modern liberalism has moved away from Adam Smith's vision. At the same time, resources are considered a primary source in satisfying human needs. Over the years many of these philosophies have undergone significant changes. Modern liberalism embraces much of the thought of John Maynard Keynes (1883-1946), who believed in enlarging the scope of government's role which he called 'demand management'.

The first Liberal government was formed in 1868 by William Ewart Gladstone (1809–1898). In the United States, F.D. Roosevelt (1882–1945) developed liberal welfarism under the 'New Deal'. This policy was eventually followed by the 'New Frontier' policies of John F. Kennedy (1917–1963) and Lyndon Johnson (1908–1973), giving rise to improvements in civil rights and the establishment of 'affirmative action'.

The 1942 Beveridge Report promoted the welfare state in the United Kingdom (UK) while advocating positive freedoms including want, disease, ignorance, squalor and idleness. In other words, modern liberals concluded that if the market could not provide individuals with equal opportunities, the government should become the enabling state, capable of exercising considerable power to take on social and economic responsibilities.

As a result, Liberals embraced social justice, which also believes in reforming, but not replacing capitalism. This notion of a commitment to social justice, gave rise to the idea that poverty should be reduced and through the redistribution of wealth from the rich to the poor, inequality between the classes would be narrowed.

Based on the above beliefs, modern liberal governments expanded the welfare state, with the Liberal Party of Canada embracing and campaigning for its adoption. The best known leader of the Liberal Party of Canada was arguably Pierre Elliot Trudeau (1919–2000), who in his early days, was interested in Marxism, as reflected in his Harvard dissertation on 'Communism and Christianity'.

Influential political parties which have embraced the liberal philosophy include: The Liberal Party of Canada, the U.S. Democratic Party and the U.K Liberal Democrats.

Socialism

With its origin in the nineteenth century, 'socialism' is made up of a number of theories and traditions. As early as the 1830's, Robert Owen (1771–1858) in Britain and Charles Fourier (1772–1837) in France started to advocate a utopian society based on cooperation and love.

The movement gained popularity as a result of the growth of industrial capitalism in the early nineteenth century. Under these economic conditions a growing group of industrialised workers who suffered from poverty and low wages started a revolution against industrial capitalism.

The *laissez-faire* policies of the nineteenth century left many workers under the threat of unemployment. Working long hours for low wages; women and children commonly toiled under very harsh conditions. Social institutions providing workers with any form of stability or meaning were non-existent. Consequently, Karl Marx (1818–1883) and Friedrich Engels (1820–1895) declared that the overthrow of capitalism was inevitable.

As workers organized themselves and improved their living conditions, the socialist movement grew through the establishment of trade unions, social clubs and political parties. In Western Europe, socialist political parties adopted a more organized movement encouraged by the right to vote for working class men. But by the First World War there was a clear schism in the movement. The western group gained power through the ballot box. In Russia, however, a different movement, based on revolutionary ideology, started to appear. The Bolsheviks, under the leadership of Vladimir Ilyich Lenin (1870–1924) eventually gave birth to the communist party of Russia.

The twentieth century saw many changes to the socialist movement. From the collectivist ideology grew other ideologies which were based on anti-colonialism, instead of worker exploitation. This change happened mostly in the former colonies of Africa, Asia and Latin America. Communism gained ground and established a foothold in China, North Korea, Vietnam, Cambodia and Laos. In Latin America the struggle against military dictatorships, often viewed as being supported by American imperialism, saw the rise of Fidel Castro in Cuba, Salvador Allende in Chile and the rise of the Sandinista guerrillas in Nicaragua. These revolutionaries were often backed by a communist Soviet Union.

The socialist movement, in the twentieth century, evolved into social democracy and democratic socialism. Social democracy originated from Marxism, and was formed to make a clear distinction between the fundamental objectives of socialism and the narrow goals of political democracy. It also took its ideals from the old liberal movement:

> *"Social democracy has never denied, but on the contrary considered it an honour to have its roots in the same intellectual soil that nourished the old liberal ideas of freedom. But it never saw the way to realise these ideas as being competition between individuals, regulated only by the free market and with the state's and the society's tasks reduced to a minimum"*[3]

After the Russian Revolution, the socialists who believed in revolution adopted the title of 'Communists', while the .followers of Karl Johann Kautsky (1854–1938), who proposed a more peaceful transition to socialism, adopted the name of 'Social Democrats and espoused parliamentary strategies. Western social democrats, instead of abolishing capitalism decided to reform or 'humanise' it. As a result, social democracy became a movement that stood for a balance between the free market economy on the one hand, and state intervention on the other. At this point it appeared that Keynesian social democracy had won the day. Unlike Marxism, this form of socialism had embraced the dynamism of the market.

Socialism in general has traditionally looked at society in terms of class struggle. To this effect, social democrats support welfare or regulated capitalism, and they regard the market as a good servant with a bad master. Consequently, socialist societies have embraced authority stemming from the collective body which has the ability to check individuality and greed. In addition, socialists have looked at religion as a form of ruling-class ideology and a distraction from the political and class struggle.

Based on these views and ideology we have seen many modern governments adopt these values. In Great Britain two men turned the Labour Party into a government under Harold Wilson (1916–1995) who won four general elections in the late sixties and early seventies; he was then followed by James Callaghan (1912–2005). In Canada, the New Democratic Party (NDP) was formed in 1961 out of a merger between the Co-operative Commonwealth Movement and the Canadian Labour Congress.

The recessions of the 1970s and 1980s created strains between the left and right-wings of social democracy. Furthermore, globalisation and the collapse of communism in the Soviet Union and Eastern Europe undermined socialist governments' ability to deliver prosperity through their policies. In effect, socialism as a means to tame or reform capitalism seemed to have failed. This sea change caused the 'modernisation' of social democracy. As a result, in the 1990s we saw a retreat from Keynesian principles which had become associated with 'tax and spend' policies. Tony Blair in the U.K, and even François Mitterand (1916–1996) in France abandoned their attempts to fundamentally transform society. But is socialism truly dead?

In the early twenty-first century it may seem that socialism is dead, but it has gradually given rise to communitarianism, which believes that the individual is shaped by the community he/she belongs to, and therefore owes the community a debt of respect and consideration. Jack Layton (1950–2011), leader of the NDP, led his party to a second place finish in the 2011 federal election, thus becoming the Official Opposition for the first time in Canadian history. Furthermore, we cannot ignore President Barrack Hussein Obama's eloquent diatribe during his campaign for the White House in 2008, when he said "We have five days to fundamentally transform America".

Since President Obama's election, recent events in the United Sates under his administration may prove to inaugurate another sea change in the movement. Therefore, we should clearly be reminded that socialism is not static, as Eatwell and Wright wrote:

> *"The whole history of social democracy has been shaped by its response to the changing nature and fortunes of capitalism, and the present period is no exception."*[4]

On the other hand, the collapse of several economies in Europe may yet be the catalyst to reverse the fortunes of socialism once again.

Progressivism

Harsh working conditions and hardships caused by industrialisation led many to believe that laws regulating child labour and tenement housing were sorely needed. These people started a 'progressive' movement to promote gradual economic, social and political change to ameliorate the situation of the working poor. Although the term 'progressive' has been used by political parties who may not be particularly left-wing, today, more often than not, the term ***'progressivism'*** is associated with a wide range of views and policies normally associated with left-wing political organizations who see themselves as heirs to those who advocated for the working poor during the west's industrial revolution.

In the United States, where the two party system is taken for granted, we often ignore the fact that in 1912, President Theodore Roosevelt (1858-1919) founded America's third party, the Progressive Party. Other notable American Presidents such as Woodrow Wilson (1856-1924), Franklin Delano Roosevelt (1882-1945) and Lyndon Baines Johnson (1908-1973) have all embraced progressivism over the course of their administration.

The progressives were largely responsible for the first restrictions on American capitalism. They viewed capitalism as evil and immoral. As a result, they created the Interstate Commerce Commission to regulate railroads, the Sherman Antitrust Act which gave the government power to break up large companies and the Federal Reserve Act, among other anti-capitalist reforms.

The most important progressive reforms were achieved by President Franklin D. Roosevelt (FDR) who enacted a number of economic policies known collectively as the **New Deal**. The results were apparent in executive orders which established relief for the unemployed and poor. Similarly, the financial system was reformed to prevent the reoccurrence of the great depression while promoting economic recovery. As a consequence of the New Deal, the Democratic Party was able to gain a majority, including the White House, for seven out of nine presidential terms between 1933 and 1969.

Roosevelt was a very clever politician who presented himself not as an opponent of the Founding Fathers' ideals, but instead as a protector of individual rights through the expansion of Big Government. The entitlement state gained its foothold in America once the Social Security Act was passed. As the entitlement culture became normative, Americans started talking about their needs and with it came the unstoppable growth of government.

> *"The entitlement state is fuelled by altruism, but it is sustained in part by a pseudo-self – interested cover-up: You are buying security, you'll be told. No matter what happens to you, the entitlement sate will make sure your basic needs will be taken care of."*[5]

Today the entitlement state has taken on a life of its own and under President Barack Hussein Obama, it is growing at an unprecedented rate. At the same time a relentless attack on capitalism and individual rights is taking place; although not openly, but certainly stealthily.

In Canada, The Progressive Party of Canada was founded in 1920 by Thomas Crerar (1876–1975), and also had a close working relationship with the United Farmers parties in several provinces. When the party could not hold its caucus together, many members joined the Liberal party while others joined what today is known as the New Democratic Party (NDP).

During the Great Depression, the oldest party in Canada, the Conservative Party, had a disastrous showing in the 1935 elections. As a result the party looked to Manitoba's John Bracken (1883–1969) to revive the party. Bracken, while beginning with the United Farmers of Manitoba, was the leader of the Progressive Party of Manitoba. His acceptance as leader was on the condition that the party change its name to 'Progressive Conservative' a name that lasted until its dissolution in 2003. The inclusion of the word 'progressive' in the party's name still causes some friction among conservatives.

While it is no longer used at the federal level, the name is still used by some provincial parties. In England, the new coalition government of the Conservatives and the Liberal Democrats also claims to be progressive. It is better illustrated by Hillary Clinton's answer to a question by Rob Porter of California, during the Democratic Debate in 2007:

> *"You know ... ["liberal"] is a word that originally meant that you were for freedom, that you were for the freedom to achieve, that you were willing to stand against big power and on behalf of the individual. Unfortunately, in the last thirty, forty years it has been turned on its head and it's been made to see as though it is a word that describes Big Government, totally contrary to what its meaning was in the nineteenth and early twentieth century. I prefer the word 'progressive'."*[6]

The proliferation of the word 'progressive' is increasing exponentially in the media and in government policies. Today, more often than not, being progressive actually means increasingly taxing people while implementing wealth redistribution policies.

Libertarianism

The philosophy of libertarianism rests firmly on the belief that the individual is free to choose his or her destiny; liberty is held as the highest political end. Its origins stem from The Age of Enlightenment in the 17th and 18th centuries. Philosophers like John Locke (1632–1704) and Isaac Newton (1643–1727) sparked the movement. The libertarianist philosophy crossed the Atlantic and greatly influenced Benjamin Franklin

(1706–1790) and Thomas Jefferson (1743–1826), two of the Founding Fathers of the United States. The ideals of Enlightenment influenced the American War of Independence and the United States Bill of Rights.

In order to properly discuss libertarianism, we must first acknowledge that there are different factions within the movement, as explained by Merrill:

> *"If we can define libertarianism at all, we will do best to characterize it as a spectrum of political philosophies which regard the state as inherently an evil."*[7]

Since liberty is at the heart of the libertarian philosophy, it is common for different approaches to arise when analysing and discussing the ideology:

The ***'Right-libertarianism'*** philosophy supports the free market, capitalism and private property rights. Support for the state rests in the position that its only legitimate function is to ensure the protection of the individual from aggression, theft and fraud. The monarchist political philosophy believes that the state has no power to use its monopoly to interfere with free transactions between people.

The ***'Left-libertarianism'*** philosophy, on the other hand, can be described as people who distrust the market and private investment. While they support the rights to personal property, they reject commercial ownership; to them, the appropriation of such wealth would be considered not as theft, but as an act of liberation. Noam Chomsky identifies himself as a left-libertarian, but his views can be identified more as anarchism.

Libertarian philosopher Roderick Long defines libertarianism as "any political position that advocates a radical redistribution of power from the coercive state to voluntary associations of free individuals"; this is the case whether "voluntary association" takes the form of the free – market or communal co-operatives. There are those who believe that political power should be shifted to local authorities. The problem with that philosophy is that local interest would dominate at the expense of the whole. And as a result, the current problems could be aggravated by collective action.

One cannot look at libertarianism without including the influence of Ayn Rand (1905–1982). With the twist and turn in her support for different political ideology, Ayn Rand has left an indelible mark on American politics. Starting with a passionate dislike for Communism, she became an outspoken anti-collectivist. Although she supported Roosevelt in 1932, she went on to support Willkie's bid for the presidency.

When Willkie lost the election and Roosevelt's New Deal was consolidated and extended by wartime controls and extensive controls of the economy, Rand joined a few right-wing intellectuals. However, she became quickly disillusioned by politicians and broke away from the conservatives when she published *Atlas Shrugged* in 1957. In the book she rejected religion, repudiated altruism and traditional ethical values and called for society to follow a pure *laissez-faire* model.

Although vilified by intellectual conservatives, she supported Barry Goldwater for the presidency. When Goldwater lost – Rand ascribed his defeat to what she claimed was Goldwater's lack of rational basis for conservative ideas – she started the Objectivist movement which was embraced by some college students. The Young American for Freedom movement never gained traction within the broader conservative movement in Rand's time; we are, however, beginning to see some form of its revival in the early part of the twenty first century with the support of libertarians, instead of objectivists. Libertarianism, with its foundation in the "non-initiation of force' principle, coupled with a strong belief in limited government, seems to be gaining traction, especially among a younger generation who regards government as an intrusion and who seek greater freedom on social issues.

Locke's philosophy and Rand's ideas are deeply ingrained in the new Tea Party movement. Followers of the Tea Party have strong ethics which espouse hard-work and self-responsibility. Adopting Rand's political stance, they believe in capitalism and abhor statism and collectivism. Governor Sarah Palin, a darling of the Tea Party, like Rand, is scorned by the establishment and the media.

Notable libertarians of today includes former House of Representative Congressman Ron Paul from Texas, who ran for the Presidency in 2012, and his son Senator Rand Paul, who may run for the Presidency in 2016.

In Canada, Danielle Smith, the leader of the Wildrose Party of Alberta, often refers to herself as a libertarian. John Stossel is a well-known journalist on Fox News who regularly presents special reports on issues that should be looked at under the microscope of a libertarian ideology.

Conservatism

Conservative in everyday language can mean a number of things. It can be used to refer to moderation, cautious behavior, an affinity for being conventional or to describe a fear to change. Contrary to general belief, conservatives do not oppose change, but rather are opposed to change that is based on preconceived ideologies.

Following the French Revolution, François-René de Chateaubriand (1768–1848) was the first to use the term 'conservative' in a political context. In the nineteenth century, those who opposed the more radical forms of democratic progress formed the conservative movement to challenge liberal ideals. By 1830, the American republicans were calling themselves conservatives, and in 1832 the term conservative was being used to describe the British Tory party.

Although in the early days, the enemy of conservatism may be readily identified as liberal ideology, currently, it has been replaced by socialism which is viewed as more radical. The conservative doctrine, however, opposes these two political ideals and has never been homogeneous. Therefore, over the years, we have seen many forms and interpretations of what a 'conservative' stands for. Nevertheless, there may still be common ground as Eatwell and Wright explain:

> *"The unifying theme of conservatism, then, is the quest for*

> *a realistic concept of order which acknowledges the inelim-inable tension at the heart of the human condition. It is the principled nature of conservative realism which provides the answer to cynics who dismiss the doctrine a nothing more than a commitment to pure pragmatism, power and success.*"[8]

In the twentieth century, conservative realism can be divided into three main schools, which form the basis for the opposition to socialism:

- The ***reactionary school*** views the universe as ordered and with an assigned place for everything. It draws its strength from its analysis of the chaos and instability of the modern democratic state.
- The ***revolutionary school*** believes that we should not suppress the inevitable trends of the century, but instead we should embrace them and construct a new dynamic type of conservatism.
- The ***moderate school*** of conservatism believes in balance, compromise and moderation.

The problem is that there are so many nuances in these interpretations that it has created factions and dissent within the conservative movement.

During the 19th century, British Conservatives rarely abandoned the influence of Edmund Blake (1729–1797). While the core of moderate conservatism is the limited state, post Second World War Britain saw a shift towards the *'middle way'* as formulated by Harold Macmillan (1894–1986), which resulted in a politics of compromise. Under Prime Minister Edward Heath (1916–2005), his conservative government created the most controls over the private industry of any government up to that point in time. Through informal consultations between the government, the Trade Union Congress (TUC), and the Confederation of British Industry (CBI), Heath created an environment that Samuel Brittan identified as "The Dangers of the Corporate State".

Greatly disappointed by the middle way, conservatives looked for a new identity. This time the movement was greatly influenced by economists like Milton Friedman (1912–2006) of the Chicago School, and others from the Mont Pelerin Society and the Virginia school of public choice. This group of liberal and libertarian philosophers challenged many of the previous conservative principles and emphasized economic issues promoted by the 'middle-way'.

Among the ideas criticized were:

- The illusion that every evil had a political root, and could only be remedied by political action.
- The naïve post war collectivist view that future economic growth would be automatic.
- That automatic economic growth would result in happiness.
- The advantages of centralised state planning
- That welfare plans created a sense of personal responsibility and the promotion of individual initiative.
- The existence of a middle ground between capitalism and socialism.
- That inflation was rooted in economics rather than in politics and morality.
- Those public officials were the disinterested administrators of Keynesian economic theory.
- That a pluralist social system was the answer to promote stability and economic prosperity.

As a result of these challenges, the 1980s saw the emergence of the **'New Right'** in Great Britain and the United States, and to a lesser extent, in Canada. The New Right draws on two schools of thought: the first being the ***economic school,*** which believes in the free market and that the legitimacy of government is contingent on the creation and maintenance of such a market; and second, the ***political school*** which supports the free market, promotes nationalism, and the authority of the state combined with a concern for moral and communal factors.

There are a number of factions that have emerged in the early twenty first century. This includes one based on a 'commons sense 'approach to fiscal policies and economics, and the 'religious right' or social conservative faction which believes strongly in morality and family values.

On one hand, the '*laissez-faire*' conservatives believe that government should refrain from interfering in the private lives of citizens. On the other hand, social conservatives believe that the social and domestic spheres should include government intervention and therefore, political enlistment.

Numerous parties have had conservatism as their ideology. These parties include the Conservative Party in Great Britain, the Grand Old Party, also known as the Republican Party in the United States, the Conservative Party of Canada, The Reform Party of Canada, The Canadian Alliance party of Canada, the Wildrose Party and the Progressive Conservative Party. Great conservative leaders include Winston Spencer Churchill (1874–1965), Margaret Thatcher (1925–2013) and President Ronald Reagan (1911–2004).

Disparities in the acceptance of conservative philosophies have contributed to fissures in the conservative movement. Too often, the establishment has moved away from true conservative principles. Just like the Progressive Conservative Party of Canada gave rise to the Reform Party and the Wildrose Alliance, in the U.S., we have seen the rise of the Tea (Tax Enough Already) Party. These are new, grassroots organizations and are strongly anti-establishment. The Tea Party is often characterized by the media as a fringe group of extremists, 'far-right' racist people. In actuality, it is a far cry from this crass description; many of its members are African Americans who have joined together with ordinary, disaffected white conservatives who no longer believe in politicians who say one thing and do another. In 2010, it was the Tea Party's growth that handed the House of Representatives to the Republicans. In 2014 and 2016, this party may play an even bigger role.

The fall of Nazism and Communism have left very few 'far left' or 'far right' politicians in the mainstream political arena. There may still be a minority of politicians who are influenced by some Marxist ideology or some form of ultra conservative ideology. However, more often than not, we continue to see politicians changing their stripes over the course of their career. Some of these people switch their party allegiance and have had a significant influence on major events in history.

It was important to define and discuss the various political ideologies to evaluate and examine their influences over history and how the media today reports on political events, affecting public opinion. The epithet ***'far'***, to describe either the right or the left is frequently used to distort and even demonize, instead of presenting the true facts. Ultimately, and quite unfortunately for the public, political labels become superfluous as the media and political pundits choose to interpret them as they please to suit their purposes.

CHAPTER 2

GREAT CONSERVATIVE LEADERS

Over the years, great leaders have come and gone. Events usually determine a leader's approach to solving problems. Some leaders are remembered for what they have done for their country and others are remembered for a wider range of deeds, including their influence on international and historical events.

Some would argue that the same leaders who have shown great leadership may also have had a negative effect on certain sections of society and even countries. However, there are three great conservative leaders who should be recognized for their contributions to their respective countries and the world in general. Despite the fact that none of them was awarded the Nobel Peace Prize, their contributions have left lasting results and their influence on history cannot be ignored, whether or not one is in favour or opposed to their actions.

Sir Winston Spencer Churchill (1874–1965)

An aristocrat born into the family of the Dukes of Marlborough, Winston Churchill had a long, turbulent and distinguished career as a British politician. An accomplished artist, historian and writer, Churchill received the Nobel Prize in Literature, and will always be remembered for his service as The United Kingdom's Prime Minister and Minister of War during the Second World War. But to understand the man, we must look at his turbulent political career.

Churchill first started as a member of the Conservative Party. During his term he opposed the government's defence budget and was a strong supporter of free trade. He stood against the protectionist policies of Joseph Chamberlain who proposed extensive tariffs to protect Britain's economic superiority. His actions were not viewed positively by the Party and he was dropped as a conservative representative. He quickly crossed the floor and joined the Liberal Party. When the Liberal Party won the next election he was appointed Under Secretary of State for the Colonies.

During his time as a member of Herbert Asquith's Liberal government he supported Liberal Reforms, which many believe was the start of the welfare state in the U.K. The Liberal Party of that time shifted from a *laissez faire* approach to a more collectivist one which created the split between modern and classical liberalism. Churchill, as president of the Board of Trade, introduced a bill which set up the first minimum wage legislation in Britain; he followed this bill with the Labour Exchange bill to help the unemployed find work and also drafted the National Insurance Act of 1911. Churchill supported the People's Budget which contained the first legislation for the redistribution of wealth and radical social welfare programs.

His greatest achievement was accomplished as Prime Minister, when he stood against Adolf Hitler. Although not really the favourite of his own party, he was called by King George the VI to be Prime Minister. His steadfastness in the face of adversity, supported by strong speeches which greatly inspired an embattled Britain, helped him gain the confidence of his nation. One of his famous speeches included the following:

> *"We shall not flag or fail. We shall go on to the end. We shall fight in France, we shall fight on the seas and oceans, we shall fight with growing confidence and growing strength in the air. We shall defend our island, whatever the cost may be. We shall fight on the beaches, we shall fight on the landing-grounds, we shall fight in the fields and in the streets, we shall fight in the hills. We shall never surrender!"*[1]

He refused an armistice with Germany and forged the British Empire's resistance which later culminated in the Allied counter attack which later helped liberate Western Europe.

After defeating Germany, deliberations were held between the three Grand Alliance countries of Britain, the United States and Russia. Trying to resolve the boundaries of Poland and the fate of many of the Eastern Europe States became a point of contention between President Truman and Winston Churchill on the one side, and Josef Stalin on the other. Despite having once said: "I will not pretend that, if I had to choose between communism and Nazism, I would choose communism', he found Stalin to be extremely difficult to deal with. When he found a new ally in President Truman, Churchill promoted an even stronger alliance with the United States which formed the basis of friendship between the two countries that we see today.

In 1945, Churchill was ousted as Prime Minister in one of the Conservative Party's worst defeats in history. As in the past, he knew that he did not need to be Prime Minister to make an impact on the world stage. From that day in July 1945, he started his ascent back to power.

This time, Churchill took the rise of communism head on. In his great speech in Fulton, Missouri, entitled 'The Sinews of Peace' he attacked the Soviet Union in no uncertain terms and laid the grounds for the start of the Cold War Alliance. Although committed to the British Commonwealth, he believed that an expansion of the coalition with the United States would provide the best foil against Russia and its allies, leading to what became known as the Warsaw Pact nations.

In a speech which he later termed 'The most important speech of my career' he concluded:

> *"If the population of the English-speaking Commonwealths be added to that of the United States with all that such cooperation implies in the air, on the sea, all over the globe and in science and in industry, and in moral force, there will be no quivering, precarious balance of power to offer its ambition or adventure."*[2]

The Fulton speech was predictably attacked by the Soviet Union. But what was really surprising, was the criticism Churchill received at home. Ninety-three Labour MPs proposed a motion of censure, which incidentally failed. The speech was also criticized in the United States, both by members of the Republican and Democratic parties who branded the speech as the harbinger of a "new British-American imperialism". The most disingenuous response came from Harry Truman, who publicly separated himself from the text of the speech, but in fact, privately agreed with it.

Churchill's position of standing firm on issues of democracy while simultaneously keeping an open dialogue with the Russians gained him favour with many leaders of the post-World War II era. President John F. Kennedy quoted Churchill in Manhattan when he said:

> *"A Democratic administration can never and will never negotiate with the Russians from a position of weakness."*[3]

Richard Nixon adopted Churchill's views and approach to Communism. He used 'superpower diplomacy' as advocated by Churchill when he twice met with the Soviet Premier Leonid Brezhnev in the 1970s. Later, both Prime Minister Margaret Thatcher and President Ronald Reagan, in their dealings with Soviet Leader Mikhail Gorbachev, followed 'Churchillian' diplomatic philosophies as enunciated in the 'Sinews of Peace' speech. Together, this triumvirate put an end to the Cold War.

Sir Winston Churchill left an indelible mark on history. This was accomplished through his resolve against the Nazis during the Second World War, and later, through his imprint on the Cold War leading to its eventual termination. His influence is best illustrated by Mikhail Gorbachev in a speech the soviet leader delivered on May 6, 1992, in Fulton:

> *"Churchill urged us to think "super-strategically," meaning by this the capacity to rise above the petty problems and particularities of current realities, focussing on the major trends and being guided by them ... In a qualitatively new*

and different world situation the overwhelming majority of the United Nations will, I hope, be capable of organizing themselves and acting in concert on the principles of democracy, equality of rights, balance of interests, common sense, freedom of choice, and willingness to cooperate."[4]

President Ronald Reagan (1911–2004)

Ronald Reagan was born of humble beginnings in Illinois, in 1911. His father was a salesman and just like Margaret Thatcher, at one stage, lived above a store. He earned a Bachelor's degree in economics and sociology. As an athlete, he played football and was captain of the swim team, which allowed him to become a lifeguard in 1927. His political career started when he was elected president of the student body, and he led a student revolt against the college president who wanted to cut back the faculty.

He started a career in radio broadcasting and followed that by becoming an actor under contract with Warner Brothers. Although he was voted the fifth most popular star of Hollywood's younger generation, he did not have the chance to really attain the heights of stardom as he was called to active duty by the U.S. Army in 1942. Due to his near sightedness he never saw active duty but he was very instrumental in the army's First Motion Picture Unit which produced 400 training films for the Army Air Force.

His political career follows a similar path to that of Winston Churchill, who started out as a Liberal. Reagan was influenced by Franklin Roosevelt and was a new Deal Democrat, but eventually supported Dwight D. Eisenhower in 1952 and 1956, and Richard Nixon in 1960. However, in 1954, and over the following years as the host of a TV drama series called *General Electric Theater*, he started to embrace conservative pro-business ideas as well as a strong anticommunism, small government stance. In 1962, the ratings for the show fell and he was dropped; thereafter, he changed his allegiances to the GOP and two years later endorsed Barry Goldwater as a presidential candidate. His speech 'A Time for Choosing' during the campaign raised $1 million for Goldwater but more importantly, launched his political career.

In 1967 he was elected Governor of California, and despite an unsuccessful attempt to recall him in 1968, he served in that capacity until 1975. During that time he was faced with a number of issues that showed both sides of his political ideology. In 1969, during the protest at UC Berkley, he sent the California Highway Patrol to quell the protest which resulted in one student death. This incident came to be known as 'Bloody Thursday'. When the protests did not subside, he called on the state National Guard troops who occupied the city of Berkley for two weeks. In 1974, following the kidnapping of Patty Hearst by the Symbionese Liberation Army who demanded the distribution of food to the poor, Gov. Reagan, as reported by the Los Angeles Times joked: "It's just too bad we can't have an epidemic of botulism".

By the same token in 1967, when the national abortion debate started, Reagan signed 'The Therapeutic Abortion Act' which was introduced by Democratic State Senator Anthony Beilenson. As a result of the bill's passing, some two million abortions would later be performed. He had been in office for only four months when he signed the bill, and later he explained that if he had been more experienced, he would not have signed the bill. From that point on, he declared himself 'pro-life' and continued to oppose abortion for the rest of his life.

He first tried to be nominated for the presidency in 1968 – he wound up third behind Richard Nixon, and Nelson Rockefeller. He once again ran for the Republican nomination in 1976 against a more moderate conservative, Gerald Ford, and was narrowly defeated by 57 votes. However, it was his concession speech, which like Winston Churchill's, warned about the Soviet Union's threat and the dangers of nuclear war that propelled him as a true conservative Republican. As Lou Cannon of The *Washington Post* wrote:

> *"But whether the Republicans win or not, it is also quite conceivable that Reagan's campaign this year and his impact on*

the Republican credo may lead Americans to conclude that the GOP, once again, really stands for something."[5]

It was at this particular juncture, that everybody believed that Reagan's prospects to become president of the United States were over. He had ran twice and lost twice, but the improbable happened: President Gerald Ford lost to Jimmy Carter who became the 39th President of the United States in a narrow win of the popular vote by 50% to 48%. For Reagan's supporters, the result gave them hope; Reagan did not, at first, discount a run in 1980, although he would be turning 70 in 1981.

Jimmy Carter moved ahead with his populist agenda. However, he seemed to have misread the American public who wanted the President to have some class and not just, as the *New York Times* called it 'show-boat populism'. He proceeded to cut regulatory red tape, and took on the oil companies. Taking on big oil companies is always easy, but telling the country that they faced sacrifice, scarcity, hardship and cutting the size of government was not a popular Democratic mantra. From then on his presidency started to go downhill.

At the same time Reagan started to rekindle conservative enthusiasm, more importantly, among disaffected democrats concerned with social issues and the younger generation. In his 1977 CPAC speech he said that the party:

"cannot be one limited to the country club, big-business image that ... it is burdened with today. The 'New Republican Party,' I am speaking about is going to have room for the man and woman in the factories, for the farmer, for the cop on the beat."[6]

It was the start of the New Right, and just like Reagan, it began to flex its muscles against the GOP establishment. Thus began Reagan's climb back to the top of the party's leadership as he became Carter's most vocal critic.

In 1980, after defeating George H. Bush for the GOP nomination, he made him his running mate for the Vice-Presidency. What was unthinkable at first happened, the Reagan/Bush ticket galvanized the GOP and Reagan's support grew. Carter, although bruised by his inadequate administration and his tussle with Edward Kennedy for the Democratic nomination, made the race for the White house even tenser.

The Iranian invasion of the American embassy in Teheran and the taking of American hostages certainly did not help at all. The majority of the polls on the weekend before the elections pointed to a close race. But at the end of the day, Reagan had a resounding win over Carter with 489 to 49 electoral votes, one of the most crushing defeats in American Presidential elections.

The previous four years of the Carter Presidency had seen America in a dire economic state and diminished its standing on the global stage. It was time for revival and Reagan made it possible.

As if the stars had aligned themselves, Reagan's Presidency benefitted from having allies in virtually all spheres. With Margaret Thatcher as Prime Minister of Britain, and Pope John Paul in the Vatican, the three staunch opponents of communism worked together to see the fall of the Soviet Union. In 1983, Reagan put into place National Security Decision Directive 75. It was a strategy to counter Communist aggression and undermine the Soviets' economy. The result was the gradual retreat of the Soviet Union from Latin America, Africa; its influence in Eastern Europe was also greatly diminished. The Cold War was coming to an end.

At home, Reagan followed the advice of economist Arthur Laffer, stuck to his principles of a free-market economy and put into place supply – side economics policies, which many leftists named Reaganomics. For Reagan the answer was simple: 'high taxes are a disincentive to production; tax cuts on the other hand stimulate production, which with lower tax rates generates more government revenues.' The result was a growing economy which brought tax rates down and interest rates tumbling from the double digits of the Carter years.

In 1981, America's air traffic controllers went on strike. Presumably, Reagan recollected the employment tactic used during the days of the movie industry strike of the 1940s and stated that if the controllers did not report to work within 48 hours, they would be terminated. When the strikers did not return to work, he fired 11,345 of them, and used military controllers until new controllers were hired.

After years of prevailing liberal attitude in American politics dominated by FDR's New Deal, Conservatism had been relegated to a fossilized status quo. But in 1980, under the most unlikely leadership of Ronald Reagan, the Grand Old Party came to life and out of the wilderness, and with it came renewed hope for a demoralized America.

Ronald Reagan, the Hollywood actor, was never given a chance when he started in politics. Just like Winston Churchill before him, he was spurned by his own party, but as it turned out, he is credited with having been the catalyst for the revival of conservatism in America and became one of the greatest Presidents of the United States.

Baroness Margaret Thatcher (1925–2013)

The longest serving Conservative Prime Minister of Great Britain was born Margaret Roberts on October 13, 1925, to a middle-class family in Grantham, Lincolnshire. Her father was the local mayor and owned two grocery shops. In an England often rife with class distinction she was often referred to as 'the grocer's daughter'.

Roberts attended Oxford on a scholarship and obtained a Bachelor's degree in chemistry. Greatly influenced by the work of Friedrich von Hayek, she joined the Oxford University Conservative Association and was elected as its President.

After losing two general elections (1950, 1951) as the youngest and first female Conservative candidate for Dartford, she became a qualified barrister in 1953 and specialized in taxation. After several attempts at representing the Conservative Party, she was finally elected in 1959 as an MP for Finchley. Prior to becoming Prime Minister she occupied a number of cabinet positions including:

- Parliamentary Undersecretary at the Ministry of Pensions and national Insurance.
- Spokeswoman for Housing and Land
- Education Minister and Cabinet Minister
- Leader of the Opposition after the Heath government's defeat in 1974

Her career was marred by controversy. A polarizing figure, her views on several issues would ruffle her opponents' feathers as well as her strongest supporters. She was a strong supporter of Israel and believed that Israel should trade land for peace, while at the same time she condemned the 1981 bombing of Osirak.

She was a supporter of birching and judicial corporal punishment. In 1966, she criticized the Labour Government's high-tax policies as being steps "not only towards Socialism but towards Communism". Thatcher's critique was merely meant to be a footnote, but it alienated many on the left. I personally supported this notion at the time, because these same policies in the 1970s turned me into an 'economic refugee' and I subsequently immigrated to Canada in 1978.

As Education Minister, she advocated for the comprehensive school system as an alternative to the grammar school system. The comprehensive system is roughly equivalent to the High school system of North America. This system offered a wider range of subjects across the academic spectrum, thus creating larger class sizes and accepting children from a wider range of abilities. She also opposed sanctions on South Africa which were the catalyst for the defeat of apartheid policies.

In 1976, she delivered a speech critiquing the Soviet Union in no uncertain terms:

> *"The Russians are bent on world dominance, and they are rapidly acquiring the means to become the most powerful imperial nation the world has seen. The men in the Soviet Politburo do not have to worry about the ebb and flow of*

> *public opinion. They put guns before butter, while we put just about everything before guns."* [7]

As a result of the January 19,1976 'Britain Awake' speech at Kensington Town Hall, Margaret Thatcher was for ever branded by the *Krasnaya Zvezda* newspaper as the 'Iron Lady', a title that she wore with great pride and which earned her many supporters.

Among her many achievements, there are three that really exemplify her leadership of the Conservative Party and Great Britain (1975–1990).

The first of the three dealt with Britain's economy, which at the time had been ravaged by the socialist policies of the Labour Party, and to some extent the policies of the failed Heath Conservative government. Because of its failed economy, Britain was commonly referred to as the 'sick man of Europe', and was being constantly audited by the IMF as well as subjected to an imposed currency control whereby no one could leave the UK with more than a few hundred pounds.

Influenced by the thinking of economist Milton Friedman, she reduced income taxes and increased indirect taxes. By increasing interest rates she was able to reduce the money supply and thus the rate of inflation. Thatcher took the bold position of limiting public expenditure, made cuts to education, housing and social services.

These policies, of course, drew the ire of not only the left but also some of the remaining Heath supporters in her own government. By December 1980, her approval rating had dropped to 23%, and as the recession deepened, she increased taxes despite a previous promise not to do so.

Two years later the UK economy started to show signs of recovery with inflation rates falling form 18% to 8.6%. In succeeding years mortgage rates and inflation rates kept falling, and by 1987 the economy was stabilized and unemployment continued to decline.

During the 1980's she used the 90% tax on North Sea Oil revenue to pay for the costs of reform and balance the economy. The 'sick man of Europe' was on the road to a full recovery.

Thatcher used privatization as a pillar of her policies, which became known collectively as 'Thatcherism'. Industries that were privatized included gas, water and electricity, all had traditionally operated as monopolies. The only services left untouched were National Health and the BBC. The introduction of competition in most cases benefitted the consumer through lower prices and efficiencies.

After being re-elected for a third consecutive term, she implemented perhaps her biggest and most unpopular policy – the poll tax which resulted in the Poll Tax Riots of March 13, 1990.

Her second major achievement can be said to be the way she dealt with the unions. In previous years, and more specifically under Labour governments, the Unions had gained enormous influence. Their power was so great that strikes were more the rule than the exception. Before her election in 1979, it seemed that every group of workers had been on strike at one time or another. Garbage collectors, transport workers, electric worker unions and many others were among the more prominent ones, until the big strike by the coal workers union. Britain lost 29 million working days during that time. Shop stewards had the ability and power to stop the publication of newspapers and the railway could even be shut down. In fact, Britain could be said to have been controlled by the unions during that period.

As a result of this chaos and union anarchy, Thatcher introduced legislation to curb the power of unions. As a result, the miners' strike became the biggest confrontation between the unions and the Thatcher government. Arthur Scargill of the National Union of Mineworkers held three ballots for a national strike and lost all of them; consequently the strike by the miners was declared illegal. Thatcher steadfastly refused to meet the union's demands and after a year-long strike, the union finally conceded without a deal. Thatcher's government closed 150 coal mines, including profitable ones, resulting in the loss of tens of thousands of jobs which devastated communities and led the BBC to label her as the nemesis of the trade union movement:

> *"Most trade unions loathed her; but she remained utterly convinced of the need to cure the nation of what had become known as the "British disease", strike fever."*[8]

Work stoppages fell drastically during her premiership and the number of trade union members fell from 13.5 million to 10 million in 1990 when she left office.

Thatcher's third significant accomplishment was her stance on national security and British sovereignty; one that ranks among the policies of the great leaders of the United Kingdom.

When she first came into power in 1979, she did not have a clear position on Northern Ireland. At the time, she supported a vague proposal for 'regional councils' in Ulster. Following bombings in both Great Britain and Northern Ireland, it became quite clear that the United Kingdom was under siege. The assassination of Lord Mountbatten and the killing of eighteen soldiers deeply affected her. Having survived a failed assassination attempt in 1984, Margaret Thatcher took a very radical approach towards terrorism, mainly from the Irish Republican Army (IRA). She said in a speech following the Brighton bombings:

> *"The bomb attack ... was an attempt not only to disrupt and terminate our conference. It was an attempt to cripple Her majesty's democratically elected government. That is the scale of the outrage in which we have all shared. And the fact that we are gathered here now shocked but composed and determined, is sign not only that this attack has failed, but that all attempts to destroy democracy by terrorism will fail."*[9]

Her government, under great pressure, worked towards the Anglo-Irish Agreement of 1985. This agreement tried to bring an end to the continued troubles in Northern Ireland. However, in the tradition of not alienating the Irish government and Irish nationalist opinion, and in the hope of gaining their support against the IRA, the agreement according to Thatcher produced disappointing results. She never wanted to give the impression that the British government was trying to lead the Unionists into a united Ireland against their will.

As the bombings continued, Thatcher believed that the failure to reach peace was rooted in the lack of the Labour Party's support for the Prevention of Terrorism Act. The continued support of Noraid by American Irish; funding by Arab revolutionaries like Colonel Gaddafi were also a factor.

Regarding sovereignty, there are two notable chapters – one national and the other international – in Margaret Thatcher's career.

In the spring of 1982, Argentina invaded the Falkland Islands in a bold move. Most Britons could care less for these islands, because most of them were not even aware of its existence or importance to the crown. These islands, 780 of them to be exact, had at the time some 1,800 inhabitants, and 60,000 sheep. Long claimed to be part of Argentina, they are known as the Malvinas in the Argentinian constitution.

For years, Argentinian politicians had stated and inferred that reclaiming the islands from the British should be a priority. Negotiations to return the islands had been underway for several years, but were marred by the misunderstanding that Britain did not really care about the islands. General Leopoldo Galtieri assumed that there would be no consequences, and landed his troops on East Falkland. Despite heavy losses, the Argentinians captured the island and deported members of the British garrison back to Britain.

While most Britons never thought that this invasion would result in a war, pressure from unlikely quarters gave Margaret Thatcher the go ahead to reclaim the islands. Older members of the Conservative Party and even Michael Foot, Leader of the Labour Party pushed the government to take back the islands. Among international supporters was France's President François Mitterrand who galvanized support from other European and franco-African countries. The United States' administration was divided at first and President Reagan was not automatically in support of British action. In fact, during talks between General

Vernon Walters and the Argentinian junta he said:

> *"The British would huff, puff and protest and do nothing. America would deal with Britain's wounded pride."*[10]

What changed the situation was the surprising decision by the Soviet Union not to veto a Security Council motion to condemn Argentina's action. – That gave the green light to Thatcher to go into war. While she never believed that she would have to order British troops to war, she wrote:

> *"The significance of the Falklands War was enormous, both for Britain's self-confidence and for our standing in the world."*[11]

The victory in the Falklands transformed Thatcher's standing in the Conservative Party, and led to the electoral victory of 1983. Her feelings about the war are better expressed in her July, 3, 1982 speech in Cheltenham:

> *"We have ceased to be a nation in retreat. We have instead a newfound confidence – born in the economic battles at home and tested and found true 8000 miles away ... And so today we can rejoice at our success in the Falklands and take pride in the achievement of the men and women of our task force. But we do so, not as at some flickering of a flame which must soon be dead. No – we rejoice that Britain has rekindled that spirit which has fired her for generations past and which today has begun to burn as brightly as before. Britain found herself again in the South Atlantic and will not look back from the victory she has won."*[12]

Her contribution to international politics was rooted in her strong distrust of Communism. She believed that the Soviet Union was a danger to world peace. Under Carter's presidency, it became clear that the West had been losing the Cold War to the Soviets. During that time, the Russians were increasingly gaining ground in the third-world.

The Thatcher-led government defence policy revolved around the constant threat posed by Russia. As a result, she aligned herself with then newly elected President Ronald Reagan, and together, worked towards the destruction of the Soviet Union. The invasion of Afghanistan by the Soviets and the Polish government's martial law to contain the Solidarity movement strengthened her determination to stop the proliferation of communism and spurred her to forge greater links with the Western Alliance. At first she opposed Reagan's Strategic Defence Initiative, believing that it would leave Europe without American defence. But later, despite political backlash at home, she supported the deployment of short-range missiles, mainly in Germany.

In late 1984, the political climate was changing in the Soviet Union. The appearance of Mikhail Gorbachev on the political scene allowed Thatcher to take a different approach towards the Russians. Her meeting with Gorbachev was a success; she concluded that Russia and the West could 'do business together'. In a 1988 interview with the *Washington Post* and *Newsweek*, Mrs. Thatcher said:

> *"We're not in a Cold War now" but in a "new relationship much wider than the Cold War ever was,"*[13]

When the demolition of the Berlin Wall started on November 10, 1989, Margaret Thatcher may have correctly – or mistakenly – taken credit for prophesizing its fall, but in retrospect, she may have greatly contributed to its final demise.

One of Margaret Thatcher's most important contributions is often forgotten. Although reviled by many left-leaning feminists, it must not be forgotten that she inspired many women who came after her. She shattered the glass ceiling to such an extent that even powerful men would be hard pressed to effect such change. Women including Hillary Clinton, Condoleezza Rice, Angela Merkel and Christine Lagarde, among many others, owe their success on the international stage to Margaret Thatcher.

In life and in her death, Margaret Thatcher remained a polarizing figure. While tributes lauding her as Britain's greatest peace-time Prime Minister, others were not so gracious. Unions and supporters of the left splashed vitriolic comments online, in the press and on the streets.

However, perhaps her greatest triumph could be how the Russian newspapers praised her in death as 'Lady Number One' and 'Iron and great'. One paper said: 'The iron step of Margaret Thatcher tread into the ground all those she wanted to get rid of, but out of the ground grew British economic prosperity'.

Even Margaret Thatcher had some of her supporters and opponents on the left doubt that she was a true Tory. There were some who believed that she did not espouse a Tory tradition which believed that social obligations were more important than market relations. But this allegation never stood the test of time, as John Nott who had first put the idea forward, recanted and wrote:

> *"it is a complete misreading of her beliefs to depict her as a nineteenth-century Liberal"*[14]

Despite the fact that historians may have different opinions about the track record of these leaders, there is no doubt that their achievements cannot be ignored. While some of them started their political careers as Liberals, it seems that at one stage or another they had an epiphany and became staunch conservatives. So much so that they espoused and defended conservative philosophies with a zeal not seen by other conservative leaders. Of course, for political reasons, they had to compromise on certain occasions, but more often than not they stayed true to conservative principles, even in the face of adversity and defeat.

These three conservative leaders had enormous influence on world history. Their successes can be found in one simple common factor: a relentless commitment to a belief in freedom. Although their leadership may in some instances be questioned, they have made contributions to the world that should not be ignored today. Rather, their initiatives should be revisited to bring economic stability, and most of all, peace in the world. All three demonstrated that where appeasement does not work, coalitions and cooperation do. They may have compromised on process but never on their principles.

CHAPTER 3

GREAT CANADIAN CONSERVATIVES

In the previous chapter we examined the contribution of conservative world leaders. We must not, however, forget the national leaders whose historical contributions have made Canada what it is today. By highlighting the deeds of two exceptional contemporary Canadian conservatives, we will better be able to understand the current framework of conservatism in Canada, which is a major theme of this book.

This does not mean that the greatest Canadian conservative leader is forgotten. I dare say such a fate would even be possible for Sir John A. Macdonald, a Father of Confederation and a winner of six majority governments. He was a beloved leader in both French and English Canada and should serve as an example to all current and future Canadian conservative politicians.

Canada's political history has been dominated by the Liberal Party to the extent that the media has labelled it as the 'Natural Political Party of Canada'. But some of the most significant achievements of the past three decades must be attributed to Conservative leaders. In this regard, two Prime Ministers come to mind. In many respects, despite some of their flaws, they have made significant contributions to Canada.

Prime Minister Brian Mulroney (1939–)

Born in Baie-Comeau, Québec, Brian Mulroney became involved in politics in 1956 as a youth delegate at the leadership convention in Ottawa. He was an ardent supporter of John Diefenbaker who was elected leader of the Progressive Conservative Party of Canada, and who later became the Prime Minister.

Mulroney eventually became the Executive Vice-President of the Iron Ore Company of Canada. As a lawyer, he garnered a strong business resume while resolving a strike at the Montreal newspaper, *La Presse*. In 1974, he was appointed to the Cliché Commission entrusted with the investigation of Canada's largest hydroelectric project, where he further gained the support of Quebec Premier Robert Bourassa.

In 1974, when Robert Stanfield's Progressive Conservatives lost to Pierre Trudeau's Liberals, Mulroney decided to run for the leadership of the PCs at the 1976 convention – unfortunately, he lost to Joe Clark. After Joe Clark's minority government's careless loss on a confidence motion, many party members began to question Clark's leadership.

Clark's loss to the Liberal Party led by Pierre Trudeau in 1979, further led to his leadership being challenged. Brian Mulroney, despite not being a member of parliament entered the 1983 PC leadership race, and wound up winning the leadership on the fourth ballot. His fluency in both official languages coupled with his understanding of Quebecois culture gave him a strong advantage for the upcoming elections.

Mulroney accomplished his goal by defeating John Turner's liberal government in September, 1984. Armed with the largest majority government in Canadian history, Prime Minister Mulroney went on to put into place some of the most important pieces of legislation of the latter part of the twentieth century.

Despite what some may construe as failures, Mulroney's actions were consistent with his conviction that Québec should be brought into the fold of Canada. In his first term he negotiated the Meech Lake Accord which was designed to recognize Quebec

Quebec had not signed the Canadian Constitution negotiated by Trudeau in 1982. The Accord devolved more powers to the provinces and attempted to satisfy Quebec's demand to be recognized as a 'distinct society'. But the Accord died a natural death in 1990 when Manitoba was unable to get a vote, and Newfoundland cancelled the planned free vote.

True to form, Mulroney tried again in 1992, when the Charlottetown Accord tried to resolve the perennial Canadian problems of the devolution of powers to provinces, including such areas as telecommunications, immigration, training and regional development, among other things. Unlike Meech Lake, Charlottetown required a referendum. Mulroney's unpopularity among almost all the major political leaders from former Prime Minister Pierre Trudeau, the Reform Party's Preston Manning, Lucien Bouchard's Bloc Quebecois to Jacques Parizeau of the Parti Quebecois, produced the 54.3% 'No Vote' that killed the Accord. Despite the fact that the agreement had been supported by every premier and different political groups, it was ultimately seen as a rejection of the political elite in Canada.

But to his credit, and more importantly as a fiscal conservative, he proceeded to privatize many of Canada's crown corporations. More importantly, he promoted the privatization of Petro-Canada which had been created and practically nationalised by Trudeau. Trudeau's handling of Petro-Canada had alienated the province of Alberta through the implementation of The National Energy Program (NEP).

Following the example of his mentor, John Diefenbaker, who influenced the Commonwealth to expel apartheid South Africa in 1961, Mulroney aggressively supported U.N. sanctions against that regime. This move against South Africa came despite the reluctance of his conservative allies, Margaret Thatcher and Ronald Reagan, as Mulroney told the *Globe and Mail*:

> *"Well, they took positions that were antithetical to those of Canada. We favoured the tightening of sanctions and indeed*

> *the rupturing of all relations with South Africa if that could bring an end to apartheid. They disagreed with that and so we had to disagree with them."*[1]

South Africa was already experiencing exclusion from many international events, but as a result of these economic sanctions, it became even more isolated, leading to immense pressure which the white supremacist government of South Africa could not withstand. It wound up abolishing its apartheid policy and brought forward a more inclusive constitution reform that saw Nelson Mandela and the ANC come to power in 1994 bringing democracy to South Africa.

Prime Minster Mulroney, also negotiated some of the most stringent environmental agreements with the United States that brought forward policies which curbed emissions and reduced the effect of acid rain in the Great Lakes region of North America. He recounted the resolve with which he approached this issue in a speech delivered March, 2012:

> *"Well, we simply wouldn't let go of it. We got in the Americans' face about it at every bilateral meeting until they realized we were serious about it, that we meant it, and that we wouldn't go away until we had dealt with it to our satisfaction ...*
>
> *But while we were talking to the Americans, we were taking action with the provinces and industry, implementing a "Clean Hands Policy" of leading from the front."*[2]

Then, in 1987, came *The Montreal Protocol on Substances That Deplete the Ozone Layer* which reduced, and eventually halted the use of CFCs that were seriously damaging the Ozone layer. This agreement prevented a potential planetary catastrophe. The Mulroney government also put into place the *cod moratorium* in 1992, despite its unpopularity in Newfoundland. As a result, we have seen the resurgence of the Atlantic cod stock. For his efforts, Brian Mulroney was honoured in 2006 as "Canada's Greenest Prime Minister" by the Corporate Knights.

While these two accomplishments were significant, his major victory is really found on the economic front. Armed with another majority, his government proceeded to advance the most important trade deal in Canadian history. The North American Trade Act saw the rationalization of trade between Canada and the United States, and was later extended to include Mexico. These agreements, despite protests from the left, have proven to be a boon for the country.

On January 2, 1988, Mulroney signed the Free Trade Agreement (FTA) with the United States. In 1994, the free trade zone was extended under the North American Free Trade Agreement (NFTA) to include Mexico. These agreements eliminated trade barriers for goods and services, created conditions for fair trade within the free-trade zone and liberalized investments within the area; at the same time rules were established for resolving disputes and bilateral and multilateral cooperation was promoted.

At first, on both sides of the border, there were many opponents to the free trade agreement. Mulroney has stated that even he was skittish during the negotiations:

> *"Canada was in many ways somewhat fearful, concerned about the size of our neighbour, and deeply concerned as well by the matter that had always been out there, namely the absorption by the United States."*[3]

The initial apprehensions and skepticism among many Canadians were ultimately dispelled; the last 25 years of free trade in North America have made this country much better off. As a nation, we have also shed some of our fears of the big neighbour to the south. Kevin Lynch, Clerk of the Privy Council commented on the decisive role free trade played in getting Canadians to

> *"believe in ourselves – to take down the tariff barriers and think we could compete with the world's largest and most competitive economy, and do well at it...All these things were made possible by thinking about the world through a totally different prism ... And free trade allowed us to do that."*[4]

After moving forward with free trade, Mulroney replaced the Manufacturers Tax with the Goods and Services tax. Despite the fact that many Canadians of different political mindsets have questioned the implementation of the Goods and Services Tax (GST), there is no doubt that it was the lesser of two evils. The Manufacturers Sales Tax (MST) was previously applied at the wholesale level on goods manufactured in Canada. This proved to be a burden for exporters because the tax made their goods more expensive in the world market. The GST on the other hand, is a tax on consumption, which in the long run is far better for the economy and international trade. Although strongly opposed by the Liberals and 80% of the Canadian public, the GST went into effect in 1989.

Mulroney's leadership of the country ended on an unfortunately sour note. His reputation was marred by allegations that he had accepted bribes in the 'airbus affair' – these allegations were later found to be unsubstantiated. The airbus affair and his association with convicted businessman Kalheinz Schreiber, tarnished the mainstream narrative regarding Mulroney's integrity and ethical conduct. However, in order to fully understand and appreciate his role in determining the future success of Canada's society and economy, it is imperative that we remember his earlier commitments to recognize Quebec and the role he played in ratifying the Free Trade agreements. For his services he has been awarded the Companion of the order of Canada, the country's highest civilian honour. He was also granted the Woodrow Wilson Award for Public Service among other prestigious accolades.

Prime Minister Stephen Harper (1959–)

There is no doubt that the inclusion of Stephen Harper as a great Canadian Conservative leader will receive criticisms and praise. Nonetheless, there are many significant reasons why Harper should be included as one of this country's most important conservative politicians.

Stephen Harper was born in Toronto, a fact which may explain why he was a member of his high school Young Liberals Club when he first started his political career. He moved to Edmonton to work for Imperial

Oil, and attended the University of Calgary where he earned a bachelor's degree in Economics.

Harper has one of the most chequered political careers. Since the mid-eighties, he has been affiliated, for various lengths of time, with every single conservative political party in Canada. These affiliations would eventually provide him with the ability to understand the true nature of Canadian conservatism.

In 1985, he served as chief aide to Jim Hawkes of the Progressive Conservatives, but quickly became disillusioned in the bureaucratic maze of Ottawa. More specifically, he was not happy with Mulroney's fiscal policies, especially the creation of the GST. Living in Alberta had made a profound impact on Harper, leading him to become a committed westerner. He was therefore disappointed in the inability of the Mulroney government to reverse the much reviled National Energy Program put in place by Trudeau. He found himself working in an environment which was filled with the trivialities of networking and a clear lack of intellectual stimulation. A follower of Ronald Reagan and Margaret Thatcher, his hopes of finding true blue conservatives in Ottawa vanished, and he left for Calgary to pursue a Master's degree in economics.

Robert Mansell, the head of the economics department at the University of Calgary, introduced Harper to Preston Manning, the leader of the then nascent Reform Party. Harper brought credibility and intellectual gravitas to the party. As the party's chief policy officer he was influential in shaping the Reform Party's 1988 election platform. He ran against his old boss Jim Hawkes in the 1988 elections, and failed. But he came back in 1993 to beat Hawkes and claimed the Calgary West seat for the Reform Party.

While being very influential and a major contributor to Reform party policies, there were fundamental differences between Harper and Manning. These included many dissentions ranging from political philosophy to political strategy. At the root of the divide lay the fact that Harper was a conservative, while Manning a populist. In his autobiography,

Manning writes that he and Harper shared Conservative values, but that Harper "had serious reservations about Reform's ... belief in the value of grassroots consultations and participation in key decisions."

In 1977, before his term as an MP expired, Stephen Harper announced his retirement from the House of Commons and joined the National Citizen's Coalition (NCC). In his new role, completely independent from any political bonds, he contributed to unique policy papers that would shape his future political career and provide fodder for his liberal critics. Harper's words became reminiscent of Jean Lesage – "*Maîtres chez nous*" – as this excerpt from a *National Post* column demonstrates:

> *"The latest dribblings from the mouth of Canada's Prime Minister suggest Alberta's wealth can be attributed to the federal government. While there is clearly no merit to the claim, we must not ignore the implied threat: If Ottawa giveth, then Ottawa can taketh away.*
>
> *This is just one more reason why Westerners, but Albertans in particular, need to think hard about their future in this country. After sober reflection, Albertans should decide that it is time to seek a new relationship with Canada."*[5]

With six other signatories, he also wrote an open letter to Premier Ralph Klein in which he implored the premier to protect Alberta's autonomy from aggressive federal policy. "To build firewalls around Alberta, to limit the extent to which an aggressive and hostile federal government can encroach upon legitimate provincial jurisdiction."

A principled conservative, Harper always believed in some form of coalition between conservative factions, including several regional conservative parties. Following the dismal showing by the Alliance Party at the 2000 federal elections, Stockwell Day, who had been leader of the new party which had replaced the Reform Party – perhaps in name only – came under scrutiny as several members wanted him out. The problem was that some members chose to form a coalition with the Progressive Conservatives. This alignment caused consternation among many true blue conservatives as they feared the possibility of a return by Joe Clark. Harper came back and won the leadership of the Alliance party, defeating Stockwell Day. Change was in the air, as described by Plamondon:

> *"Under Harper's leadership, the Alliance party emerged from the populist roots of the disgruntled westerners advocating economic and social policies that were out of touch with mainstream Canadians, and became a more focussed, thoughtful, and intelligent conservative party. Harper brought recalcitrant Alliance MPs back into the fold, then reached out to Joe Clark to seek a merger of the parties or some other form of agreement that would end vote splitting."*[6]

Once elected leader of the Alliance Party, there was still an obstacle to uniting the right. The other faction, the Progressive Conservative, was still lead by Joe Clark. But when Joe Clark resigned as leader in 2003, a new leader emerged. Peter MacKay, a young conservative from Nova Scotia, who over the years had fulfilled many roles under Brian Mulroney, Jean Charest and Joe Clark, won the PC leadership over Scott Brison, Jim Prentice, and David Orchard an anti-free trade activist. There were definite signs of optimism for the PC party. But, given the poll numbers for the Alliance and the Tories, it was unlikely that either of them would unseat the Liberals at the next election.

MacKay was a team player and a man who recognized that collaboration was better than division. Making the first move, he asked Harper to sit down and talk: enter Magna International CEO Belinda Stronach who arranged the meeting between the two leaders. The deal between Orchard and MacKay to review the Free Trade Agreement ended without an Alliance merger. This was not only surprising at the time, but was also a potential obstacle to any talks with Harper. Nevertheless, talks between emissaries of both parties were started. The first barrier was eliminated when the suggested name of the new party would be the Conservative Party of Canada, with no reference to Reform or Alliance. The second and most important obstacle was removed when the Alliance emissaries accepted the principles of the Progressive Conservative constitution, as explained by Plamondon:

> *"In fact, the founding principles of the new constitution of the new Conservative Party were lifted virtually verbatim from the PC party constitution – the same words, the same order ... Short of a merger, Stephen Harper had few firm conditions. Because the PCs had a constitution that reflected conservative values, Harper saw little point in debating the issue."*[7]

The only condition that could prevent an agreement was the leadership selection. Mackay wanted an 'equal weight' system, whereby each constituency would receive an equal number of votes no matter the member population size. Harper wanted a one-member, one-vote system. The emissaries could not reach an agreement. Ultimately, Harper accepted the 'equal weight' system which would receive final approval at the party's founding convention. Mackay refused. On October 14, 2003, Harper and MacKay agreed in a telephone conversation to move forward, sealing the fate of the merger. Still, the deal would have to wait for ratification by members of both parties.

The majority of Alliance members backed the deal, while the PCs were a bit more hesitant in accepting MacKay's decision. In an expected move, David Orchard and the ever-disgruntled Joe Clark and their supporters opposed the merger. When the final ballots were counted, 95.9% of Alliance members and 90% of delegated PC members backed the deal.

In January 2004, Harper announced his candidacy for the leadership of the new party. While extremely popular in the West, he had no organization in Quebec and carried some baggage stemming from his previous statements about Atlantic Canada. However, he had the support of Brian Mulroney and Mario Dumont. Not surprising was Joe Clark's last and desperate salvo against Harper on CTV's *Question Period*:

> *"The issue is going to be which leader is better, which leader is worse, and I think the question is a very tough one ... .I*

> *would be extremely worried about Mr. Harper. I personally would prefer to go with the devil we know. I'm that concerned about the imprint of Stephen Harper."*[8]

On March 20, 2004, the leadership vote went ahead, with Belinda Stronach and Tony Clement as the other candidates. When the results came in Harper had won overwhelmingly in the West, along with a 33% backing in Quebec, 35% in the Maritimes and surprisingly, 57% support within Ontario. Harper was the new leader of the Conservative Party of Canada.

With only three months remaining, Harper had little time to prepare for a general election. While he was not successful in defeating Paul Martin's Liberals, and although the Tories did not increase the combined percentage of popular vote of the old PC and Alliance parties, Harper won 99 seats and became the *de facto* leader of Her Majesty's Loyal Opposition.

The details behind his policies and track record in Parliament will be discussed in a later chapter. What entitles Harper's selection within this pantheon of conservative greats are the consecutive general election wins which brought the Conservative Party from the brink of disappearance to two minority governments ending Liberal rule after twelve years. Even more important is Harper's astounding accomplishment in establishing a majority government with representation in every region of the country, thus putting himself and the PCs firmly in control of Canada.

- January 26, 2006: Minority government with 124 seats
- October 24, 2008: Minority government with 143 seats
- May 02, 2011: Majority government with 166 seats

Both Mulroney and Harper are somewhat controversial figures. Mulroney had his accomplishments tarnished by his alleged involvement in dubious transactions concerning the airbus affair. His dealing with

Karlheinz Schreiber, certainly added a black mark to otherwise great contributions to Canada's status in the world.

Harper who at the time of writing this book is still Prime Minister of Canada, has his fair share of flaws, which we shall examine in greater detail in a chapter which will analyze his policies during his tenure as prime minister. Despite their blemishes, these two men have consistently revived the moribund Canadian conservative movement. They were both able to snatch power from the Liberals who had spent many years prior, running the country into the ground.

CHAPTER 4

CANADA'S DIVIDES

Both Canada and the United States continue to experience internal historical conflicts which are a cause of tension and concern, both for current and future generations. While the divisions are not the same, they are still very similar. The main issue concerns the treatment of minorities in both countries, namely the French and First Nations members in Canada, and of course, the black descendants of slaves in the United States. Even today, resentments which originate from these conflicts greatly influence policies and politics in both countries.

For Canada there are two issues that still cause great consternation among the general public; they are sometimes racial, but very often, culturally-based. On the other side of the border, the United States' legacy of internal conflict includes the experience of a bloody civil war between the Southern and the Northern states on the issue of slavery.

Too often, political discourse has been marred by how the right or the left is perceived to have addressed these issues. The Liberals on the one hand, have always portrayed themselves as the champions of the French and First Nations in Canada, while American democrats continue to represent themselves as the more tolerant party that has always looked after African Americans' interests and well-being. Conservatives and Republicans, on the other hand, continue to be depicted as being the opponents and sometimes even assailants of these minorities. This misconception continues to dominate politics in both countries. A further look into the nature of these divides will provide us with insight into the political role played by Left and Right political parties.

The French Canadian Conundrum

As we say in Canada, we have two solitudes. Much of the unreasonableness in any discussion over the relationship between French and English Canadians may well stem from a lack of knowledge about Canadian history. To many Quebecois, the rest of Canada is another nation which does not share their values. Over the years, politicians from Québec have tried to redefine the province's relationship with the rest of Canada on this basis.

Québec is one of the four founding provinces of the Canadian Federation. As part of the British North America Act, the Quebec Act of 1774 guarantees the maintenance of its language, although English and French were both recognized as the official languages of the province. It seems that ever since that time, a division of sorts has existed between English and French Canada.

There have been attempts to secede and to form a separate State, if not an entirely independent Nation within Canadian borders; some francophone believe the solution to the French/English divide is a complete break from Canada. At the heart of the separatist challenge is the belief held by many French Canadians, that if they can control their language, culture and laws they will survive as a distinct society. However, in reality the puzzle is more complex, as it entails several factors beyond politics such as demography, geography and economics.

In the 1930s, Maurice Duplessis created the Union Nationale after the collapse of the Conservative Party of Quebec and the Action libérale nationale, which was the remnant of the Liberal Party of Quebec. The alliance was based on a common hostility towards the Liberal Party. Duplessis convinced Quebec voters that the only way to maintain autonomy was to keep the provincial Liberal party out of power, and aligned himself with Conservatives in English Canada. However, under his government, Quebec found itself in an era under the rule of an authoritarian regime called the 'Great Darkness'. During that period, Duplessis implemented laws that gave the Montreal-based Anglo-Scot business elite and other American and British-based capital the freedom to run the province's economy. He also banned unions, communism and books which were proscribed by the Catholic Church. He also refused federal funds from Ottawa earmarked for health, education and social programs. All of these policies were designed to jealously guard his provincial autonomy.

As a result, many young professionals found that they had to adopt both the culture and language of the English speaking minority. These young people belonged to the middle and working class and desired better education opportunities, higher welfare benefits, improved housing and labor laws that showed preference to the state over the church. This change and the search for nationalism are at the root of the conflicts between the federal and provincial governments. It is better expressed by René Lévesque who described the state in the following way:

> *"It must be more than a participant in the economic development and emancipation of Québec; it must be a creative agent. Otherwise we can do no more than we have been doing so far, i.e., wait meekly for the capital and the initiative of others. The others, of course, will come for their own sake, not for ours. It is we alone, through our State, who can become masters of our own house."*[1]

In 1959, the death of Duplessis and the rise of a young intellectual Liberal Jean Lesage changed the dynamics of Quebec politics. In June 1960, when the Liberal party under Lesage won the elections, it was the beginning of the end of the Quebec federal Conservatives.

This domestic feud has been brewing for at least a century, but has become more acerbic since 1962 when the Progressive Conservative (PC) government, who had won a majority four years earlier, was reduced to a minority government. In 1963, the PCs lost a few more seats and gave the Liberals under Lester Pearson the opportunity to form a minority government. Since then, the result has been a constant ebb and flow in Canadian politics with several attempts through referenda to make Quebec an independent nation.

Quebec has approximately a third of the population of Canada, and with this demography and electoral power, they practically control who forms a government at every federal election.

Quebec has often objected to Ottawa's control of policies, including welfare and economic development. In 1960, newly elected provincial premier Jean Lesage appointed René Lévesque (1922–1987) as his Minister of Natural Resources from 1961 to 1965. While in office, Lévesque played an important role in the nationalisation of hydroelectric companies, greatly expanding Hydro-Quebec. This was an important reform that was part of the Quiet Revolution, which later brought Lévesque to national prominence during his long-time feud between his province and Ottawa.

But not everyone in Quebec was, or is, a separatist. Mr. Gilles Boyer expressed his opinion regarding this phenomenon in the 1961 September edition of *Le Soleil*:

> *"that secession would be unconstitutional and might well be opposed militarily. Even without resorting to arms, the surrounding continent could exert all kinds of pressure against the new state, for the Americans would favour it no more than they do Cuba. Economically, Quebec would be a "small, isolated market of five million consumers", walled in by the high tariffs of its angry and vengeful neighbours … separatism is a last resort only premature in a province that is just beginning to exploit the power and liberties it has under the Constitution."*[2]

In 1963, three days before federal elections, Lesage delivered an 'ultimatum' speech. Fully expressing his opinion on the autonomy of Quebec, regardless of what government – Liberal or Conservative – was in power in Ottawa.

Emboldened by this declaration of '*independence*', several factions began to appear in Quebec politics. Moving away from the Lesage interventionist state, younger radicals with a variety of orientations, took to the political stage. There were Marxists, advocates of secularization, those whose focus was anti-clerical, far-right clerical corporatists and even fringe terrorists who began to make known their anti-nationalism yearnings. This period marked the beginning of explicit separatist movements in the province.

A series of bomb attacks ensued. Her Majesty's military barracks in Montreal was the first target, followed by the Wolfe monument in Quebec City, a railway track to be used by Prime Minister Diefenbaker, an RCMP building, a military recruiting centre, a Black Watch depot and several mail boxes.

Events escalated as the separatist movement gained support in the province. It was further emboldened by the unusual 1967 interference by then France's President Charles de Gaulle in Canada's domestic politics, when he proclaimed: "*vive le Québec, vive le Québec libre.*" Federalists were found scrambling to find answers to the ever-growing problem of Quebec separatism. This resulted in the Mackenzie Commission Report which contained words like 'subversion' and 'sedition', and perhaps worse still, Trudeau's 'crime against humanity' statement.

The situation got worse in October 1970, when British trade commissioner James Cross and Quebec's Labour minister Pierre Laporte were kidnapped by the ***Front de libération du Québec*** **(FLQ).** While Cross was released two months after his abduction, Pierre Laporte's body was found just seven days after he went missing on October 10.

Despite the fact that the FLQ was involved in the bombings of 1963, it was the events of October 1970 that triggered some of Canada's darkest hours as Prime Minister Trudeau invoked and declared the War Measures Act (WMA) of 1970.

Three reasons were given to invoke the WMA: the request by the Quebec government, the kidnappings, and 'confused minds'. These reasons are suspicious at best, as Bouthillier and Clottier point out:

> *"the RCMP was opposed to invoking the War Measures Act as a means to free the two hostages and arrest the kidnappers. Though the Quebec government provided a letter, it is well known that Pierre Elliot Trudeau was never one to automatically give in to Quebec's demands, and finally, since when and in what countries is there no confusion as long as democracy and freedom of expression exists?"*[3]

During these dark days, the streets of Montreal were patrolled by some 7,500 troops. There were massive arrests of approximately 450 people, these were sometimes violent and at times conducted 'in the middle of the night'. Yet, Canadians accepted the WMA willingly without any questions about the loss of their basic rights and protections under the law. The conclusion is that Canadians were not happy about what was happening in Quebec and wanted the problem solved despite the level of fascistic totalitarianism exercised by Trudeau, the same man who before becoming prime minister had argued for the entrenchment of fundamental freedoms and placing limits on police power.

Another wedge between English and French Canada, is of course, language. Quebec Liberals had demanded that Quebec be granted a 'particular status'. Nationalist politicians from the NDP and the federal Conservatives, for political reasons, accepted some accommodation for Quebec, which Trudeau had said should be made, although his official position belied the truth of his conviction. As Byfield writes:

> *"To him, any unique recognition of Quebec was unacceptable, whether it was called "special status," "compact federalism," "deux nations" or anything else. During his meteoric rise to power, he had described Quebec's ever-growing demands as a "time bomb," and his first act as prime minister was to defuse it."*[4]

However, in order to accommodate French Canada, the government introduced the Official Language Act (OLA), which gives Canadians everywhere the right to communicate in French with the federal government and crown corporations, and to be able to read all official documents in both French and English. Opposition to the Act was fierce among conservatives. While the Conservative leader Robert Stanfield supported the Act, he was strongly opposed by Alberta MP Jack Horner and Diefenbaker. Nevertheless, the Act passed 191 to 17 (all but one conservative from the West, opposed the Act by 70%.)

If the OLA was passed to integrate the French language across Canada or to appease Quebec's fear of assimilation, it certainly did not achieve its purpose. Over the years the divide has grown wider. First, in 1977, came Bill 101, and since then, The Parti Quebecois (PQ) has introduced legislation to limit the use of English in the province.

Reciprocity of language recognition has not worked very well. Many businesses are under the scrutiny of L'Office Québécois de la Langue Française (OQLF), commonly known as the "language police." The department has the task of making sure that French is the predominant, if not the only language used in certain circumstances. Furthermore, Quebec is the only place where there exists distinctions between French speaking citizens. Everywhere else in the world, French speaking people are described as francophone, yet in Quebec if you are from a different French speaking country, you are labelled as an ***allophone***, because your mother tongue is not pure French as defined by the OQLF. More recently employees of Haitian origin working at the Hôpital Rivière-des-Prairies were reprimanded for speaking creole among themselves. Johanne Gagnon, the hospital's director of communications said:

> *"Employees can converse in the language of their choice during breaks and lunch hour, but the hospital told them to be mindful not to make their coworkers feel excluded ... Is it interpersonal, a racial problem, a misunderstanding?"*[1]

The French Language Charter has created more division and frustration among English speaking residents of Quebec, further dividing the nation – this time along language lines.

In 1979, the Parti Quebecois released a paper proposing the negotiation for a 'sovereignty association' with Canada entitled *Québec-Canada: A New Deal. The Québec Government Proposal for a New Partnership Between Equals: Sovereignty-Association.* As a result, we had the first province-wide referendum on May 20, 1980.

On one side were the federalists and 'NO' supporters: Prime Minister Pierre Trudeau, Justice Minister Jean Chretien, Provincial Liberal Leader Claude Ryan and Jeanne Sauvé, the Speaker of the House of Commons. On the 'YES' side were: René Lévesque, Jacques Parizeau, Camille Laurin and Lise Payette of the government of Quebec. The proposal for secession was defeated by a margin of 59.56% to 40.44%

In 1982, the Canadian Constitution was patriated. When the Supreme Court of Canada ruled that the Prime Minister did not require the consent of the provinces to do so, provincial premiers stood united against the amendments, until an agreement was reached – this occurred without the input of the Premier of Quebec. Thus, the accord on the Constitution Act of 1982 was signed by all provinces except Quebec. Despite refusing to sign the agreement, Quebec was bound by the ratified amendments, to which Premier René Lévesque warned of awful consequences as a result of the betrayal.

In 1994, the sovereigntist Parti Quebecois, under the leadership of Jacques Parizeau came back into power. As promised, Parizeau called for another referendum in 1995. This time, the question was different and was presented in the two official languages as well as in First Nation languages.

The English version asked:

> *"Do you agree that Quebec should become sovereign after having made a formal offer to Canada for a new economic and political partnership within the scope of the bill respect-*

ing the future of Quebec and of the agreement signed on June 12, 1995?"

The supporters of the 'NO' side included: Prime Minister Jean Chretien, Federal Ministers Lucienne Robillard, Brian Tobin, Federal Progressive Conservative Party Leader Jean Charest and Quebec Liberal Party Leader, Daniel Johnson.

On the 'YES' side were: Quebec Premier Jacques Parizeau, Federal Bloc Quebecois leader Lucien Bouchard and Mario Dumont, provincial leader of the Action Démocratique du Québec (ADQ).

Sovereignty for Quebec was rejected by a narrow margin of 50.58% **No** votes against 49.42% of **Yes** votes. Despite this second defeat, many francophone still support a separate Quebec. This popular sentiment hangs like the sword of Damocles over the heads of Canadians!

Pauline Marois made the latest attempt to revive the independent Quebec issue. She called an election in 2014 and recruited one of the most powerful businessmen in the country to run as a PQ candidate. By doing this, Marois forcefully pushed the envelope of separatism. We can be sure that had the PQ won a majority, with billionaire star candidate Pierre Karl Péladeau in the new government, the Parti Québécois would have sought, once again, to separate from Canada. But under what conditions?

Madame Marois may have been delusional in thinking that an independent Quebec would keep the dollar as its currency, and be granted a seat on the Bank of Canada. Such a move verged on lunacy because Canada would still bear the risk of any insolvency and liquidity to Quebec's banking system. The rest of Canada should never accept such a request.

However, it is almost certain that the great divide will continue despite Marois' loss. Just like her predecessor Jacques Parizeau, she quickly invoked the claim of fraud by Anglophones and the allophones, and never considered that it was her policies of separation, and social policies that caused her failure. Fortunately, on April 7, 2014, the Parti Quebecois and Madame Marois suffered a resounding defeat at the polls, which included her own seat.Quebecers are the savviest electorate in Canada. They vote according to what is best for them, not necessarily the country. This time, they chose to vote against the possibility of a referendum, but this is not over yet. The spectre of separatism still exists; it will be revived when Quebec decides that it is time to do so.

First Nations within a Canadian Nation

The other divide that constantly preoccupies Canadian politics is the status of First Nations. Today there are 630 bands and recognized governments representing Aboriginal people who are neither Inuit nor Métis.

Trade was at the heart of the first relationship between First Nations peoples and Europeans, starting as far back as the 17th century. But over the years the relationship took several different turns. Tribes fighting each other started to sell conquered enemies as slaves and were handed out as gifts to the citizens of New France. This practice continued until the 1793 Act Against Slavery came into effect, establishing the gradual abolition of slavery.

On the other side of the coin, First Nations of Acadia aligned themselves with the French and fought six colonial wars against the British, which ultimately ended in the conquest of Canada by the British.

The late 18th century saw the policy of 'assimilation' come into force. It was the belief that First Nations would be better off if they could change their culture. The attempt into forced assimilation saw its expansion in the 19th and 20th centuries. Under the Indian Act, Indian and Northern Affairs Canada funded the development of a Canadian Indian residential school system. This period of residential schooling turned out to be one of the worst times in the history of Canadian First Nations. The Canadian federal government's Indian Affairs department promoted the assimilation of Native Canadians into the European/Canadian society. Under the system, schools were run by churches of different denominations. To achieve the goals of assimilation, these institutions implemented some of the vilest practices, which included physical punishment, sexual abuse, and some of the worst living conditions resulting in malnutrition, overcrowding, poor sanitation and increased levels of tuberculosis. These conditions were so poor that in the 20th century they led to allegations of cultural genocide and ethnocide.

Amendments to the Indian Act made it possible for the government to expropriate Indian lands. Eventually, the 1930 Constitution Act provided the recognition of indigenous rights:

> *"Indians shall have the right ... of hunting, trapping and fishing game and fish for food at all seasons of the year on all unoccupied Crown lands and on any other lands to which the said Indians may have a right of access"*[5]

Over the years many concessions have been made and governments of different leanings have made changes to previous treaties. Today, First Nations have negotiated devolution powers for the delivery of some services.

The 1979 Indian Health Transfer Policy provides for the provision of health care under the control of each community based on their specific requirements and capabilities. First Nations enjoy several exemptions from taxation under the current Indian Act which states:

> *"87 (1). Notwithstanding any other Act of Parliament or any Act of the legislature of a province ... the following property is exempt from taxation*
> *I(a) the interest of an Indian or a band in reserve lands or surrendered lands; and*
> *(b) the personal property of an Indian or a band situated on a reserve.*
> *87 (2). No Indian or band is subject to taxation in respect of the ownership, occupation, possession or use of any property mentioned in paragraph (1) (a) or*
> *(b) or is otherwise subject to taxation in respect of any such property"*[6]

Many left-leaning academics believe that these tax exemptions are detrimental and in many cases serve to oppress natives rather than provide a privilege. On the other hand, many Canadians feel that these exemptions should be curtailed as they seem to be discriminatory and promote a sense of entitlement which does not help the economy.

Land disputes and jurisdiction over natural resources have been at the centre of the division between First Nations and changing Canadian governments. The proposed *First Nations – Federal Crown Political Accord* promotes a partnership between First Nations and Canada. The Supreme Court stated that treaties: "served to reconcile pre-existing Aboriginal sovereignty with assumed Crown sovereignty, and to define Aboriginal rights,"[7] The problem with this statement is that First Nations see these agreements as lasting forever, regardless of circumstances, and coupled with the beliefs that the agreements are between themselves and the Sovereign not with the government of Canada.

This belief has been at the root of many failed discussions on changes to the status of First Nations. In 1969, then Indian Affairs Minister Jean Chretien proposed the abolition of the Indian Act of Canada, including the rejection of aboriginal land claims while redefining the status of First Nations people as 'another ethnic minority' and not 'a distinct minority group' within Canada. When Harold Cardinal and the Indian Chiefs of Alberta strongly objected to these changes, the Trudeau government backed away from the proposed changes.

In 1990, Elijah Harper of Manitoba refused to accept the Meech Lake Accord, because it failed to recognize aboriginal grievances. In 1987, Harper also scuttled the third constitutional conference on Aboriginal people, by preventing Manitoba to ratify the accord through procedural rules. He also opposed the Charlottetown Accord of 1992.

While several Canadian governments have made suggestions to effect changes in the relationship between First Nations and Canada, the chasm continues to grow. The 1994 Royal Commission on Aboriginal Peoples chaired by René Dussault and Georges Erasmus proposed discussions on a 'Nation-to – Nation' basis. A year later, the Chretien government accepted the report's recommendations and apologized for the forced acculturation of aboriginal people by the federal government accompanied by an 'initial' payment of $350 million.

Over the years, agreements between federal, provincial governments and First Nations have been signed. But unrest has grown as aboriginals have become more political. Conflicts are no longer just verbal but have developed into militant and sometimes violent demonstrations. The 1990 Oka conflict resulted in one person's death. The 1995 Ipperwash Crisis in Ontario saw the death of Dudley George, an unarmed protester who was shot by the Ontario Provincial Police. On the other side of the country in British Columbia, we saw the Gustafsen Lake Standoff, which resulted in the non-life threatening shooting of a non-indigenous protester, Suniva Bronson; the shooting occurred in an extensive exchange of fire between protesters and 400 RCMP officers and military personnel. In 2001, a dispute about lobster fishing caused the Mi'kmaq blockade of Highway 11 in New Brunswick. The conflict cost the federal government $15 million, not including legal expenses.

As First Nations have become more organized and also more political, they have affiliated themselves with various radical groups. While some believe these connections are good for their cause, the tactics used are actually further alienating Canadians from First Nations peoples. Environmental groups and 'occupy' movements are now entrenched in First Nations politics. They even propose to disrupt the country's economy.

There is no doubt that there has been mistreatment of First Nations members in the past. However, it is time to face reality in the 21st century and find a new model to resolve the disputes. The continued 'handouts' are not helping anyone, as individual members of some nations live in relative squalor, their chiefs are basking in thousands of dollars, provided for by the taxpayer. We cannot solve the existing problems if we refuse to acknowledge the misbehaviour and lack of accountability that prevail in some instances.

A clear example of the type of unconstructive tactics used in this conflict was Chief Spence's 2013 hunger strike. After many demands to meet with the Prime Minister and the Governor General, resolving any dispute become next to impossible in an environment dominated by the spirit of blackmail. While some would argue that this latest episode was about the treaty between Queen Victoria and First Nations, it is more likely to be the perennial debate about finance, either in dollars or resources.

More significantly, we have the 'Idle no More' movement, which threatens to create havoc with the economy through blockades and civil disobedience if aboriginal demands are not met. The problem is that very few members of the Assembly of First Nation (AFN) actually understand the content of the demands. At first sight the protest is very reminiscent of the 'occupy' movement: both movements seem to be made up of radical left anarchists who lack group structure and leadership.

Chief Spence's eventual refusal to meet with the Prime Minister while only briefly attending the meeting with the Governor General showed that even the poster child for the protest had no clear idea as to what her demands were really about.

In reality, Chief Spence of the Attawapiskat reserve had been under public scrutiny since the demise of the reserve was reported; an independent audit called to examine the financial affairs of the reserve only cast more of a bad light over the situation. As it turned out, expenditure in the millions of dollars do not have any paper trail. Over the past six years, the reserve received some $100 million from the government. While the Chief and her spouse/partner received hundreds of thousands of dollars, many residents still live in virtual squalor. The release of the audit was immediately branded as a ploy by the government to embarrass the Chief. By that same token, shouldn't we also say that the Chief's hunger strike may have been a ploy to pre-empt the findings of the audit?

To add to the outrage regarding the Chief's ingratiating herself, it is disclosed that for the fiscal year 2013/2014 Chief Ron Giesbrecht of the Kwikwetlem First Nation 'earned' close to $1 million in bonuses and expenses. It must be nice to earn three times the equivalent salary of the

Prime Minister and be responsible for 85 people. Of course, we must not forget that the earnings were tax free.

The watershed decision by the Canadian Supreme Court to grant land-title rights to First Nations provides native groups with enormous bargaining power. In so doing, the Supreme Court has granted rights to aboriginals that are not available to ordinary Canadians. No doubt, these new powers will be used to erode governments' and corporations' standing in matters of economic growth – such as right of way for pipelines. To counter balance this decision, a Conservative government approach would be to cut back subsidies. With fewer handouts, First Nations will be forced to generate their own revenue. Perhaps then, agreeing to Economic development on their land would then become a necessity instead of a hammer with which to extort more funds from Canadians.

Most Canadians are sympathetic to the problems of First Nations peoples, but by the same token, they are also aware of the amount of money being allocated by the government without any accountability in many cases. Let's be clear: not all reserves have the same problems or are managed in the same way. However, since it is taxpayers' money, it would be nice to have greater accountability. It is time that First Nations should be viewed as another form of local government. They may be independent, yet they require funds from the federal government. In this case, they should be subject to the same accounting rules as any other recipient of government funds. Financial reports under current accounting standards should apply. The public deserves more transparency and accountability.

The latest failure in First Nation accommodation and reconciliation is Bill C-33 which was designed, ostensibly, to return control of First Nations education to the First Nations themselves. Despite the backing of the Act by Shawn Atleo, the national chief of the Assembly of First Nations (AFN), many First Nation leaders opposed the Bill. The infighting among members of the Assembly is the real obstacle to this bill, and in fact to any other bills affecting Canadian Aboriginals. The failed acceptance of Bill C-33 resulted in Shawn Atleo's resignation as Chief of the AFN. This latest failure clearly exemplifies the divisions within the AFN. The perennial opposition to the Act by First Nation Leaders was "that if passed, the bill would strip away their rights and give the federal government too much control over the education of their children." The reality is that some members are not concerned with the state of their children's education, but rather the financial control of the $1.9B allocated by the government.

We shall never resolve these problems, since many chiefs do not want to be at the table. The prime minister, who has agreed to meet again with Aboriginal leaders, should come to a new agreement which addresses the issues put forward by those who are willing to attend. Chief Atleo should be given credit for agreeing to discussions and changes. To acquiesce to the request to meet with the governor general or the Queen, for that matter, shows that the 'Idle no More' movement has no intention of ever coming to a final solution.

The treaty may have been signed by Queen Victoria, but times have changed. The Queen of England has also been stripped of many of her royal powers. Decisions of importance are made by elected officials and not the monarchy. So let us get off this horse and move on!

Certainly, there are grievances to be addressed, but it should be done in a more consensual manner and with more respect for First Nations with an acknowledgement of a new era. The media has a role to play in reporting the facts and not just the sensational and political issues. Former or current political figures use First Nations conflicts to further their agenda or undermine the current government. Former prime ministers who make their views public are equally guilty, since they did not solve the problem when they had the chance; to come out now and critique, is purely hypocritical.

Over the years, First Nations have received enormous amounts of money from different levels of government, and yet many of them still live in poverty and sometimes squalor. Just increasing funding for one reason or another is not the solution to the plight of Canada's aboriginals. This situation is clearly stated in an article by Ravina Bains and Mark Milke of The Fraser Institute who write:

> *"Canadians have financed growth in the aboriginal welfare state at a pace that eclipsed even the growth of the Canadian welfare state – and unfortunately with little improvement in the well-being of aboriginal Canadians to show for it. That makes it critical to track existing spending and to offer up policy reforms for federal and provincial governments. That is vastly preferable to the tried-and-failed approach of simply throwing more money at failed aboriginal policies."*[8]

Not all members of First Nations are destitute. Many of their members thrive in the current economy. Most First Nation members who live off the reserves are better off economically. Staying on the reserve under the rule of chiefs who exploit them may be the real cause of the problem. It is said that to give a man a fish, feeds him for one day. Teaching him *how to fish*, feeds him for a lifetime.

Any new agreement, while addressing land and resource sharing, should help to create viable independent First Nation communities through education, proper housing and proper utilities with greater transparency. The AFN must also take responsibility for the current failures. Welfare without proper accountability is no longer the solution.

The two Canadian gulfs discussed in this chapter are a huge millstone hanging around the nation's neck. Despite all the acrimony, history shows that both Quebec and the First Nations have been treated fairly. The Royal Proclamation of 1763 recognized First Nations and Indian land title rights. The Quebec Act of 1774 recognized the French in Canada. In the face of a strong disagreement by the British merchant class, the Constitutional Act of 1794 established the legislature in Lower Canada, including a majority of French Canadians. The British North America Act of 1867 confirmed Quebec's unique place in Canada.

The conflicts must be resolved as they constantly create political and economic risk. In the past, conservative politicians have been more willing to collaborate and make amends, and yet they seldom receive the recognition they rightfully deserve.

CHAPTER 5

RACE – AMERICA'S GREAT DIVIDE

Slavery is one of the most heinous crimes against humanity. It has been practiced for centuries and is still perpetrated today in some areas of the world. At the turn of the 19th century, slaves and serfs made up approximately three-quarters of the world's population. It is reported that there are between 12 to 27 million in servitude today. Most of these indentured humans are in South Asia under debt bondage that may last for generations. There also exists a wide trade of women and children forced into sex industries.

Slavery in the United States was firmly established as a legal institution in the 18th and 19th centuries. After the 1776 Declaration of Independence, there was a gradual abolitionist movement in the North, while the South strongly supported slavery and even tried to expand it to the Western Territories. Thus, the country was separated into Maryland as a slavery state and Pennsylvania as a free state; in fact, the country was clearly divided along the Mason Dixon Line.

Abraham Lincoln, the Republican President of The United States, led his country through the one of the most turbulent times in history. His fight against slavery caused the American Civil War, as he said in his inaugural address: "Both parties deprecated war, but one of them would make war rather than let the Nation survive, and the other would accept war rather than let it perish, and the war came." After four years of brutal war, the Confederacy, which was led by many Democrats, collapsed and slavery was abolished.

It took many years before the emancipation of the descendants of the slaves was fully accepted in the United States. Racial discrimination persisted in many southern states until the passage of the Civil Rights Act of 1964. This landmarked piece of legislation "outlawed major forms of discrimination against racial, ethnic, national and religious minorities, and women"[1]. It was started by John F. Kennedy, but his assassination left it the implementation process up to his successor, Lyndon B. Johnson. Despite being a Democrat, many members of his party, mostly from the South, opposed the bill. Using his political capital as president, he had the support of a majority of Republicans in both Houses, and was able to pass both the Civil Rights Act (1964) and the Voting Rights Act (1965).

Despite the official signing of these two ground-breaking pieces of legislation, the U.S. still had rampant racial discrimination. This gave rise to the Civil Rights movement led by Martin Luther King Jr. who, until his assassination, used nonviolent civil disobedience to push for civil rights for African-Americans. But between 1964 and 1970, a number of inner city riots in black communities undermined the support from white Americans. The rise of the Black Panther Movement challenged the black establishment's nonviolent approach and cooperative attitude – this did not help the situation. In fact, it caused dissention among those who believed in segregation and others who supported self-determination. This division still exists today among certain black leaders.

Over the years, and through much struggle, African Americans have made much progress. Thurgood Marshall was the first African-American appointed to the U.S. Supreme Court. He was part of the majority decision in favour of the right to abortion in the landmark 1973 case of *Roe v. Wade*. Marshall consistently supported rulings upholding a strong protection of individual rights and liberal interpretations of controversial social issues. He is revered as one of the first civil rights crusaders of the last century. When he retired, he was replaced in 1991 by Justice

Clarence Thomas. During the scrutiny hearings, Thomas was accused of sexual harassment by Anita Hill. The committee did not find sufficient evidence and appointed him in a narrow 52-48 margin. To this day, Justice Thomas, considered a conservative, is vilified by some black leaders and the liberal left.

Thomas, who rarely makes speeches outside of the Supreme Court, recently delivered a speech at Palm Beach Atlantic University:

> *"The worst I have been treated was by northern liberal elites. The absolute worst I have ever been treated."*[2]

In fact, as the 2014 mid-term and 2016 Presidential elections approach, a new movie on the subject of his Senate appointment hearings will be aired for what can be inferred as purely political reasons.

Unfortunately, the treatment he refers to, is not only festered upon Justice Thomas, but is increasingly used to attack any black conservative in America who dares to speak up against Obama's policies. In this vein, it is noteworthy to mention the NAACP's disgraceful record of having never defended a black conservative.

Today, the fields of sports, entertainment, media and politics can count many African-Americans among the elites of these fields. Among the most recent ones are Secretary of State Condoleezza Rice and Colin Powell, athletes Tiger Woods and Michael Jordan, to name but a few. However, many black leaders, rightly or wrongly, are not satisfied with what they see as slow progress, and they are fixated on 'race' as a factor for every issue they choose to fight for.

The race card has been played by the Democrats for years:

- Al Gore, on July 16, 1998, speaking at an NAACP convention said: "They are in favor of affirmative action if you can dunk the basketball or sink a three point shot, but they are not in favor of it if you merely have the potential to be a leader in your community ... And bring people together and lift people up and make this a better country. Don't tell me we've got a color blind society."

- A Missouri Democratic Party Ad., in Nov. 1998 read: "When you don't vote you let another church explode. When you don't vote you allow another cross to burn. When you don't vote you let another assault wound a brother or a sister. When you don't vote you let the Republicans continue to cut school lunches and head start".
- Julian Bond, Former NAACP Chair, said the following in February, 2006: "Their idea of equal rights is the American flag and the Confederate Swastika flying side by side."

This brings us to the election of Barack Hussein Obama as the first black President of the United States. According to the Central Intelligence Agency's World Factbook, the United States' Demographic profile in a July 2007 estimate was as follows:

"White 79.96%, black 12.85%, Asian 4.43%, Amerindian and Alaska native 0.97%, native Hawaiian and other Pacific islander 0.18%, two or more races 1.61% ... a separate listing for Hispanic is not included but about 15.1% of the total US population is Hispanic."[3]

Race was certainly not a factor in the overall result, because his majority could not have been reached without a substantial percentage of the white vote.

Accountability does not exist without transparency. To obfuscate issues, thereby discarding transparency, is common in politics and more frequently the word 'racism' is being used to that effect. Having promised to be a conciliator and not a divider, President Obama has only succeeded in exacerbating the divisions along economic, and still racial lines.

Certain political pundits and peddlers of racial divide have taken to the air waves to portray any opposition to the President's policies as being of a racist nature. The 'race card' is being used by the Democrats to promote or defend their liberal policies, which under Obama, continue to fail to address the real problems that affect America in general and the black community in particular. The African-American community had high hopes when Obama was elected, but the race rhetoric has not stopped, so much so that Rep. Andre Carson (D-In), in an address to the black congress caucus on Aug 22, 2011, said: "We have seen change in congress, but the congress *(intelligible)* point the Tea Party is stopping that change, and this is beyond symbolic change, this is, this is the effort that we're ... seeing of Jim Crow, some of these folks in congress right now would love to see us as second class citizens. Some of them in congress right now with this Tea Party movement would love to see you and me, – I'm sorry *(unintelligible)* hanging on a tree, some of them right now in congress ... are comfortable with where we were fifty and sixty years ago. But this is a new day with a black president and the congressional black caucus."

Racism exists. But it is not just blacks who suffer: there is anti-Hispanic, anti-Semitic, and even ageist sentiment in the country.

In 2013, a highly publicized trial that virtually everyone watched on CNN and left-wing media, introduced a new racial category when describing George Zimmerman, the accused in a shooting of a black youth in Florida – Zimmerman became the first man in America to be described by media as "White-Hispanic". Florida has a 'stand your ground' law, which allows the use of a gun when threatened. An FBI investigation prior to the trial showed no evidence of racial bias.

When a lawyer for the Martin family said that she was a 'social engineer', it certainly changed the role of lawyers within the justice system. Should we interpret the law based on social circumstances? One of the more noble goals of modern democracy is to erect clear boundaries between politics and the criminal justice system, especially in cases as politically loaded as the Zimmerman/Martin case.

This same justice system saw the acquittal of O.J. Simpson, who allegedly murdered a white woman and a white man and was found not guilty. But finding Zimmerman not guilty was apparently a travesty of justice because the victim happened to be black?

The media turned the Zimmerman case into a race-baiting frenzy, which as horrible as it may have been was in no way extraordinary, according to American cultural standards.

Even the president found his opportunity to play the race card. In an unprecedented White House briefing on July 19, 2013, a week after the verdict, the president made some contradictory remarks when addressing the continued protests and marches in the U.S. Among the remarks, he said that: "When I said that if I had a son, he would look like Trayvon *(the victim in the case)*, what I meant was he could have been me 35 years ago ... If a white boy were involved the outcome and aftermath might have been different." He also concluded that: "each successive generation is making progress in changing attitudes. Things are getting better – we are becoming a more perfect union."

Not having learned a lesson from the Zimmerman case, the media and the peddlers of racism did it again in the unfortunate case of Michael Brown in Ferguson, Missouri. When an 18-year old black man was shot by a white policeman, once again it was turned into a racist act. Without any of the facts being known, thousands of protesters looted the town and conducted violent protests for several nights. While the disparity between whites and blacks continues in the United Sates, what we should be concerned about is the role of the media in the United States and around the world as concerns race relations and its role in politics.

On August 14, 2014, one of Canada's major news outlets, CTV, broadcast a 'report' on the troubles in Ferguson. In the 11 p.m. national edition news story, the reporter clearly editorialised on the riots that had been raging in the town for three days prior. Looting and Molotov cocktails were not uncommon in Ferguson, but the anchor's comments were focussed on the use of pictures of the alleged victim by the U.S media. The reporter took the position that these pictures showed Brown as a gang member. Presumably, his suggestion was that pictures of the angelic college boy should have been used. This report gave the wrong impression here in Canada that blacks are being killed by white cops with complete abandon.

All wrongful death is wrong. In the U.S the police are quick to use weapons against unharmed civilians. However, reporters should not express either personal opinions or make statements that may later, when full investigations are concluded prove to be wrong.

In fact, on August 15, it was reported that the name of the officer had been released together with further information about a possible robbery that took place before the confrontation between the police and the victim. The 'angelic' boy, who was over six feet and 200 lbs, was seen shoving the owner of the store after stealing his cigars.

The news media has a responsibility to wait for the facts before editorializing. Racism already a huge problem does not need further exploitation by an opinionated biased media. . Canadians receive the majority of their news feeds from U.S. sources. To be sure we are getting factual data and not sensationalism that sells ads, we need to ensure that all the facts are checked and re-checked. We want to make sure that certain factions, here in Canada, do not get inflamed by the media. We have a moral obligation to wait for all the facts to be known, before judgement is passed. Responsibility should be the priority, not sensationalism.

As the race for the White House got tighter during the 2012 elections, the claim of 'racism' was used as an excuse for Obama's decline in the polls. The question is: which art of the president is being targeted by racists? Is it his mother's white side or his father's African side?

Obama could not have been elected in 2008 and 2012 if a substantial percentage of the white electorate had not voted for him. Those claiming racism for his decline in popularity should instead look at his failed policies rather than the colour of his skin.

After his re-election in 2012, as the President's abysmal policies continued to plague the economy and other areas of government, the 'race card industry' went into overdrive. Led by many in the African-American community, and backed by the DNC and mainstream media, every opportunity was taken to poison the political arena with ideological nonsense.

Many black leaders have made a career of the civil rights movement; they have to perpetuate the status quo despite the fact that times have changed. And even more cynically, the racism excuse is used to portray legitimate criticisms of the president's policies.

President Obama has not delivered on many of his promises, but the one demographic that has sustained the most disappointment from his lack of initiative is the black population who so adamantly supported him. Indeed, unemployment is rampant among the black American youth. Race relations continue to suffer. Statistics paint a very grim portrait of Obama`s failures in the black community.

How are race relations in the United States?

	July 2013	*Jan 2010*
Very or fairly good	*52%*	*72%*
Fairly or very bad	*44%*	*23%*

Source NBC News WSJ Poll of 1.000 adults

The virtual collapse of family and its values is a major cause of problems in the black community. The outdoor drug trade is a huge problem for blacks. Drug gangs on Chicago's South side are the reason for such a high number of black on black murders. There seems to be a disconnect between the black community and black leaders. They refuse to believe that some responsibility lies with the community as they ignore some startling facts: "While the black community makes up 13% of the population, African Americans committed more than half of all murders, and 93% of black murder victims were killed by other blacks (Bureau of Justice Statistics 1976-2005)."

The media is dedicated to the narrative that whites continue to hold blacks back from achieving success. Many media outlets are invested in the problem to increase their audience. In the world of cable news, MSNBC has taken a prominent role in perpetuating the race divide. The majority of opinion hosts on the channel's programs make some of the most outrageous statements, either to gain notoriety or to build a shield for Obama's failed policies.

On June 15, 2013, Salamisha Tillet of the University of Pennsylvania made the following comment on the MSNBC show, *Melissa Harris-Perry*:

> *"Well, I think, the Census just released data, so part of it is the changing racial demographics in the United States. For the first time in American history, children born under the age of five are racial; the majority of them are racial and ethnic minorities in the U.S.*
>
> *So I think that there's a kind of moral panic, a fear of the end of whiteness that we've been seeing a long time in that I think, you know, Obama's ascension as President kind of symbolizes to a certain degree. And so I think this is one response to that sense that there's a decreasing white majority in the country and that women's bodies and white women's bodies in particular are obviously a crucial way of reproducing whiteness, white supremacy, white privilege. And so I think it's just a kind of clamping down on women's bodies, in particular white women's bodies, even though women of color are really caught in the fray."*[4]

When the media encourages these types of comments, it is no wonder that the fringe can make their statements even more vitriolic. On a "Black Power Radio" broadcast, New Black Panther Party Chief of Staff, Michelle Williams, made the following comment:

> *"The Republicans hate black people, and for all the black people that are republicans I ask you on this day. This 12th day of August 2012. I ask you this day when did you lose your dignity and lay down for these damn crackers who mean this black community no good. They have shown this, their history has shown this so if white people are mad because I continue to call them crackers on the day that you stop referring to me as a n*** … and treating my black community as a n*** I let (inaudible) my damned pinkie toe let up off your honky asses. But other than that you'd better believe my foot on your god damn mother f***necks"*[5]

This type of comment is not only reserved for fringe activists, but even respected elected officials are emboldened to make outrageous comments about race in America. On the John Fredericks Show of July 20, 2012, Louise Lucas, Virginia State Senator (D-Portsmouth) said:

> *"Let's be really clear about Mitt Romney is speaking to a group of people out there who don't like folks like president Barack Obama in any elected or leadership position ... he is speaking to the fringe out there who do not want to see anybody other than a white person in a leadership position... I absolutely believe it's all about race and for the first time in my life I've been able to convince my children finally that racism is alive and well."*[6]

As the president's signature policy, the Affordable Care Act continues to face increasing problems; many Democrats are quick to pull out the 'race card' to explain his failures. For example, here is Senator Reid on a KNPR Radio show:

> *"My counterpart, Mitch McConnell, said at the beginning of the presidency of Barack Obama that he had one goal, and that is to defeat Obama and make sure he wasn't re-elected and that's how they legislate in the Senate. It was really bad, and we've been now seven months into the second term of the President's and they haven't changed much. It's been obvious that they're doing everything they can to make him fail. And I hope. I hope, and say this seriously, I hope that it's based on substance; not the fact that he's an African American."*[7]

Oprah Winfrey, a model of success, who has made millions of dollars, mostly from a huge support base of white women went to England to promote her movie '*The Butler*' and gave an interview to BBC's Will Gompertz and said:

> *"There's a level of disrespect for the office that occurs in some cases and maybe even many cases because he's African*

> *American," ... There's no question about that. And it's the kind of thing no one ever says, but everybody's thinking it."*[8]

She followed the above comment with:

> *"There are still generations of people, older people, who were born and bred and marinated in it, in that prejudice and racism, and they just have to die."*[9]

The president, while at first not openly playing the race game, has started to do so to revive his failing popularity. As we approach the 2014 elections, the tone is getting more acerbic. It is actually beginning to sound like his presidency is no longer viable as his policies fall by the wayside. His comments seem to be more pessimistic than his renowned 'hope and change' campaign statements. In an interview with David Remnick of *The New Yorker*, Obama said:

> *"There's no doubt that there's some folks who just really dislike me because they don't like the idea of a black President," ... Now, the flip side of it is there are some black folks and maybe some white folks who really like me and give me the benefit of the doubt precisely because I'm a black President."*[10]

We should not be surprised about this turn of events; in fact, maybe we should have taken a warning when on September 16, 2009, former President Jimmy Carter said on nightly NBC's "*Nightly News*": "I think an overwhelming portion of the intensely demonstrated animosity towards President Barack Obama is based on the fact that he is a black man. That he is African-American."

There was so much hope when Obama was elected. People of different ethnic backgrounds expected so much from him. However, he brought criticisms upon himself by making grandiose promises during his campaign. Now, even the black community is beginning to question whether he has done enough. Marcia Fudge, a U.S. Representative for Ohio's 11th District a Democrat, (D-OH) and Chair of the Congressional Black

Caucus complained to Obama in a March 11, 2013 letter: "You have publicly expressed your commitment to retaining diversity within your cabinet, however, the people you have chosen to appoint in this new term have hardly been reflective of this country's diversity."

Unfortunately, for some members of the black community in America, not enough has been done. It is true that it is extremely difficult to erase the abominations of the past, and that the indignities of slavery cannot be glossed over. However, much change has happened over the years. Many African-Americans have risen to the challenges and have been successful in many aspects of civic, economic and artistic life. Continuously playing the race card to justify bad policies is not the road to reconciliation.

Too many black leaders view race as an opportunity to make themselves seen and heard. They quote Martin Luther King and Nelson Mandela, but they ignore the fact that these two great leaders professed reconciliation during their fight for freedom and human rights. Instead of perpetuating the great American divide, they should heed the message of Nelson Mandela's May 10, 1994 inauguration speech as South African president wherein he stated:

> *"We understand it still that there is no easy road to freedom. We know it well that none of us acting alone can achieve success. We must therefore act together as a united people, for national reconciliation, for nation building, for the birth of a new world. Let there be justice for all. Let there be peace for all. Let there be work, bread, water and salt for all. Never, never and never again shall it be that this beautiful land will again experience the oppression of one by another and suffer the indignity of being the skunk of the world. Let freedom reign."*[11]

Regrettably racism will continue long after Obama leaves office, because in some U.S. academic circles it is seen, by definition, as a white only problem: "A racist is one who is both privileged and socialized on the basis of race by a white supremacist (racist) system. The term applies to all white people (i.e., people of European descent) living in the United States, regardless of class, gender, religion, culture or sexuality. By this definition, people of color cannot be racists, because as peoples within the U.S. system, they do not have the power to back up their prejudices, hostilities, or acts of discrimination. (This does not deny the existence of such prejudices, hostilities, acts of rage or discrimination)." [12]

The disapproval of President Obama is not about skin color, but rather about his failed policies. Once in office, he could not fulfill his promises, and if he did, he used a dictatorial approach to do so. Those who believe that he has not done enough will continue to play the race card. His original aspirations of "hope and change" could quickly make him the frontrunner to replace Jimmy Carter as the *'worst president of the United States'*. At that point, he will be accused of being the wrong president for the African American community. It is too bad that buyers' remorse has already set in, as famed actor Morgan Freeman informed his host Michel Martin on the NPR show, "*Tell Me More*":

> *"Contrary to the prevailing wisdom, Barack Hussein Obama is* not *America's first black president ... He is the country's "first mixed-race president." The first black president, Freeman continued, has not as yet "arisen."*[13]

With race being made by some into the predominant issue of his presidency – as opposed to achievement – Obama's overall dismal performance may produce an environment where the notion of electing another Democrat African-American President in the foreseeable future, becomes improbable.

Racism cuts both ways. There are both white and black racists. It is unfortunate that this belief and resulting actions still exist today. The actions and statements of prominent people like Cliven Bundy, Donald Sterling and Rep. Bennie Thompson (D-MS), who called Justice Thomas an 'Uncle Tom', should be condemned by both the right and the left. In this diverse world there is no place left for this disgusting and shameful behaviour.

In the United Sates there is a paradox where racism is concerned. Democrats generally benefit from a greater proportion of the African American vote. But too often, history is ignored. For example, Abraham Lincoln was the first in a long-line of republicans who helped President Johnson pass the Civil Rights Act while Richard Nixon desegregated Southern schools. They were all republicans who do not receive the proper credit for what they did for the African-American community. Is this conservative humility or plain stupidity?

CHAPTER 6

THE CARBON WAR

The state of the environment has become a very important issue, and in the past two decades it has reached quasi-religious proportions. The world is now divided into two camps: those who believe that climate change is man-made and those who believe that it is a natural cyclical occurrence.

Whichever side of the argument one may stand on, there is no doubt that something must be done to decrease pollution and its effect on the planet. But the question of how to do that remains a bone of contention. The left believes that we should ban everything which is carbon based; the right, on the other hand, is less inclined to jump onto a bandwagon for drastic policies to curb pollution or pay for it through taxes and other measures.

The right has, however, proposed many alternatives, albeit mostly market-driven, to abate the rate of pollution. And yet, the debate rages on, because seemingly the left wants an 'all or nothing' solution, but in reality they are hiding a much larger agenda.

In order to be able to have a constructive debate, we must first examine the two sides of the argument. This is exactly what this book will do by exploring the issue in light of both the environmentalist and the conservationist point of view. Each side has its own set of beliefs, but over the years it is the interpretation of terms used to describe the problem which has caused much of the differences.

Sustainability has become a term for division rather than a starting point for problem solving. One would have thought that conservation and conservative ideology would be a good fit. But this has not been so. Given these stark ideological differences, it is important that we examine how the environmental movement evolved into a leftist cabal, and how the conservatives have or have not responded to a barrage of criticisms which have at different times been justified and others, totally misrepresented.

What do environmentalists want?

To start understanding where environmentalists come from, we should look at the history of environmentalism and its origin, and how the whole issue has been used by some to further a totally different agenda. We are not going to discuss the merits or controversies generated by scientific reports prepared by both sides of the argument. Rather, we shall examine the effects of policies and consequences emanating from international conferences on the environment.

In 1969, U-Thant, then Director-general of the United Nations declared:

> *"The Third World War will be the war to save the environment"*

These words may have been the catalyst for the creation and existence of the ever-growing number of U.N. conferences, committees and reports which today dominate the often one-sided discussions on the environment. The most significant of these conferences are the **Stockholm Conference** in 1972, and the **United Nations Conference on Environment and Development Earth Summit (UNCED)**, held in Rio de Janeiro in June, 1992. Many environmental agreements were established there, including the **United Nations Framework Convention on Climate Change** (**UNFCCC** or **FCCC**). Maurice Strong, a Canadian, was Secretary-General of that conference. The Kyoto Protocol on greenhouse gases was subsequently negotiated, and came into force in 2005.

One of the most contested terms that has come out of these U.N. conferences was the notion of ***'sustainable development'*** which was first defined in 1987 when the U.N. World Commission on Environment and Development published Gro Harlem Brundtland's report *Our Common Future*:

> *"development that meets the needs of the present without compromising the ability of future generations to meet their own needs."*[1]

After the Rio conference, Strong took a lead role in advancing the notion of sustainable development through his involvement in many organizations including: Earth Council, the Earth Charter movement, the World Resources Institute where he acted as chairman, the Board of the International Institute for Sustainable Development, the Stockholm Environment Institute, The Africa-America Institute, the Institute of Ecology in Indonesia, the Beijer Institute of the Royal Swedish Academy of Sciences, and others. These organizations are responsible for contributing momentum to the climate change/global warming movement. This movement has no doubt given rise to the proliferation of research and reports that ultimately wind up promoting – even if only implicitly – a 'cap and trade' system and a market for the trade of carbon dioxide emissions.

What followed was a slew of policies, protocols and regulations to control carbon emissions, and of course, tax increases in another form. The left embraced these policies because it suits their agenda of redistribution of wealth.

In summary, the idea behind carbon emission trading is that those who emit greenhouse gases (GHG) do not bear the full costs of their actions; therefore, to be fair to the welfare of others, they should be made to bare additional costs to mitigate the costs of GHG that will be borne by future generations.

This idea, however, has not done anything to improve the environment but has made some people extremely wealthy through the trade of emissions mainly through the Chicago Climate Exchange (CCX).

Interestingly, the formation of CCX was funded by the Joyce Foundation who had Barack Obama as its director. In an excellent article by Judi McLeod, she explains:

> *"The 'privately-owned' Chicago Climate Exchange is heavily influenced by Obama cohorts Al Gore and Maurice Strong ...*
>
> *For years now Strong and Gore have been cashing in on that lucrative cottage industry known as man-made global warming."*[2]

While some supporters of carbon trading have made millions, governments have been forced to enact policies and regulations to combat so-called climate change. Millions of dollars are being diverted from the economy to support programs such as carbon capture, solar and wind energy production. While the use of alternative sources of energy is a worthwhile endeavour, it should not be done with a single purpose in mind – that is the use of taxes to fund these projects. Too often tax payers' dollars have either been squandered or lost due to a lack of demand or the high costs of producing energy from these alternative sources.

Examples of failures abound:

- Spain in the late 2000s offered large subsidies to promote the growth of solar-energy projects. In addition, banks loaned the renewable-energy companies an estimated €30 billion. As a result, the amount of solar-power capacity installed in Spain far surpassed official government targets, increasing the tariff.[3]
- Dalton McGuinty's Green Energy Act was a spectacular policy blunder, based on a string of faulty premises: that coal emissions were killing us (they weren't), that we'd soon be running out of fossil fuel (we aren't, and Ontario doesn't use much anyway), and that switching to green energy would help save the planet (not in our lifetime). As the price of fossil fuels went up and up, the accepted idea was that competition for renewables would only increase. Just one problem: The price of fossil fuels has plummeted ... Today, the wind power generated in On-

tario is both expensive and useless. The province actually pays hundreds of millions of dollars to other jurisdictions to take surplus power off its hands.[4]

- In Britain, a new analysis of government and industry figures shows that wind turbine owners received £1.2billion in the form of a consumer subsidy, paid by supplementing electricity bills in 2013. Through this 12,000 people were employed to produce an effective £100,000 subsidy on each job ... The level of support from subsidies in some cases is so high that jobs are effectively supported to the extent of £1.3million each. [5]
- In a 245 to 161 vote, lawmakers passed the No More Solyndras Act, named for the solar panel manufacturer that declared bankruptcy in 2011, shortly after receiving a $535 million loan guarantee from the Obama administration.[6]

When these investments fail, governments seek alternatives to make up for their losses. As revenues from gasoline taxes decrease because of the use of electric cars, politicians seek to raise taxes somewhere else. Under the guise of promoting the reduction of carbon dioxide emissions, Rep. Ed Orcutt of Washington State declared the ludicrous notion that cyclists somehow endanger the environment:

> *"increased heart rate and respiration," the act of riding a bike "results in greater emissions of carbon dioxide from the rider ... bicycling is bad for the environment and bike riders should have to pay a tax to help maintain the state's roads."*[7]

These types of ideas seem to have their origins from way back in the late sixties. Spurred by the events of the last half of the twentieth century, many young people gathered together to protest everything from the Vietnam war, poverty, a possible nuclear holocaust and of course, all things that threatened the environment. From this awareness of the environment's health grew an organization known as Greenpeace.

In all fairness, the early activities of Greenpeace gave the world a lot of food for thought. Through their protests and with the help of the media, they raised awareness about nuclear proliferation, the killing of baby seals, the dumping of toxic waste and other environmental calamities. Greenpeace must be given credit for bringing environmental awareness to the masses. Unfortunately the common environmentalists' point of view that humans are the problem became the center piece of their mantra as Patrick Moore writes:

> *"There is an unfortunate tendency among environmental activists to characterize the human species as a negative influence on earth. We are likened to a malignant cancer that is spreading, threatening to destroy biodiversity, upsetting the balance of nature, causing the collapse of the global system."*[8]

Over the years, Greenpeace evolved into a more extreme and intolerant organization as its members abandoned logic and science as the bases for their arguments. They became radicalized and have been taken over by Marxists and far-left groups who use the environment to promote anti-capitalism and anti-globalization. Indirectly, they derive a lot of strengths from the 1988 creation of the United Nations Intergovernmental Panel on Climate Change (IPCC), which together with Al Gore, were awarded the 2007 Nobel Peace Prize for warning the world of the dangers of climate change caused by humans.

Many of these young environmental activists from the 1970s are now adults and are often part of today's academia. Indoctrination by these environmentalists is now entrenched in schools and universities. Many institutions now offer programs that embrace 'sustainability' as the basis for their courses. The problem is that 'sustainability' today can cover a multiple number of interpretations. Education is good, but do we use science and logic in the courses taught or just rhetoric? More importantly, who teaches these courses? Are they engineers, economists, biochemists, biologists and other scientists, or are they just human-hating humanities academics and historians?

For instance, at the University of Delaware the environmental program contains no science at all. Kathleen Kerr, the head of the residence program uses a program on sustainability to:

> *"debunk the "myths" that sustainability is mostly about the environment" and that "sustainability is primarily a scientific and technical problem." Rather, in their view, sustainability has over a dozen "social justice aspects"*[9]

Numerous academics are now injecting 'environmental racism'(ER) into the discourse. Although a pure definition of the term is still debatable, the intent however is to link the effect of environmental degradation on minorities. According to this 'idea' racial discrimination is a major aspect of environmental policymaking and enforcement. While this rhetoric is popular in the U.S., it is gradually being inserted into the Canadian discourse. The Centre for Environmental Health Equity (CEHE) is certainly promoting it through their published papers, under the guise of environmental justice:

> *"In Canada's urban centres, where populations are not so clearly defined along lines of race, ER is not so apparent–and possibly not present at all. However, in many of Canada's more remote First Nation communities the same cannot be said."*[10]

While it is true that in Canada environmental racism is not too apparent, it did not stop Calgary Alderman Gian Carlo Cara, to label those who did not agree with his views on the environment as 'environmental racists', and at the same time expand social engineering policies.

The central point about the legitimacy of the 'sustainability' claim is whether it has more to do with politics than the environment. Perhaps only time will tell.

Conservatives and Conservation

Often ignored in the debate about the environment is the commitment that conservatives have made to improve the environment over the years. Sadly, the media does not report on the achievements or policies of conservative politicians when it comes to this subject.

The focus of any discussion is always about how the environment is being destroyed by conservatives because of their commitment to free market solutions. The views and arguments made by conservatives are minimized to suit the rhetoric of environmentalists, who by the way, very often use violence to support their cause. To this effect, it is important to look at the contribution made by conservative politicians to abate pollution while providing solutions that improve quality of life without using taxpayers' money to promote their ideas.

In 2006, Brian Mulroney was honoured as the greenest prime minister in Canadian history.

- His most acknowledged accomplishment is the (1980) Canada/United States treaty on acid rain. Our lakes were dying due to heavy pollution from emissions from U.S. industries, which caused the water to become too acidic. Ontario lakes are the most vulnerable because of the geology of the Canadian Shield. He negotiated and persuaded a somewhat reluctant President Ronald Reagan to have U.S. industries reduce their levels of acid emissions. Our lakes are in recovery due to this agreement.
- The use of chemicals like ***chlorofluorocarbon*** (CFC) was damaging the ozone layer. Through the 1987 *Montreal Protocol on Substances that Deplete the Ozone Layer*, Mulroney was able to convince the nations of the world to halt the production of these chemicals, and as a result the damage to the ozone layer has been greatly reduced.
- The cod stocks were vanishing due to overfishing, Mulroney took the unpopular decision to halt overfishing. The 1992 Cod Moratorium has helped promote the slow recovery of the species.
- He also created eight new national parks and ushered in the Environmental Act.
- In October 2006, the Harper government released the Clean Air Act which promoted the reduction of GHG by as much as

20% by 2020; also announced were tax credits and $345 million of funding and other measures to promote the use of biodiesel and ethanol.

- The Conservative 2006 budget included a 15–25% tax-credit on monthly passes for transit users.
- There have been several agreements with provincial governments that provide funding for the expansion of transit and commuter infrastructures.
- In the 2009 Federal Budget the government introduced billions of dollars in spending on the environment and green initiatives.

Contrary to popular belief, the Republican Party in the United States has been very active on environmental issues. Newt Gingrich, the former House Speaker has been an advocate of green conservatism, which stands for efforts to conserve natural resources while protecting human and environmental health.

Conservation has long been a tradition of the Republican Party. The conservation movement thrived under President Theodore Roosevelt as he promoted a crusade to protect natural resources. This included fisheries, wildlife management, water and soil conservation and the preservation of forestry. Today the conservation movement has broadened its goals to include biodiversity.

Ronald Reagan, the president who once opposed the treaty on acid rain, is often misunderstood for his stance against the environmentalist movement. He did not believe that the environment was a priority, but he also defended it when he said there is an:

> *"absolute necessity of waging all-out war against the debauching of the environment ... The bulldozer mentality of the past is a luxury we can no longer afford. Our roads and other public projects must be planned to prevent the destruction of scenic resources and to avoid needlessly upsetting the ecological balance."*[11]

Reagan established agencies to protect the environment and address many pressing environmental issues; these include the California Air Resources Board to combat smog and the Tahoe Regional Planning Agency to protect Lake Tahoe. He opposed the construction of two dams on the Eel River and the Feather River. He merged two wilderness areas which will forever prevent the expansion of highways through the Sierra Nevada Mountains.

In addition, the United States Environmental Protection Agency (EPA) was proposed and created by none other than President Richard Nixon. It was first formed to protect human health and the environment by enforcing the laws written and passed by Congress. However, the EPA has been hijacked by President Obama to promote a socialist enforcement of laws to promote his policies on climate change through what is known as 'command and control' mechanisms.

Canada's Prime Minister Stephen Harper is often regarded by environmentalists as the proverbial boogie man. Despite the fact that his government withdrew from the Kyoto Protocol in December 2011, his government has put in place many policies to address environmental issues. The reasons for the withdrawal were based on sound economic data that saw Canada going into a possible recession if the protocol parameters had been accepted. What is often ignored is that the Harper government has passed a number of legislative measures to improve the environment.

The actions of the Harper government may be criticized and vilified by environmental groups, however it is inaccurate to say that this government is ineffective when it comes to environmental protection. Conservatives around the world have taken action to minimize the effects of a changing environment. Can they do better? Of course, but to have an informed debate there must be a clear reporting of the facts.

Do we have a balanced future?

The great debate of the past 45 years has revolved around climate change and global warming. The problem is that there has been no real solution because the protagonist cannot agree on the source of the problem and therefore cannot find common ground for a solution.

Environmentalists clearly use the environment to reshape the economic landscape. Conservatives, however, want a solution which is more economical and market-based. Unfortunately, many also choose to ignore solid scientific data, fearing interference with a profit-generating economy. Can we find a balance for the sake of humanity? Is the debate truly about the environment or is it about politics? The real question is how do we find equitable solutions to address complex environmental issues, without the use of rhetoric?

The fact is that we are a carbon-based species. After all, close to 90% of what we consume contains carbon-related content. Transportation, plastics, virtually every household good has a carbon/oil component. We cannot just dismiss this fact and decide to use alternative sources of either energy or materials to please environmentalists. It can be a gradual process, and should not be an excuse for more regulations and control that favour some and discriminate against others. In this debate, there is an economic component that must not be ignored.

It is becoming more difficult to reconcile the two sides as the public becomes ever more skeptical about the effects of climate change. Despite apocalyptic reports by the media who seize on every natural catastrophe as proof of global warming, people are becoming fatigued with the increase of rhetoric and deterioration of solutions. In the midst of a world recession, it is hard to ask the public to pay more taxes or higher commodity prices to correct the 'ills' of climate change.

Fossil fuels have become the culprit behind global warming. Scientific reports, albeit often paid for by organizations that support climate change theory, continuously produce data that shows a continued path towards an environment apocalypse – contrary findings by other scientists are either ignored or demonized.

The latest pronouncements by President Obama on climate change are nothing but a power grab which is established by exerting more government control. His position that coal should be eliminated will cause enormous harm to the economy. Ironically, all his regulations will have absolutely no effect on global carbon emissions as the third world continues to use coal.

Part of the debate centres around the approval of the Keystone XL pipeline which will deliver oil from Alberta to refineries in the United States. This move is actually approve of by 74% of Americans and 68% of Canadians. This issue is very controversial because for environmentalists, the oil sands have become their preferred target, while on the other side, the economy is the priority. Obama has taken a curious approach to the issue. In a speech on Climate change delivered at Georgetown University in June, 2013, Obama stated that Keystone will be approved: *"only if this project does not significantly exacerbate the problem of carbon pollution."*

Obama's grandiose speeches are full of rhetoric and platitudes but contain little substance. The oil in Alberta will not stay in the ground whether he approves the Keystone pipeline or not. Alberta will extract the oil and simply ship it somewhere else. The rest of the world is not entirely on his side on this issue. While he was making his big speech, on the other side of the world German Chancellor Angela Merkel, backed by England's Prime Minister David Cameron, was spoiling the EU's plans to set a maximum limit on vehicle carbon emissions. Merkel believes a maximum limit could damage the German auto industry, especially luxury carmakers:

> *"At a time when we're spending days sitting here talking about employment, we must pay attention not to weaken our own industrial base despite the need to make progress on environmental protection."*[12]

But mostly ignored by the media, is a serious and unbiased reporting of who is behind the opposition to the pipeline. Tom Steyer, founder of Farallon Capital and a friend of President Obama, is opposed to Keystone, despite the fact that he made his millions from investments in fossil fuels. As reported by Fox News:

> *"One of Farallon's biggest holdings is in U.S. pipeline company Kinder Morgan, which has plans to expand a major competitor to Keystone – the TransMountain pipeline. It carries tar sands oil from Edmonton to British Columbia's west coast for export to Asia. If Kinder Morgan gets approval for the expansion, TransMountain would carry 900,000 barrels of tar sands oil every day."* [13]

Furthermore, environmentalists use the term 'tar sands' in their rhetoric to further their viewpoint and make the source sound more dirty. The reality is, the oil companies are cleaning a toxic wasteland contaminated by oil. As Patrick Moore writes:

> *"Is it not a fact they are leaving the sand cleaner than when they found it? If it is desirable to clean up an oil spill in the sea or underground, surely it is acceptable to clean up the oil sands."*[14]

Unknown to most people, some environmental activist funding is cloaked in secrecy. Environmentalists are well funded by several organizations around the world who give money to causes that oppose everything that they believe may harm the environment. But in so doing they are just playing into the hands of organizations that either have a political or economic agenda.

Vivian Krause has brilliantly investigated and exposed many environmental organizations for their duplicity, especially their funding sources. The many organizations include:

- The Rockefeller Brothers Fund
- The Dogwood Initiative
- The Tides Foundation
- The William & Flora Hewlett Foundation
- Training Resources for the Environmental Community (TREC)
- The Pew Charitable Trusts ("Pew"), created by the founder of Sun Oil

- The Hewlett foundation and the Gordon & Betty Moore Foundation
- The Canadian Boreal Initiative (CBI), largely supported by the forest industry
- The San Francisco-based Consultative Group for Biological Diversity (CGBD)
- Securing America's Future Energy Foundation

These organizations have an ulterior motive as Krause points out:

> *"American foundations aim to reduce fossil fuel dependence to stop global warming and strengthen U.S. national, energy and economic security. That's clear. What's unclear is whether they fund conservation initiatives in Canada, in part, to foster U.S. energy security."* [15]

So, if this assertion is correct – which it most likely is – what can Canada and the rest of the world do to safeguard both their sovereignty and economic future?

First and foremost, aggrandizing politicians must tell the truth. What they have done in the past has amounted to no improvement; in fact, carbon emissions are still rising. Secondly, scientists must take responsibility for their 'end of days' threats and their assertions that all extreme weather and natural disasters are caused by climate change. While scientists produce the data, they unfortunately never challenge radicals' use of their findings to advance their own agenda. And more importantly, scientists must demonstrate that their findings are always supported by peer reviews, which in the past have been less than ingenuous. And lastly, economists must produce evidence of the true costs of decarbonisation. After all, there is no such thing as a free lunch, and in this case, consumers will have hell to pay for it.

The answer may well be found in an international approach to the problem, not a Kyoto-like protocol. It must be one that gets everybody to sign on the bottom line. For example, every year, China adds twice the equivalent of Japan's yearly emission. As a result we cannot have carbon reductions in the industrialised world and not in the developing world. Shifting production from industrialised countries to developing countries does not produce fewer emissions, but in fact, may produce more because their technologies may not be as efficient.

Nobody denies that the planet has experienced a warming of less than one degree centigrade over the past century, as reported by the World Meteorological Organization. Nobody denies that there has been an increase in GHG; the key dispute is the correlation between the two. What is often ignored is the research of University of Guelph economist Ross McKitrick who found there has not been any statistically significant warming of the climate for the past 19 years; a discovery reinforced in a recent report by the United Nations Intergovernmental Panel on Climate Change that recognised this global warming "hiatus"

Recent natural disasters – a flood in Calgary, flash floods in Toronto, frequent floods in China and hurricane Sandy in the United States have immediately been linked to climate change. To infer from these scenarios that we are going to die soon as a result of global warming is nothing but an alarmist position.

What we should be doing instead is accept that climate change is a constant and learn from the past by adapting accordingly. This means that we should also look into the findings of Richard Harrison who is the lead of space physics at a laboratory in Oxfordshire, England. Harrison is worried because our Sun appears to be falling asleep, as it were, and a mini ice age could be on the way.

If we believe the green activists, we should be changing everything in our lifestyles: eat local, stop using electric bulbs, ride a bicycle and discard all human made technology that has brought us to where we are today. Maybe we should even go back to living in caves, since in their view, advances by humans are the root cause of our problems. Their answer to getting us where they want us to be is to impose punitive taxes. We cannot tax people to death in the guise of helping the climate. Instead, we must come up with incentives rather than punishing taxes which do not lead to reductions. Unless we institute border taxation there is no equitable solution. As Dieter Helm explains:

> *"What precisely the tax is levied on matters a great deal, carbon consumption is what matters, and explicitly or implicitly raising prices and costs at home with a carbon production tax, but not on imports, leads to carbon leakage. A border carbon adjustment is essential if the tax is to do its work properly"*[16].

We need policies based on conservation coupled with carbon reductions. After all, sustainability is not just based on a policy of carbon curbing and the dire doomsday predictions of green NGOs who use exaggerations and often loose scientific assertions to make their case. Instead, we should encourage nations to meet their obligations under the Convention on Biological Diversity. Canada, a long-time supporter of the U.N's 1992 Convention should be a leader on this front, especially now that the world views Canada as the worst polluter because of the Oil Sands.

After all, Canada has long had a strategy on biodiversity that creates:

> *" A society that lives and develops as part of nature , values the diversity of life, takes no more than can be replenished and leaves to future generations a nurturing and dynamic world ... rich in its biodiversity."*[17]

Obama's latest polices and platitudes are not going to solve the problems, but will only hamper his relationship with his neighbours to the North. Conservative governments around the world should adopt conservation policies which support biodiversity instead of fighting left-wing environmental agendas; in most cases they are nothing more than an attempt to redistribute wealth and continue to fill the pockets of rich environmentalists like Gore and Strong. A climate policy which is not global but regional is not going to reduce GHG.

Then there are those who claim that the climate change issue is an established fact because the scientific evidence is conclusive. How preposterous! Science is never settled, otherwise we would still believe in a flat earth, and that the sun revolved around the earth. Furthermore, Einstein's theory of relativity would not be open to challenges. If scientific evidence was always conclusive, why are some of the same scientists who proclaimed that climate change science is settled are still getting grants to further their research. Better still, remember the 1970s, when scientists warned of a global cooling and 'great freeze'?

Conservatives can better serve the world by shifting the imposition of taxes on 'desirables' such as income, investments and hard work, to taxing 'undesirables' like consumption, pollution, loss of biodiversity and waste. Conservation instead of taxation is the path to resolving the carbon problem.

CHAPTER 7

HEALTHCARE

The issue of healthcare is of paramount importance on both sides of the 49th parallel. Both Canada and The United States had similar healthcare systems, until Canada made changes to its system in the 1960s and 70s. The changes have created many problems, most notably the ever increasing wait times, among other issues. Canadian conservatives would like to see a mix of private and public delivery services, just like the United States had prior to the Patient Protection and Affordable Care Act (ACA) commonly known as Obamacare. On the other side of the border, for years some Democrats like Bill Clinton and others, have tried to change the Medicare and Medicaid system to look more like the universal Canadian health system. However, the ambiguity between the two systems still exists. A *Harper's Magazine* report quotes President Obama:

> *"There are those on the left who believe that the only way to fix the system is through a single-payer system like Canada's. On the right, there are those who argue that we should end employer-based systems and leave individuals to buy health insurance on their own. There are arguments to be made for both these approaches. But either one would represent a radical shift that would disrupt the health care most people currently have. Since health care represents one-sixth of our*

> *economy, I believe it makes more sense to build on what works and fix what doesn't, rather than try to build an entirely new system from scratch."*[1]

The debate on healthcare will rage on, and it is important to look at the history and development of this essential service on both sides of the border. In Canada, for political reasons, the debate is always muted and more often than not, any discussions end up with the statement "we do not want an American system." The problem is that most Canadians do not know anything about the American system, and are often given the wrong information and therefore cannot make an informed decision.

The unfortunate predicament is that the implementation of ACA may disrupt both systems without providing any improvements; instead, it will result in more long term problems in both countries. The question is whether healthcare should be viewed as a political issue or a human rights issue.

This chapter discusses the background, evolution and pros and cons of healthcare on both sides of the border. It will examine the significant role of political ideology in the delivery choices for this important service. Therefore, I shall attempt to provide an unbiased explanation of both systems and the various effects of changes made under Obamacare. This chapter will also offer some solutions for the Canadian system, while discussing some of the alternatives to Obamacare.

Medicare in Canada

Canadians love their healthcare system. This is true despite the fact that it costs a lot and in many cases, under delivers services and is also plagued by long wait times. Polls constantly show that the general public strongly supports the public system rather than a private system. Whether they understand it or not, they overwhelmingly prefer their healthcare system to that of the United States. To be able to discuss this issue, we must first define the term 'Medicare' in the Canadian context. Generally it means: *"all universally provided public health care services"*.

The current system originates from the Province of Saskatchewan's introduction of a near universal system in 1946, when the Co-operative Commonwealth Federation government of Tommy Douglas passed the Saskatchewan Hospitalization Act. The government of the day had hoped to provide a health care system and financial protection to all its citizens, but failed to do so because they did not have the financial means.

Saskatchewan was followed by Alberta in 1950, and by 1961 all provinces had agreed to start the hospital Insurance and Diagnostic Services Act (HIDS) which had been passed by the Liberal government of Louis St. Laurent. The government funded 50% of the costs of the program for any province that accepted the protocols of HIDS. The Act contains five conditions which today still form the pillars of the Canadian Health Act, they are: public administration, comprehensiveness, universality, portability and accessibility.

In 1966, the Liberal government of Lester B. Pearson introduced the Medicare Act which extended the cost sharing between the Federal and provincial governments. Subsequent government Acts have been passed to re-affirm the five principles and prohibit the use of fees and extra billing by doctors.

Universality, one of the five principles of Canada's Health Act, has a well-meaning goal, but in reality it does not work very well. The level of service from province to province varies, because the system, although funded mainly by the Federal government, it is delivered according to the discretion of each province. This causes some problems and is the source of many disputes between the federal and provincial governments. Of course, politics plays a major role as the left and right argue for the continuation of the system or the possibility of reform to allow private care. Unfortunately for the patient, the result is always negative.

Several unsuccessful attempts at improving the system have been made by different governments; the original mandate and cost sharing seem to always prevent a successful consensus. To be able to understand the road blocks we should analyze the system and its workings.

The Canada Health Act provides insured health services without any co-payment for all legal residents and permanent residents who are not Canadian citizens but who have a permit to work and stay in Canada. Approximately 70% of the expenditures are paid for from public sources, the remainder is funded through private insurance and/or out-of-pocket expenses. The delivery of services is provided by physicians and hospitals, funded from public sources to the tune of 99% and 90% respectively.

Most doctors in Canada are small independent businesses and operate on a fee-for-service basis. Even hospital physicians use the billing system, since unlike many other countries, Canada does not consider them as employees of the hospital. For tax purposes, many provinces have allowed doctors and physicians to incorporate. An additional complication is that because delivery is under provincial jurisdiction, there is in effect no such thing as a 'Canadian healthcare system'.

While the Canada Health Act mandates coverage of all necessary care provided by doctors and hospitals, each province has its own program rules and issues its own health care card. The level of drug, dental, eye care, mental health and long-term care coverage vary from province to province. In most cases, these services are paid for either privately or through private insurance and out-of-pocket.

While provinces have reciprocal arrangements for hospital services, inter-provincial imbalances exist. Because health insurance plans are administered by the provinces, there are inequities in revenues and expenses. For example, a resident of Newfoundland working in Alberta is contributing to Alberta's revenues but his healthcare costs are borne by his home province. Furthermore, a Quebec resident who requires health care in another province is not automatically covered because Quebec has no physician agreement with other provinces. Therefore, the Quebec patient has to pay for his care upfront and then make a claim for reimbursement from the Régie de l'assurance maladie du Québec (RAMQ). Unfortunately, the claim is often denied and has to be covered by a private insurance plan.

Similarly, patients from other provinces receiving care in Quebec must make claims through their own provincial health plan. Having looked at the complexity of the current system we have identified the first misnomer regarding the 'universal' Canadian healthcare system.

The Health Canada web site states:

> *"Canada's national health insurance program, often referred to as "Medicare", is designed to ensure that all residents have reasonable access to medically necessary hospital and physician services, on a prepaid basis. Instead of having a single national plan, we have a national program that is composed of 13 interlocking provincial and territorial health insurance plans, all of which share certain common features and basic standards of coverage."*[2]

Since the system is managed independently by each province, inconsistencies in the delivery of certain services exist. Once care moves away from the prerequisite of the Canada Health Act, the extent to which certain services are covered vary from province to province. While pharmaceuticals, nursing care and physical therapy are covered for in-patients in hospitals, continued coverage for them varies after they have been discharged from the hospital. This issue was addressed by the Romanow Commission when it issued its final report, *Building on Values: The Future of Health Care in Canada,* on November 28, 2002. There were 47 cost recommendations, including the following themes:

> *"Medicare requires strong leadership and improved governance to ensure it remains a national asset.*
>
> *The health care system should be more responsive, efficient, and more accountable to Canadians.*
>
> *The health care system requires short-term strategic investments to address priority concerns, as well as long-term investments to make the system more sustainable."*[3]

Further variances in delivery exist when it comes to drug coverage, dental, eye care and other services. Limited or no coverage is provided for dental care. In some provinces dental care is subsidized for young children or elderly citizens, but generally, dental care is covered by some form of insurance either private or through employee/employer programs.

Similarly, eye care for each province is provided in varying degrees. The majority of provinces do not provide eye care but some do cover certain surgeries like cataracts and diabetes-related vision problems. Eye care is primarily paid for by the patient. As for other services like chiropractic, cosmetic surgery, psychological and mental health, the provinces either provide partial or zero coverage. In all these cases the service level and funding may be altered by the province.

The disparity in the delivery of healthcare among provinces is only the tip of the iceberg when it comes to the problems that plague the current system. The decentralised nature of healthcare delivery in Canada often prevents proper evaluation of the system. The acute lack of co-ordinated data does not allow for good comparisons between locales. While Canadians support the system, there are many concerns and it is a growing political issue, as Stuart Soroka stated:

> *"Herein lies one of the puzzles of Canadian health care: Canadians increasingly view the health care system as unsustainable and under threat, even as their own experiences with the system are mostly positive."*[4]

Provincial Ministers and representatives of the federal government have meetings to discuss how to improve the system, however very little progress has been made over the years. There have been attempts at the provincial level to make changes, but they have generally resulted in more problems rather than improvements. Cost cutting or searching for efficiencies have often resulted in less supported services, fewer hours of operation and in some cases loss of facilities. Delisting, which is a provincial practice of removing a procedure from the list covered by Medicare, is increasing. In the hope of saving money, provinces are continuously reviewing their list of covered services, and they are delisting services which in some cases may be considered as 'medically necessary'.

There is a growing shortage of physicians as a result of cost cutting in the early nineties and ironically we have a number of foreign physicians waiting for years to be admitted to the profession. The system of evaluation and accreditation done by provinces is extremely slow and onerous, having physicians wait for years to be integrated in their profession, even after they have passed the required examinations. With the number of retired physicians growing, the pressure on the system is acerbated, more specifically because the desire to enter family practice continues to decrease at an alarming rate. Increasingly it is becoming difficult for Canadians to access general practitioners. Small towns cannot find doctors to serve their growing needs. The result in all cases is that the system is plagued by long wait times, which not only affect the economy but also contributes to the decreasing state of services. This state of affairs is not only caused by the lack of physicians but there are ongoing issues with nurses. Once again schools are not re-qualifying foreign nurses quick enough, due to more barriers being erected.

Over the years there have been several attempts to modernize Canadian Medicare. For example in 1986 a federal report called *Achieving Health for All* made an attempt at de-medicalization. As explained by Terry Boychuk:

> *"the report made a distinction between health-promotion and implementation strategies that gave added credence to health services reorganization on a local level."*[5]

Despite the many attempts at reform, unlike other countries similar to the United States or the United Kingdom, Canada has been reluctant to introduce market competition to promote efficiencies and patient control over health care. Many think – tanks and politicians have proposed removing the barriers to a parallel private system, but although polls show that there is an increasing acceptance for a two-tiered system, politicians of either parties have yet to adopt such a policy in their platform. The exception has been the province of Quebec, which has experimented with the use of for-profit hospitals, when in 1961 the government started to signed contracts with for-profit hospitals. The experiment however was generally considered a failure.

However, we must take note of the 2005 ***Chaoulli v. Quebec (Attorney General)*** case which was decided by the Supreme Court of Canada in a 4/3 majority decision. This particular decision is only binding in Quebec and states that the *Quebec Health Insurance Act* and the *Hospital Insurance Act* which prevented private medical insurance in the face of long wait times violated both the Quebec Charter of Rights and Freedoms, and section 7 of the Canadian Charter of Rights and Freedoms. This decision is viewed by some as a call for the reform of the current Medicare system. Others believe that this could lead to the dismantling of the Canadian Medicare. Either way the door is opened to have a serious discussion about the delivery of health care in Canada. Unfortunately, not many politicians have the intestinal fortitude to attack the problem, and they are reluctant to open a Pandora's' box, despite the fact that the current system continues to deteriorate and wait times continue to lengthen. We need political leadership that can offer straight talk. As Jeffrey Simpson said:

> *"The talk will mean tackling the two most difficult task in public life. First, place unpalatable truths in front of the people. Second, alert people to the looming problems that will require hard decisions today and outline options for these decisions."*[6]

Health care in the United States

For many on both sides of the 49th parallel, the question of health care has been the subject of many debates. In Canada the proponents of private care have always regarded the U.S system as a model to be adopted in the country. By contrast left leaning Americans have argued for a long time that their system should be changed to one reflecting some of the universal care system of Canada.

According to a World Health Organization report, the United States in 2011 spent more per capita and a higher percentage of GDP on healthcare than any other nation. Yet the Commonwealth Fund ranked the U.S. last in the quality of health care among similar countries. The question is why?

Prior to the Affordable Care Act, healthcare in the United States had a system that involved private insurance and which in many cases was revered and loathed by Americans depending on which side of the political spectrum one was. For Liberals it was always their desire to have a single payer system similar to the socialist European model. For Republicans the free market system was their favoured model.

To understand the debate we should look at the American system pre-Obamacare to understand the continued debate and why the majority of Americans reject the Affordable Care Act passed into law by the Obama administration and Democrat majority.

Medicaid/Medicare

In 1965, Medicaid was created to help states provide health services to low-income families and related individuals, who met certain requirements, such as the blind, the aged and disabled members of society. In essence Medicaid is the main source of insurance coverage for the United States low-income population. Recipients must be U.S. citizens or be legal permanent residents

Poverty is not the only criteria for qualification. It is a means-tested program funded by both the state and the federal governments, and is administered by the states. Each state establishes its own rules, eligibility and type and scope of services provided. The state also sets the rate of payment, and benefits vary from state to state. The system must conform to federal guidelines to receive matching federal funds and grants; which depends on each state's respective per capita income. Wealthy states receive 50% matching funds, while poorer states may receive a larger percentage.

Medicaid does not pay benefits to recipients but rather pays health care providers for services provided. Some states require that the patient pays part of the fees under a co-pay agreement. Medicaid services are limited to 'medically necessary services', as mandated by federal laws.

According to the federal Centers for Medicare and Medical Services (CMS), in 2009 the Medicaid program provided was responsible for the provision of services to approximately 50.1 million Americans, of whom 46 % were children. The federal government pays in average 57% of Medicaid expenses, and with the recent recession the number of participants has increased putting an additional burden on the overall costs. As a result this program is becoming a major budget issue both at state level where Medicaid accounts for 22% of the state's budget, and at the federal level where in 2008 the federal portion amounted to $204 billion.

Medicare, is a federal insurance program created by President Johnson in 1965, to provide health insurance for people aged 65 and over, notwithstanding of income or medical history. Title XVIII of the Social Security Act was put into place because approximately 35% of people over 65 faced high insurance premiums, which made it either unaffordable or unavailable. The Act also made payments to health care professionals conditional on desegregation. This opened up hospitals, waiting rooms and access to physicians available to the black community.

Since its inception Medicare has undergone many changes, and to the initial benefits many others have been added over the years. President Clinton formalized the relationship with Health Maintenance Organizations (HMO), and President George W. Bush added the coverage of almost all drugs to the entitlement.

Medicare is administered by the Centers for Medicare and Medicaid Services (CMS). It has four parts. Part A is Hospital Insurance. Part B is Supplementary Medical Insurance, Part C is Medicare Advantage plans, and Part D is Prescription Drugs plans.

Health Insurance

Prior to the Affordable Care Act (ACA), The United States is the only industrialize country which depends on a free-market, for-profit medical insurance system to provide basic healthcare. Some 55% of employees receive coverage through their employers, while another 10% purchase it for themselves. Insurance companies provide more policies with higher deductibles and require patients to cover a higher percentage of their expenses. As the costs of insurance has risen over the years many more citizens have dropped out, either cut off from their employer's program or can no longer afford the premiums due to economic hardships.

The other factor that really impedes the current insurance program is the practice of insurance companies' refusal of coverage for patients with pre-existing conditions. For those who could not qualify for private insurance had to pay the cost of healthcare out of their own pockets. According to the Kaiser Family Foundation:

> *"21 percent of those who apply for health insurance on their own are turned down, charged a higher price or denied coverage for their pre-existing condition"*[7]

This denial of coverage for pre-existing conditions may be one of the strongest arguments for the initial implementation of the ACA. But the often ignored factor is that legal costs and settlements in increasing lawsuits involving healthcare puts an enormous burden on insurance companies and therefore is a large contributor to the constant increase in premiums. Furthermore the inability to transfer coverage from state to state is another added encumbrance on the delivery system.

There is no doubt that with increasing costs and the growing Medicaid deficit; there are reasons to reform the current system. But from there to have a complete turnaround to a fully government administered program is another issue. A great majority of Americans reject a government program, as seen by the initial negative response to Obamacare.

Reform of both the existing Canadian and United States systems are badly needed. While we shall look at the pitfalls of the implementation of Obamacare, we shall also look at some ideas how to improve the Canadian system.

The purpose of this discussion is very simple. A look at the implementation debacle of the ACA and the real intent behind its forceful enactment should provide a good example for Canadians as to why we need a change towards a more 'choice based' system of delivery, and more importantly that Canadians must be more open to an unbiased form of change of the current system. We shall have this opportunity when we undertake the 2014 Accord.

The Pitfalls of Obamacare

One of the most telling presidential campaign promises made by then Senator Barrack Obama was, "to fundamentally transform America". Undeniably, a complete reform of the United States healthcare system was on his mind. Armed with political capital and supported by a majority of Democrats in both the House and the Senate, in his first term he proceeded to pass the Affordable Care Act, now better known as Obamacare. The Act was passed on a fully partisan basis with no Republican voting for it. At first it was seen as a complete repudiation of the President's agenda by the right, but since implementation on October 1st 2013, we have seen the flaws, the deceit and the upcoming problems of healthcare in the U.S.

A perfect example of how not to reform healthcare starts at the very beginning. During the President's electoral campaign and at least 30 times since then he has consistently promised or lied to the American public. Here is a chronology of what he has said to promote his policy:

- Bristol, VA. June 5, 2008: "So you're going to have a clear contrast, John McCain's, Bush light healthcare plan or a plan that lowers premium by $2,500."
- Unity NH. June 27, 2008: "It's time to bring down the typical family premium, by $2,500. It's time to bring down the costs for the entire country."
- Hempstead NY. Oct. 15, 2008: "We estimate we can cut the average family's premium by about $2,500 per year."
- Hempstead, NY. Oct 15, 2008: " If you get insurance through your employer, you can keep your insurance, keep your choice of doctor, keep your plan"
- Chicago. Il. June 15, 2009: "If you like your healthcare plan, you will be able to keep your healthcare plan. Period."
- Portsmouth. NH .Aug.11, 2009: "Under the reform we're proposing, if you like your doctor you can keep your doctor. If you like your health care plan, you can keep your health care plan."

- Belgrade MT. Aug.14, 2009" And if you do have health insurance, we'll help make sure that your insurance is more affordable and more secure"

When the bill was passed, then House Leader Nancy Pelosi on March 8, 2010 said: ***"We must pass the Bill, so that you can find out what is in it"***. From then on it has been obfuscation, denial, excuses and accusations by the Democrats to justify the implementation of the ACA.

We only have to take Senator Dianne Feinstein's (D.) statement in an interview with CBS on November 3, 2013 when she tried to explain the President's position on 'keeping your insurance if you like it' this is what she said :

> *"As I understand it, you can keep it up to the time ... and I hope this is correct, but this is what I have been told, up to the time the Bill was enacted, then after that it is a different story. I think that part of it if true was never made clear."*

Since its implementation in October 2013, the reform has been marred by multiple system problems, and more importantly increases in premiums and higher deductibles, and in many cases loss of insurance coverage. In some cases it could be cheaper for employers to pay the penalty rather than provide insurance for workers.

With the higher costs, small businesses are choosing either to reduce the work hours of their employees or reduce the size of their businesses to 49 workers, which is below the participation threshold of 50 employees as imposed by the Act.

To get 2.7 million young people (millennials) to sign up for Obamacare is costing $700m in advertising. Problem is, young people over 26 years of age are not signing, which in the long run will prove to be very costly, since their participation is crucial to maintain the sustainability of the new program.

The price of increasing insurance is the reason that in a reversal of his policy the President chose to delay the implementation for businesses and not individuals.

Under enormous pressure and dwindling approval ratings in the polls, the President remains defiant in the defence of his policies.

On April 14, 2011 he was overhead on a CBS News off mic.:

> *"I mean on health care, cutting, cutting, eliminating the health care bill would cost us a trillion dollars. It would add trillion dollars to the deficit so and when Paul Ryan says priority is to make sure that we're you know, he's just being America's accountant, you know trying to, you know be responsible. This is the same guy who voted for two wars that were unpaid for, voted for Bush tax cuts that were unpaid for, voted for prescription drug bill that costs as much as my health care bill, but wasn't paid for"*

Once implementation started in October of 2013, it seemed that all hell broke loose. The website did not work and many found out that their premiums were increasing rather than decreasing. In many cases ailments previously covered were denied. Moreover they were being asked to pay for coverage of services they did not require, and in some cases insurance companies just dropped them.

The President continuously in campaign mode, continued to blame everybody but himself, and his administration instead of rectifying the problem. As problems grew the implementation went awry with many of his supporters questioning the system, but not the program. But even before the debacles of the launch, there were already many questions from diverse quarters. Here are some of the concerns raised:

Senator Jay Rockefeller, in April 2013 told the *Washington Press*:

> *"The law is so complicated and if it isn't done right the first time, it will just get worse.... up to the point it just beyond comprehension."*[8]

NBC investigative correspondent Lisa Meyers found buried in 2010 Obamacare regulations language predicting: ***"A reasonable range for the percentage of individual policies that would terminate is 40% to 67%.***

Another report from the New York Medical Society states that a survey of doctors participating in Obamacare exchanges is:

Not participate 44%, May not 33%, and only 23% will

Despite the problems the President continues to push for implementation and in a speech on October 30, 2013 in Boston. The President said:

> *"Now if you have one of these sub-standard plans before the ACA became law, and you really like that plan you are able to keep it. That's what I said when I was running for office. That was part of the promise we made. Today the ACA requires insurance companies to abide by some of the strongest consumer protections this country has ever known. A true patients' bill of rights ... No more discriminating against kids with pre-existing conditions. No more dropping your policy when you get sick and need it most.*
>
> *I don't think we should go back to dropping coverage for people when they get sick, or because they make a mistake on their application. I don't think we should go back to the daily cruelties and indignancies and dignities, and constant insecurity of a broken healthcare system. And I am confident most Americans agree with me. The debates about the role of the individual and society our rugged individualism, and our sense of self – reliance, our devotion to the kind of freedoms whose first shot rang out not far from here, but there are also debates tempered by a recognition that we are all in this together. And when hardship strikes and it could strike any of us at any moment, we are there for one another. And that as a country we can accomplish great things that we cannot accomplish alone"*

The Fix for both countries

After years of discussions, reports and commissions, Canadians are still not getting the level of health care they demand. While we demonize the U.S. system, we have yet to improve ours.

Reports by Manzankowski and Romanow made several suggestions to improve the ever increasing problem of Canadian healthcare. With no political will, there has been no great progress, but empty political rhetoric. In 2010, the Alberta government produced yet another report – Putting People First.

This report and its recommendations are full of the 'motherhood and apple pie' rhetoric of every single previous report. The proposed Seven Patient Charter Statement is once again full of platitudes. We do not need a Charter. All these seven points are a right under our current legislation. What is clearly missing is an eighth statement: ***"I have a right to access and receive treatment from a supplier of my choice, including a private one."***

In the mean time we continue to build hospitals, and spend more money on programs and administrative costs which do not deliver required services. We keep insisting that Canada should not have a two-tier system, commonly called the American system by the opponents of progress, but in reality a two-tier system already exist in most provinces.

The Wildrose Alliance has a comprehensive alternative to the current system. It mirrors most of the European system, which has proven to be less costly and better than ours. This is a good start, but the Institute for Public Sector Accountability believes that in the 21st century, Canadians need to stop sticking their heads in the sand when it concerns the delivery of health care. We must instead acknowledge the following:

- The use of private health care in Canada
- Allow those who can pay to buy services as they see fit, and spend the money in Canada
- To ensure that public and/private delivery works, governments should find a compromise balance in the delivery of services
- All private practice and practitioners must sign a contract that ensures that at least 40% of their work is done in the public sector.

- Public sector work is paid according to government rates, private rates are subject to market forces.
- Speed up the review and certification of foreign health workers and doctors.

Canadians lose by not having enough health professionals. We lose millions of health care dollars to foreign deliverers like Benefits Health System in Montana. What we need is a system that delivers services effectively and efficiently. It does not matter whether the system is private or public; Canadians just want to stay alive!

The Alberta government, the largest provider of health care in Canada, has tinkered with its health system so many times and repeating the same mistakes that one can see that our health care management is verging on insanity. In general, this situation is repeated across the country.

Waiting times in ER are getting longer, suicidal patients are made to wait hours without assistance, and we build new facilities, without ensuring that they can be staffed properly. Even a fool can see the system is clearly broken. Canadian governments do not like dissent and cannot take constructive criticisms from anyone.

To add insult to injury, Premier Stelmach of Alberta suspended a member of his government for critiquing his policies. Dr. Raj Sherman is not only better qualified than the Premier on matters of health, but he also took the Hippocratic Oath: "First do no harm" and is quite right in defending the right of Alberta's patients. On the other hand, Canadian governments have taken a 'hypocritical oath' and continue to spend money without accountability and more distressfully without any improvement in service delivery.

Stephen Duckett, the much maligned former President and CEO of Alberta Heath Services, has some good ideas that we agree with, they are:

- The 2014 Accord should be for 10 years. It should establish a Federal/Provincial/Territorial Advisory Committee, consisting of consumer representation as well as health care professionals. The role of the committee is to make recommendations to the government, and its status should be reviewed after the first two years of its inception.

- The 2014 Accord should provide that if a pharmacare program is introduced, federal funding to the provinces should be reduced to offset any provincial savings.
- Federal, provincial, territorial governments should agree on a limited set of performance measures to be published annually. The partners should commit to achieving access to a national linked data by 2020.

Furthermore, in their book *Canadian Medicare*, the authors Stephen Duckett and Adrian Peetoom state:

> *"There is no need to change the 5 criteria of the Canadian Health Act. There is no need to play with access-quality-sustainability trade-offs: all three are achievable. Taking action means investing money, but investing wisely with a view to achieving social efficiency."*[9]

According to Duckett and Peetoom: In 2009, Canada spent $25.4 billion on prescribed medications, of which $11.4 billion came out of the public pot and $9.4 billion from insurance companies; $4.6 billion had to be coughed up by individual Canadians. Based on these facts we believe that pharmacare should be included in a revamp of Canada's medicare. Notwithstanding the gains in economies of scale, we support Duckett and Peetoom when they propose:

> *"Prescriptions drugs should be an insured service under medicare. Federal, provincial, and territorial leaders should immediately commission an independent study to determine the most practical way of introducing prescription pharmaceuticals as an insured service under medicare."*[10]

While these proposals seem to be pragmatic, it will require much political will to make them happen. This is where a conservative approach would help greatly.

In the United States, the situation seems to have taken a turn for the worse with Obamacare. The Democrats used their majority in Congress to nationalize one-sixth of the economy. Not only will this action have economic repercussions but it looks as if that providing health care for the so-called uninsurables, some 15 million will now cause some 100 million to be without insurance. The fix could have been made simpler by eliminating some loopholes, and making changes to the portability of insurance.

The following are some ideas that are out there: but have been rejected outright by the President, who is protecting his signature legacy.

- Tax all employer provided healthcare plans as compensation
- Give large tax credits to spend on health insurance
- Allow the health insurance to be purchased across state lines
- Encourage health savings accounts
- Delay for a year
- Amend requirements for compliance
- Universal tax credits for health insurance
- $2,500 /individual and $8,00/family
- Let people shop for coverage for both private and Medicaid
- Acknowledge progress is incremental repeal & fix health care piecemeal
- Allow sale of health care across stateliness
- Eliminate insurance mandates
- Tax code fairness for private health care plans
- Make deal with insurance companies that protects them from losing money
- No federal regulations of health care
- Allow states to regulate health care

Unfortunately these ideas are mostly from Republicans or right leaning pundits. Despite the fact that the President constantly challenges the Republicans to bring forth alternative ideas, any suggestions that may deviate slightly from his socialist reform are rejected outright by the President, who is protecting his signature legacy.

Not only has Obamacare been implemented in the most incompetent way, it will result in one of the greatest chaos in government nationalization of a service. While the previous system penalized or left unprotected some 15 million people, the new system may penalize a whole nation, albeit at different levels. As the debacle grows Obama keeps amending the law by 'decree'. Not because it is the right thing to do, but rather so that the implementation does not affect the 2014 elections.

A repeal of the Act is not in question, but significant changes have to be made to address the nationalization of healthcare in America. The financial implications resulting from the chaos will really be felt in future years, when Obama would have left office. Those who supported Obamacare will have a heavy burden to bear and more importantly it should serve as an example of socialist bungling. Canadian conservatives should seriously take heed of what is happening next door.

CHAPTER 8

EDUCATION

One of the pillars of a country's economic growth is undoubtedly education. Individual success cannot be achieved without a modicum of education, and in a world dominated by technological advances, education is even more important. However, it seems that in certain industrialised countries, instead of progress, we see a decline in the quality of education. The 2013 OECD's Programme for International Student Assessment report which assesses 15-year olds aptitude in math, science and reading placed countries like Singapore, Korea and Japan, as well as Switzerland, Estonia and Finland ahead of the pack. Canada's education system is failing and our children are now ranked 13th in math. The United States does not fare any better, as their students were ranked even lower at 26th in math, 21st in science and 17th in reading. These rankings do not bode well for the future because skills attract investments and create jobs. We must explore the reasons behind the continuous decline in education and seek solutions as we fast approach a national crisis.

Why should we examine Canada's education, in parallel with that of the United States? There are two reasons for this analysis. One, most of our education books are published in the United States. Too often the contents of books are amended or even re-written for politically correct reasons; in effect causing the loss of literary interpretations and historical facts. For example a text book entitled "*Introduction to Social Work and Social Welfare*," is used for an introductory social work class at several University of South Carolina classes. In it, the author Karen Kirst-Ashman states:

> *"that conservatives 'tend to take a basically pessimistic view of human nature' with 'people conceived of as being corrupt, self-centered, lazy, and incapable of true charity'.*
>
> *The 40th president, it is stated, 'ascribed to women primarily domestic functions' and 'failed to appoint many women to significant positions of power during his presidency."*[1]

What Ms. Kirst-Asman forgets to mention is that President Reagan appointed the first woman, Justice Sandra Day O'Connor, to the Supreme Court, and Jeane Kirkpatrick as the first woman U.S Ambassador to the United Nations. The point is that academic freedom is one thing, but it is this type of blatant distortion of facts for political reasons that make some text books and some scholars so dubious, and more importantly the education of our children so questionable.

Two, like it or not, teachers' unions have a great influence in the design of curriculum and the delivery system in both countries. Whenever there is a discussion about the quality of education. Unions will contend that it is not about money, but rather it is about providing the best for the children. But at the end of the day it is always about money – it is about government funding, infrastructure, class size an most of all compensation, and working hours. The real problem though is about the reform of education in a new era of technology and demographics. Parents in many cases have relinquished many of their responsibilities to school teachers, and teachers are now overwhelmed by demands made by parents who in some cases treat schools like day care facilities. As a consequence true education has suffered. To remedy a chronic disease we must start with an examination of the design of curriculum, the assessment of students and how education is delivered today.

As population increases, class sizes increase, but it is not a widespread increase. Depending on location, class sizes and the demand for both teachers and infrastructure will vary. But too often governments respond as if the solutions are 'one size fits all'.

In the formative years, class size matter more than in high school. The early years of education are the most important, and we should not be afraid to change the way that children are taught, we must compartmentalize in order to provide the best education to our kids.

In kindergarten, our goals for our children are to be nurtured and taught proper social skills, how to communicate and learn in a fun-filled environment that allows them to specifically care for themselves. In elementary school, children should be taught how to read, write, and the basics of arithmetic, which include times tables. They should be encouraged to learn about nature and the environment. The size of classes should be limited to no more than twenty students per class, there should be less emphasis on assessments but parents should be given clear guidance and report on their children's performance.

As children move to middle and high school the emphasis shifts to a curriculum that includes reading, writing, mathematics and sciences. In addition to social studies, students participate in physical activities and sports, as well as the opportunity to learn about the arts. Students' performance should be subjected to a rigorous assessment process. Standardized tests should be used to provide a sense of competitiveness to prepare children for the real world. Teachers and schools should be judged based on the results of these tests. This is extremely important, to prevent 'grade shock' when they enter the college and university stage. Students accustomed to high school grade inflation may have a rude awakening when they do not receive the equivalent grades in university. Grade shock may also be the cause of so many drop outs after the first year. Why waste so much, money, time and potential, when we can have realistic remedies, which we shall discuss later.

Another concern is the role of universities and how they admit students to their programs. Too often unlike the United States, Canadian universities do not have a proper admission test. American universities use a combination of the Standardized Aptitude Test (SAT) and high school GPA. Instead in Canada, universities rely on grades allocated to students by high school teachers over whom they have neither jurisdiction nor control.

In addition the grading system is coming under attack because, many jurisdictions have adopted different assessment methods including the controversial no-zero policy.

The debate about the no-zero policy came to the fore mostly because of the suspension of Edmonton high school teacher Lynden Dorval, who defied the no-zero policy of Ross Shepard High School. While public outcry precipitated a review of the policy in Edmonton and other jurisdictions, Dorval received very little representation from his union, and was ultimately fired by the School Board. Two years after the incident, a provincial appeal board found that the Edmonton Public School Board "did not act fairly" when they suspended and then fired Lynden Dorval. Despite these finding some continue to dispute the use of the no-zero policy.

Some twenty years ago, researchers started looking at how teachers graded their students. Assessments are usually based on unit tests, project marks, and final grades. But today a greater emphasis is being put on formative assessment which provides students with feedback about their progress and is generally not included in their final marks.

Many education consultants believe that to make grades reliable and viable there must be a separation between data for achievement and data for behaviour and attitudes. This belief stems, in part, from The Principles for Fair Student Assessment Practices for Education in Canada which was developed in 1993 by a working group of representatives from a variety of professional organizations and ministries of education across Canada. One of the principles (4) separates achievement from effort and it states:

> *"Combining disparate kinds of results into a single summary should be done cautiously. To the extent possible, achievement, effort, participation, and other behaviors should be graded separately. A single comment or grade cannot adequately serve all functions. For example, letter grades used to summarize achievement are most meaningful when they represent only achievement. When they include other aspects of student performance such as effort, amount (as opposed to quality) of work completed, neatness, class participation, personal conduct, or punctuality, not only do they lose their meaningfulness as a measure of achievement, but they also suppress information concerning other important aspects of learning and invite inequities. Thus, to more adequately and fairly summarize the different aspects of student performance, letter grades for achievement might be complemented with alternate summary forms (e.g., checklists, written comments) suitable for summarizing results related to these other behaviors"*[2]

The proponents of this policy will argue that a no-zero policy better serves the student. For example the Alberta Education Learner Assessment Branch stated: "No-zero policies support student learning outcomes and consequently the report recommended that teachers should accept late assignments without penalty."

> *"The theory behind the no-zero policy is that students should be given every opportunity to complete work in order to allow them the best chance to succeed and move on to the next level of their education. The idea is that students should not be allowed to fail. But is this policy ultimately failing kids?"*[3]

Others rely on the information that no empirical evidence has shown that assigning a zero is effective in improving student achievement. Incidentally, there is no empirical evidence to show that no-zero policies have improved student scores on standardized tests.

Those opposed to the policy include teachers and parents and often businesses. They put forward that no-zero policies fail to prepare students for the realities of the world that awaits them after graduation. We must not discard the very important point about failure. The policy creates a false sense of security. Failure is part of life; it should not be glossed over or ignored. Instead we should take it as an opportunity to learn about responsibility, accountability, and more importantly about consequences. Many great people in all walks of life and sports have failed at one stage or another. But when they failed they got up and moved on, they embraced it as an opportunity to face adversity and become more resilient.

To add to the grading controversy, is the decision by certain school boards to do away with letter grading. Instead of the traditional A, B, C, and F evaluation, they propose to use a system called 'constructive feedback'. Proponents of the system argue that it helps both students and their parents to discuss strengths and weaknesses. The other side of the coin is that the system is no longer quantifiable and therefore it is more difficult to know whether a student is passing or failing. Opponents believe that the new system removes any incentive for a child to work harder to achieve better grades, and that in the long run we may be using a system to hide failure. The deterioration in North America's education prompted Amy Chua, professor of Law at the University of Yale to write, what some may consider a controversial book. She claims that Asian parenting as opposed to Western parenting produces academic success, she wrote:

> *"The fact is that Chinese parents can do things that would seem unimaginable – even legally actionable – to Westerners, Chinese mothers can say to their daughters, " Hey fatty, lose some weight." By contrast Western parents have to tiptoe around the issue, talking in term of "health" and never ever mentioning the f-word, and their kids still end up in therapy for eating disorders and negative self – image … Chinese parents can order their kids to get straight As. Western parents can only ask their kids to try their best."*[4]

Furthermore, we are taking away the right of teachers to punish unruly students. Gerald Pedron, the principal of Sundance Elementary in Alberta is reprimanded and fined $1,000 by the Alberta Teachers Association for locking unruly, out-of-control students in a room to cool off. Is this not sending the wrong message to students? Aren't we saying you can get away with anything? Students can be rude, disruptive, and have no respect for authority, and yet a teacher cannot make them accountable for their actions. This is the result of the cult of self-esteem that now permeates the education philosophy

With a growing attitude that we should treat children with kid's gloves to shelter them from disappointment, we are constantly removing the rewards for success and denigrate competition. When every child gets a medal and some teams are not allowed to score too many points or goals so as to shelter their opponents from disappointment, are we not creating a new generation of wimps and non-achievers?

Our universities are also failing us. In many cases they have abandoned the traditional disciplines, of literature, history, social, physical and natural sciences. In all fairness it is not all their fault, because in the past twenty years, students have demanded courses that would allow them to have a lucrative career. Consequently, many universities have become a factory for degrees, many of them in the liberal arts and other nebulous disciplines.

In a world dominated by science and technology, Canadian universities have not kept pace with the rest of the world. Not enough students are taking math-based courses. The reasons are numerous: poor teaching at elementary and high school levels, not enough emphasis and instruction at university level. In addition math seems to be unappealing, because it demands hard work, repetition (times table), and discipline. As a result universities are attracting more foreign students than Canadians in their math-based programs. The future for Canada will be bleak if we do not remedy this growing lack of Canadian mathematicians.

The growing failure of education can be attributed to the growth of the student as customer. In the old days of traditional education, universities offered specific programs and degrees. Today students' demand dictates what courses are offered. As a result instead of requiring that students take 'core and foundation' courses, universities design curriculum to fit the students' wishes. In many cases graduates end up with ill-defined degrees that more often than not do not even provide them with the ability to fulfill the demands of a future career.

There is a growing belief that everyone needs a university degree; the question is does it matter what the degree is for? All of these changes have turned universities into businesses instead of sites of learning. The focus is on making money, and therefore the desires of eighteen year olds are determining what programs are offered. Universities have drifted into more programs geared towards the humanities instead of core disciplines.

In a global economy dominated by technology, we need more science and technology graduates. Unfortunately Canadian universities are not producing them, as in Canada the top priority is now dictated by student choice.

We need technicians as well as scientists; we cannot all be doctors, otherwise who would build our houses? Many students go to university to build up a resume, but more often than not, what they study is not suited for the demands of the real world. Very few consider attending colleges and trade schools, because getting a diploma in the discipline offered by these institutions are not viewed as sexy or valuable enough in the eyes of many employers. Trades are not given the respect they deserve; in high schools student should be advised about the benefits of both a university and a trade's college training. They should be encouraged to follow their passion, and the use of their abilities to participate in the economic growth of the country. If there is any doubt about the value of a trade's school diploma, consider Southern Alberta Institute of Technology's contribution to the Sochi Olympics:

> *"John Fairbairn and Eric Neilson will represent Canada in the sport of skeleton during February's Olympic Games in*

> *Sochi, Russia on sleds designed and built by SAIT Polytechnic's Applied Research and Innovation Services"*[5].

Another alarming trend is the growing incidence of cheating at Universities. With the constant increase in the costs of attending universities, student debts are rising, and there is an enormous pressure to succeed, in some cases by any means. More and more students are involved in cheating. Plagiarism is the number one offence. According to a survey by *CBC News* of 42 Canadian universities, more than 7,000 students were formally disciplined for academic cheating in 2011/12. Problem is that the penalties are not severe enough, which begs the question: What value do today's university degrees have?

Changes need to be made if we want to safeguard the future of education. Fortunately, today there is a growing movement to reform education in both Canada and the U.S. Parents and other organizations are mobilizing to counteract the decisions of School Boards and Teachers' unions. As *Global News* reports:

> *"Grassroots movements based in Ontario, British Columbia, Manitoba, Saskatchewan and Alberta believe the problem is starting early, in elementary school, and are now lobbying their provincial leaders to rethink how teachers are instructing math."*[6]

In Alberta Dr. Nhung Tran-Davies, a mother who is asking the province to have teachers go back to basics when teaching math, has been able to garner over 5,000 signatures for a petition to the deputy minister of education which stated:

> *"The issue is that it provides students with multiple strategies with the hope that the students will discover a strategy that works for them to do calculations, but it's convoluted, it's overly complicated, it's counter-intuitive and it's not practical," says Tran-Davies. "Students are left confused and frustrated and losing confidence in their ability to do math, when they are bright students who are capable of doing math."*[7]

Pedagogy has gone to the dogs, mainly because education is dominated by liberals and union leaders who have ignored the true reasons for teaching. A once revered profession is turning into a factory of lesser qualified people who cannot find entrance in university programs that demand a higher level of grades and proficiency. Michael Gerson wrote: "(American liberals), often defend the educational status quo – even though it is one of the nation's main sources of racial and economic injustice".

It is becoming almost impossible to fire or even suspend teachers with poor performance. Even those found guilty of crimes against children are being protected by unions. As widely reported in the Canadian media, the liberal view never ceases to amaze. "In Ontario, sex education is provided to the youngest students starting in grade 1. The curriculum includes detailed anatomy and vocabulary. At eight they progress to discussions about homosexuality and its legitimacy. In Grade 6 they graduate to learning about masturbation and in Grade 7 as part of a curriculum in abstaining from sex they are taught about anal sex as an alternative to vaginal intercourse. One would think that parents would be concerned about the content of the sex education programs, but they were sold this bill of goods by Ben Levin the former deputy minister of education and current University of Toronto professor. At the time of implementation nobody was concerned with his qualifications, but now we find out that he has been charged with making and distributing child porn as well as arranging for sexual offences against a child."

To add to the problems caused by the lack of accountability in education a report by the Atlantic Institute for Market Studies showed that teachers' union control over disciplinary actions have created an environment where bad apples are protected. The report authored by Paul Bennett, Director of Schoolhouse Consulting, stated:

> *"The system has created an impression of a cadre of teachers who have immaculate records – even though this may be far from the case."*[8]

Then we have the indoctrination of future leaders through movies like Al Gore's "*An Inconvenient Truth.*" This Oscar winning movie has been shown to children all over the world as a 'conclusive' analysis on climate change. But now we know that the movie was rife with mistakes. Justice Burton of the British High Court found that there were nine scientific errors[9]. He also stated that the movie could be shown 'as long as updated guidelines were followed'. Unfortunately, in other jurisdictions this movie is still being shown, too often without the caveats.

A barrier to change in education has been the notion that parents' occupation and money have an impact on student performance. The left always believe that more money is required to improve education, in fact according to the latest OECD report this is not always the case as they concluded:

> *"Students whose parents work in professional occupations generally outperform other students in mathematics, while students whose parents work in elementary occupations tend to underachieve compared to their peers.*
>
> *The strength of the relationship between parents' occupations and student performance varies considerably across countries: for example, when it comes to mathematics performance, the children of cleaners in Shanghai-China outperform the children of professionals in the United States, and the children of professionals in Germany outperform the children of professionals in Finland, on average"*[10]

When politicians say that it is important to invest in education, what they really mean is we must support teachers' unions to get their votes. The funding for education goes up, the cost of getting an education is constantly on the rise, and student loans, and debt get larger, but the fact remains that over the years, the quality of education has gone down. Too much of government funding is going towards administration costs and fancy infrastructure, instead of education delivery.

How do we move forward?

The current approach to curriculum design known as Inspiring Education, open area classrooms and discovery math are all manifestations of the same failed educational philosophy – progressivism. To remedy the problem we must approach reform of education in a politically conservative way. The Oxford dictionary defines conservative *adj.* 1.a – averse to rapid change. Unfortunately, the change in education has been rapid and ineffectual, it is harming children.

Since most liberals support the status quo, it is time for political conservatives to make the necessary change. The actions must be bold, and in fact radical. In some instances these changes have taken place in the United States.

Since 1955, when Milton Friedman of the University of Chicago proposed the use of vouchers, conservatives have embraced the idea. Education reformers believe that parents should be allowed to take government money to the school of their choice, albeit public, private, charter or religious school. However the idea was tainted because in the U.S. the idea of school choice was often associated with segregation. Over the years the atmosphere has changed and more parents today are looking at vouchers as a means to improve the education of the children.

Under George W. Bush, the "No Child Left behind" (NCLB) policy was introduced to ensure test-based accountability and choice in education. The law states that all children in grades 3 through Grade 8 must be tested in reading and mathematics. All test scores must be reported by race, ethnicity, income status, disability status and English proficiency. When Obama was elected those who did not like NCLB, thought that the policy would be reversed by the President's 'Race to the Top'. Opponents of his policy maintain that the new policy was more drastic in that it tied teachers' evaluation to test scores, and that it expanded the number of subjects tested and the frequency of the tests. In fact the new policy created competition between the states for the $5 billion available in education grants.

There are some, including Alberta's former Minister of Education, David King who now wrongly advocates for funding only for public schools., as he wrote :

> *"Only public education exists to be a deliberate and universally accessible model of a civil democratic community. Only public education is inclusive as a matter of right rather than by invitation. Only public education is inclusive of all students and inclusive of the entire community."*[11]

Competition in education is a concept that has been advocated by many conservative institutions, including Canada's Fraser Institute. Some would argue that education policies of both the Bush and Obama administrations have encouraged the privatization of education in urban districts. They also lament the participation of corporations in the funding of education. They use the support of the Gates Foundation's support for 'Common Core' (CC) standards as an example of corporate interference.

The Common Core State Standards Initiative is an education initiative in the United States that details what K-12 students should know in English language arts and mathematics at the end of each grade. The initiative is sponsored by the National Governors Association (NGA) and the Council of Chief State School Officers (CCSSO) and seeks to establish consistent education standards across the states as well as ensure that students graduating from high school are prepared to enter two or four year college programs or enter the workforce.[12]

However, Common Core is being criticized for the heavy involvement of corporations in the program. It is alleged that Apple, Pearson, Google, Microsoft and Amplify are all cashing in on the federal standards/testing/textbook racket. But the most significant opposition to CC is the amount of data collected to make the program efficient and measurable. As Michel Malkin wrote:

> *"Assessing Common Core is inextricably tied to the big business of data collection and data mining. States that took the Race to the Top bribes in exchange for adopting Common*

> *Core must now comply with the edutech requirements of two private testing conglomerates, the Partnership for the Assessment of Readiness for College and Careers or the Smarter Balanced Assessment Consortium. Common Core states also agreed to expand existing statewide longitudinal database systems that contain sensitive student data from pre-kindergarten through postsecondary education."*[13]

No matter which curriculum is chosen we cannot ignore that technology plays an increasing part of our daily lives. In education technology has the potential to revolutionize the learning process. With interactive software and other developments such as McGraw-Hill Education's SmartBooks teachers can modify and questions based on students' responses.

> *"Using such technology, teachers can now engage their students in a more personalized, individual manner rather than the traditional, one-size-fits-all approach."*[14]

An example of the use of technology in a school is East Mooresville, where they reallocated funding to spend $7,400 per year, and have $50 user fee. The classes range from 17 to 30 students per class, and provide more individual teaching, through technology. The students are more engaged, they have constant participation through the computer, and real time assessment. The system provides achievement data for teacher evaluation that monitor student progress; and individual students get immediate feedback. Graduation rate improved from 77% to 91% in 5 years, and they do not have a teachers' union.

In Canada, change in education is slow, due to the heavy involvement and influence of large teachers' unions. Canadian education requirements for teachers vary. Some provinces require a minimum three year undergraduate degree plus a year of teacher training; others require a four year degree plus one or sometimes two years of training. When you add a requirement for M.Ed., the total education and training may take six to seven years.

There is no doubt that qualifications are important and should be required, but are we sacrificing the benefits to students for higher paid teachers, or should we be looking at different ways to compensate teachers?

The answer is that teachers should be proficient in the subject they teach. High school teachers should have a university degree, but do we need Grade 2, and elementary school teachers to have six or seven years of post-secondary education?

The real reason for those high qualification requirements is that over the years compensation has been tied to qualifications and unions have pushed for higher academic requirements. Rodney A. Clifton wrote:

> *"Public school teachers are paid on the basis of salary schedules that differ across school districts and provinces. In fact, all Canadian public school districts use salary schedules that pay teachers based on their years of post-secondary education and their years of teaching experience (Canadian Education Statistics Council, 2012: 87-92), and almost all public school districts in the United States use similar salary schedules to pay teachers (Podgursky & Springer, 2011)"*[15]

A recent report by the *Frontier Centre for Public Policy* goes further to prove that government education spending is not going in the right place. As Rodney Clifton, professor emeritus at the University of Manitoba and a senior research fellow at the Frontier Centre for Public Policy wrote:

> *"I wasn't surprised that [education spending] was increasing faster than the consumer price index, but I was surprised by the variations across the country, mostly in terms of what the cost per student is and by the increases over time … Unions try to lower student teacher ratios, because they like to have more members; members are happier if they have fewer students to deal with. But there's no evidence that a student-teacher ratio of oneto-22 or one-to-17 makes any difference in the performances of kids."*[16]

Teachers' pay should no longer be associated with their number of years of service, but rather they should be linked to the academic success of their students. In addition, it is time to reconsider tenure policies in education. There is also growing support for the re-certification of teachers on a regular basis – say every five years.

Continuing reports prove that education standards are falling, parents should not only complain, but take an active role in the reform of education. They should not accept that their child is trapped in a failing institution. Parents' attention to whether a school is public, private or charter is not as important as long as their children receive the right education. Parents should demand that their tax dollars be spent more efficiently. Education funding must be based on needs and performance. Taxpayers should embrace and support the use of vouchers to give them the opportunity to remove the shackles that prevents choice in education.

We should listen to students. Often they are more reasonable than adults. Contrary to current beliefs, students like competition. To change the assessment criteria to no-zero policies and no letter grades does not improve education. In fact it prevents students from aspiring to higher goals. Why should I do more if I get the same grade as the next student who does less? Students want to be accountable for their work. As Michelle Rhee states:

> *"To restore the competitive spirit, we need to have high expectations for all children. We have to fully acknowledge the challenges that we face, yet not let those serve as an excuse for a lack of achievement. We have to ensure that all students who graduate from high school or college are ready and able to compete in the global place."*[17]

Last but not least, we must ensure that good teachers are heard. Too often we ignore that there are many teachers out there who do not believe in the status quo. We must strive to remove the veil between teachers and their unions. Not all teachers agree with what is happening in their profession, they should be encouraged to speak up.

Governments and unions, too often reach collective agreements as political expediency. Education suffers because the problem is not about teachers, but rather because we do not put students first. We should embrace competition, reward success over failure, and make both students and teachers accountable. A small 'c' conservative common sense approach to education would better serve our future generations.

CHAPTER 9

BUILDING A NATION

Both Canada and the United States were built by immigrants. Since the discovery of North America, it has been people from foreign lands who have colonized and made both countries prosperous. Today both countries are under enormous pressure to re-examine their immigration policies. To understand the history of immigration in both countries we need to contrasts their respective history and their evolving policies on immigration.

While both countries rely on immigration for growth and economic stability, their issues, problems, strategies and policies differ greatly. However Canada and the United States can learn from each other as they move forward and develop new immigration policies in a new millennium. From a political point of view it will be important to contrast how the different political parties in power have dealt with the issue of immigration. The political approach of Conservatives and Liberals in Canada as well as the differing policies of Republicans and Democrats in the United States are to be examined to provide us with a clearer understanding of immigration, its consequences and varied results in a new century.

Canada the Welcoming

With the exception of Native Indians, all Canadians are either immigrants or sons and daughters of immigrants. At the turn of the twentieth century there was a massive exodus from Europe, and to a lesser extent, Asia to North America in search of a better life. In 1899, Sir Clifford Sifton, the Canadian Interior Minister open Canada's door to the rest of the world when he declared in the House of Commons:

> *"I don't care what language a man speaks, or what religion he professes ... If he is honest and law abiding, if he will go on that land and make a living for himself and his family, he is a desirable settler."*[1]

With these words Sifton started a vigorous immigration policy which encouraged people to settle in the West. Immigrants came from Britain, the United States, Ukraine, Scandinavia and other groups from the Austro-Hungarian Empire. At the time, Sifton's immigration policy excluded Asians, Blacks and Jews. Nevertheless, his actions were the first salvo in a number of policies by different governments to formulate immigration policies for Canada.

Canada, a vast country with natural resources but lacking in population has over the years invited people from other parts of the world. The invitation to Canada is always accompanied by the marketing of its abundance of opportunities and resources, but too often, either by design or by omission, immigrants were not told about some of the realities of life in Canada – the harshness of its winters, the lack of proper recognition of foreign professional qualifications, and the possibility and existence of racial discrimination.

Immigration in Canada is driven by the need for economic growth and nation-building. The future of the country depends on a well-constructed immigration policy, but for years through the tinkering of successive governments we have seen, to the detriment of the principles of nation-building, a progressive deterioration in regulations, statutes and administration of the country's immigration programs. So much so that there are some who believe that for political expediency, Canadians were being misled by their governments. Charles Campbell wrote in 2000:

> *"Current immigration and refugee policy exhibits contempt for the will of the majority of Canadians. Canadians resent their government's tolerance of tens of thousands of illegal immigrants; the uncontrolled opportunities for systematic abuse and growing criminal activity; the discrimination against the able; and the mismanagement of the process."*[2]

How did we get there? How did Canadians become so skeptical of their government? And what changes have been made to improve the process; these issues will form the basis of our discussions.

The 1966 White Paper initiated the principles of the government's immigration policy. The intent was to attract as many well-educated and skilled immigrants as Canada could absorbed. In 1967, with the establishment of the Department of Manpower and Immigration under the Hon. Jean Marchand, the policy divided potential immigrant into four groups: Independent applicants, Nominated Relatives, Sponsored Dependents and Entrepreneurs. Admission was to be based on a points system weighted towards productive ability.

In the late sixties the rules became more lax. The criteria of high standards were gradually dropped; the government allowed visitors to apply for landing in Canada, which allowed them to stay in the country after the expiration of their 'visitors' permits'. Further relaxation of the underlying principles of the White Paper, and the recognition of a new refugee system, made Canada the desired destination for immigrants around the world. So much so that *The Economist* magazine stated:

> *"Canada's generous refugee system is open to abuse – and foreign crooks know it. Under the Charter of Rights and Freedoms, anyone who arrives claiming to be a refugee has the same legal rights as any Canadian. That can mean a lengthy sequence of hearings and appeals, while the newcomer remains in Canada, living on social benefits … or crime."*

Immigration during the Trudeau years is somewhat misleading. Many believe that under his government immigration increased. In fact statistics show that the number of immigrants actually decreased. What changed was the demographic composition of immigrants. In the past the majority of immigrants to Canada came from Britain and Europe, The recruitment of immigrants was based on skills sets, labour shortage and the economic needs of the country. Under Trudeau, immigration quotas were filled by immigrants from Asia and other under developed countries of the Commonwealth. He also restricted the number of immigrants who were not sponsored by families or were refugees. The number of immigrants decreased under Trudeau, but the shift from economic needs to the 'family class' or sponsored relatives expanded drastically, while individual immigration decreased. The emphasis towards family reunification proved to be a political boon for the Liberal Party. Using the family reunification and multicultural policies of his government as political tools, Trudeau chastised the Conservatives as being anti-immigrant, As a result for many years to come many constituencies with large immigrant population cast their votes for the Liberals.

As the demographic composition of immigrants changed Trudeau saw the opportunity to use his policy of multiculturalism as the counterpoint against Canada's great divide – English v/s French. He used taxpayer dollars to fund cultural festivities in ethnic communities; knowing full well that it would repay him at election time. Multiculturalism thus benefitted Liberals politically.

While Trudeau believed it to be fair to support any group of immigrants who wanted to maintain its culture and preserve its mother tongue there were and still are many who question the expenditures and impact of this policy. From the start, the *Toronto Star* questioned this policy:

> *No immigrant should be encouraged to think that Canada is essentially a chain of ethnic enclaves."*[3]

Despite the grumbles of some Canadians, multiculturalism has been embraced by successive governments, because it is a vote getter. This policy entrenched in the Charter of Rights and Freedom is today the source of many controversies as Canada faces a more diverse population. The attacks of 9/11, on the United States have further uncovered the problems of multiculturalism. Germany's Angela Merkel and Britain's David Cameron have both denounced multiculturalism, as a barrier to immigrant integration. Ezra Levant goes even further:

> *"Multiculturalism doesn't work. You can't have two competing cultures at the same time."*[4]

Due to the radicalization of youths in western countries, any immigration policy should take into account the impact on cultural values. Salim Mansur, a Professor of Political Science at The University of Western Ontario, and an immigrant, summarized the cultural threat to Canada in this way:

> *"There is a limit to reasonable accommodation, just as there is limit to how much water may be poured into a glass of wine before the wine loses its properties. A liberal society based on individual rights and the rule of law cannot indefinitely accommodate demands from non-liberal cultural groups without subverting its own identity."*[5]

One can argue that the multiculturalism policy of Pierre Trudeau benefitted the liberals, and helped his government's immigration policy. The fact remains that under the Progressive Conservative government of Brian Mulroney immigration tripled and continued to increase under Harper's Conservative government. In effect removing any veracity in the – 'anti-immigrant' label often assigned to conservatives.

While the Liberals may have used multiculturalism as a seemingly positive tool for their immigration policy, it is the Hon. Jason Kenney MP, who held the post of Minister for Citizenship, Immigration and Multiculturalism form October 30, 2008 to July 15, 2013, who turned the table on the Liberals. In one of our interviews he said:

> *"The Liberal approach, I would argue was categorized by a certain kind of naiveté and political correctness. The Liberals refuse to recognize that just as there is an obligation for*

> *Canada as the host country to be welcoming and provide an opportunity to new immigrants, so to there is an obligation on new comers to integrate and to accept Canada's core historically grounded values."*

Jason Kenney became known as 'Minister 'curry in a hurry' as he courted the immigrant population of Canada. The affectionate moniker came from the fact that he attended every possible festivities and gatherings of immigrant communities. He garnered tremendous respect among immigrant community leaders as he developed a policy that was based on merit as demanded by the majority of legal newcomers.

In an anecdote, he told me that he was inspired by a comment made by Mrs. Johnson of Scarborough who told him: *"thank you for all the changes you have made. I came to this country the legal way forty years ago. I worked hard and paid my taxes. And I have seen far too many people in subsequent years sneak in through the back door, and climbing the side window. Then you came and shut the door and nailed the window. You said you have to come in the right way."*

Over the years there have been many issues with government immigration policies. Canada's 21st Century immigration policy can largely be attributed to Jason Kenney who has disregarded both the opposition NDP's demand to significantly increase the quota of immigrants to 1% of the population each year and requests by others to reduce the number of immigrants. His position is quite clear – immigration is about quality and not quantity, the determining factors being the kind of economic results and success the newcomers are achieving. Many of his changes will change Canada for years to come. The impact of his policies should be examined to put to rest any doubt about the idea that Conservatives do not like immigrants.

Many of the Harper government immigration policy have for origin the work of Charles M. Beach Professor of Economics and Director of the John Deutsch Institute at Queen's University. During the course of this discussion, reference is made to "Canadian Immigration Policy for the 21st Century."

Early in his position as Minister for Citizenship, Immigration and Multiculturalism , Kenney declared that he was ready to reform the country's immigration policies, including the points system, major issues such as fraud marriage, human smugglers, unfounded refugees, and the billion-dollar bill of health and social benefits claimed from them. At the same time his focus shifted towards attracting more international students who qualify as a graduate in the program, increasing the focus on youth, job skills and most importantly fluency in English or French. These changes in his view would fulfill Canadian immigration goals as identified by Beach *et al*[6]:

- The aging of population that is, an attempt to ease, through immigration, the fiscal burden associated with a rising share of non-working to working population.
- Responding, through immigration, to the need for additional skills (human capital), associated with the expansion of the knowledge economy.
- Promoting economic growth especially. At present, regional growth, by dispersing immigrants to small centres across the country.

Right from the start Jason Kenney was convinced that the Liberals' *naiveté* failed to recognize the integrity of the system. He strongly believed that immigrant fraud existed and it was his goal to make changes. He wanted every asylum claimant and application for marriage sponsorship to be *bona fide* and legitimate. He wanted to select people who would come through the front door with the willingness to integrate. He wanted to close the back door and stopped the abuse of the generosity of the great Canadian immigration policy

To fulfill his promise of reforming the system, Kenney introduced a number of Bills that would not necessarily please his opponents, but in the end, the decisions made sense. Among the more controversial ones are:

- Kenney radically reformed Canada's refugee system. When two boatloads of Tamil refugees arrived on the shores of British Columbia in 2009 and 2010he was prompted to change the law and gave the Minister of Public Safety the ability to designate specific refugees as "irregular arrivals" – which allows for mandatory arrest and detention for up to a year. *The Protecting Canada's Immigration System Act* also made it easier to prosecute human smugglers, improve mandatory minimum prison sentences on convicted smugglers and hold both ship owners and their operators to account when their ships are used in human smuggling operations.
- He also eliminated certain premium health benefits for unfounded asylum claimants; including dental work, vision care and prescription medication. The government expects to save taxpayers $100 million over 5 years. Refugee claims from Hungary have fallen 97% and have risen for states like Afghanistan, Congo and Somalia.
- He brought forth the *Faster Removal of Foreign Criminals Act*, making it easier for dangerous foreign criminals to be removed from Canada, also making it harder for those who pose a risk to Canada to enter in the first place, all the while removing unnecessary barriers that existed for legitimate well-meaning visitors.
- Kenney has tightened up the rules around spousal sponsorship and conditional permanent residence status, triggering criticism from human rights lawyers, refugee groups and women's groups.
- Under the new law for spousal sponsorship, foreigners sponsored to enter Canada as spouses must stay in the relationship for two years before they're granted permanent residence.
- Increasingly we find that a shortage of workers exists in certain industries. The shortages are often related to the reluctance and lack of mobility of Canadians to provinces where

jobs exists. To this effect recent immigration policies have been changed to attract more skilled newcomers to Canada.

Despite constant criticisms from the left who believed that his changes were harsh, Kenney stood steadfast in his plans to reform immigration policies. He said:

> *"I was often criticized for not using evidence based information, but every change was made with the best data available. My opponents refuse to admit that the status quo was deficient. I was willing to take the risk to be called names; I took the risk to implement the needed change to the system, based from what I learnt through my constant communication with new immigrants."*

Most of all the policies of Minister Kenney are based on the long ignored detail that most immigrants are in fact conservatives in their belief. Trudeau brilliantly monopolized symbolic diversity with the point system in the early seventies. He brilliantly closed the door for blue color workers from Europe and improved the white colour quota from non – European countries. Loyalty developed among immigrants, resulting in their support for the Liberals.

Most newcomers share values to the right of center, they are entrepreneurs, they take risks to advance themselves, and are twice as likely to start small businesses. Their decision to come to Canada is entrepreneurial. Most are against high taxation and respectful of tradition and family values. They are usually against anti – social behavior and they support a strong foreign policy due to the suffering under dictatorial regimes.

In effect immigrants have a matrix of values more aligned with conservative values. But, at first immigrants did not understand that, and the Conservatives did not recognize that immigrants are more closely aligned to their values and did not really develop a relationship of trust until recently. Until Jason Kenney that is.

Despite efforts by successive governments, Liberal or Conservative one deficiency in the system remains – for example the recognition of foreign qualifications.

According to Jeffrey G. Reitz:

> *"Occupational change, particularly in the most highly-skilled professional and managerial fields, is also a key part of the emerging knowledge economy. Occupations vary in the procedures that employers use to assess job qualifications … Professional occupations have developed elaborate and often highly bureaucratized procedures for credential assessment, and the prevalence of these occupations has grown as a component of the workforce. Management occupations also often have very educational requirements – and even higher earnings – but less codified procedures."*[7]

Too often as a result of these 'elaborate and bureaucratized' procedures masquerading for 'professional protectionism' many immigrants are under employed. The federal government has little power in enforcing the recognition of foreign professional qualifications. In Canada most, if not all, professional bodies operate under Provincial laws and therefore have and make their own rules.

In 2003, at a conference called by the Hon. Jane Stewart, Liberal Minister of Human Resources Development to discuss the mobility of foreign professionals Michael Sleigh and I presented the following conclusion:

> *"The GATS, signed by 55 countries (including Canada), is the first multilateral, legally enforceable agreement covering trade and investment services. It has provisions that support the contention that foreign qualified professionals, including accountants such as the ACCA, should have increased recognition in Canada. The GATS is also aimed at bringing more transparency into the services field. It asks the World Trade Organization members to make market access commitments in specific sectors, thereby opening the door to foreign*

service-providers. The enforcement of GATS, however, has been difficult due to jurisdictional problems: the Federal government signed the agreement but the provinces regulate the professions. To be fair the Federal government is at a loss to enforce its signed commitment unless the provinces agree to treat professionals equally across the country. This remains a dilemma for foreign professionals. Signed agreements between nations exist but are they enforceable in Canada?"[8]

While the left continues to oppose the foreign workers' policy, there is no denying that in certain regions of the country, mainly in western Canada, there is a shortage of certain types of skilled workers. In the past, the cumbersome requirements for labour market validations have driven skilled immigrants to other destinations like Australia and the United States. The new rules by the Conservative government require foreign applicants to include an assessment of their education to measure whether their degrees and diplomas are relevant to Canadian standards. The other side of the coin must be that the temporary foreign workers program should not be used to drive wages down or to fill low-skill jobs. The temporary foreign workers' policy is an integral part of the countries immigration policy. Canada has been a welcoming country for years; it is not the time to close the doors for political reasons. The policy must be one that ensures the economic growth of this country in a proper context. As Terence Corcoran wrote:

"Canadian economic history is filled with the success of free trade and the free movement of people. Today, more than ever, the world is a global market for goods. A global labour market is the next frontier. It will take a while, but it should become part of Canada's national mission. The temporary foreign worker program was part of the mission."[9]

No matter which government initiates a system, there are those who will abuse it. The revelation that the Royal Bank of Canada, and possibly the owner of a McDonalds franchise have misused the Temporary Foreign Worker Program (TFWP), has caused Minister Kenney to review some of the program's rules. On June 20, 2014, the Government announced an immediate overhaul of the TFWP meant to restore the program to its original purpose: a last limited resource for employers when qualified Canadians are unavailable for jobs. To prevent further abuse, including paying foreign workers 15% less than the average wage for a job, by 2015 hefty penalties will be imposed on employers who abuse the program.

Minister Kenney, who was awarded the "Moral Courage Award" by UN Watch, may have just made his first '*faux pas*' as a conservative. In reforming the TFWP, Minister Kenney may have gone too far. By curtailing many of the previous rules and putting more restrictions, his decision may have contributed to hurt small companies. There is no doubt, as seen above, that some will abuse the program, but in the main there still is a need for foreign workers in the fast growing provinces of the West and in many service industries. There is a Canadian problem of labour mobility. Too often Canadians are reluctant to move from one province to another and in addition there are still certain jobs that some Canadians refuse to perform. The Minister's new rules have been opposed by small businesses and organizations like The Canadian Federation of Independent Business, and the Canadian Taxpayers Federation, but supported by Unions. It is strange for a strong conservative Minister to do something that pleases the labour movement.

Canada was built by immigrants. Different governments have had diverse policies, and in recent years the Conservative government has taken an opposite approach from their Liberal predecessors. New rules have been put in place and changes, not always perfect, have been implemented. One way or another, immigrants are part of the fabric of this country and a balanced policy that offers new opportunities and promote economic growth must continue to work hand in hand.

The American Dream

The United States have long been a beacon and a safe haven for victims of ethnic, and religious intolerance for immigrants. Starting from the first settlers to today's immigrants from all over the world. Ellis Island saw the arrival of an estimated 120 million immigrants between 1892 and 1954. For many, if not all, their new country offered a new beginning and the opportunity to reach the American dream.

A complex issue, immigration has been a major source of population growth and cultural change throughout much of the country's history. Over the years, changes to the law have resulted into controversy concerning ethnicity, economic benefits, and jobs for non-immigrants, and settlement patterns. Today's political aspects of immigration have an increasing impact on crime, and voting behavior, and division within both the Republican and Democrat parties.

Prior to 1965, immigration to the U.S was restricted to people from Western Europe. As a result of the Civil Rights Movement of the sixties, immigrant quotas based on ethnicity were replaced by The Immigration and Nationality Act of 1965. As a result the bulk of today's immigrants to the United States is made up of persons born in Mexico, India, China, and the Philippines. Every year approximately two-thirds of legal immigration to the U.S is through family reunification.

The majority of immigrants are from Mexico. The Census bureau estimates that by 2050, almost 25% of the population of the United States will be of Hispanic descent due largely to immigration from Latin America. There are several factors for this shift. There are many jobs that American citizens won't take; they include agricultural and menial low paying jobs. Hispanics have been the main source of labour to fill these positions. The agricultural industry employs immigrants, including in many cases illegal immigrants, who earn a very low pay. While it may be good for the economy, unlike immigrants from other ethnic demography, Hispanics tend to be less financially secure. Foreign laborers have to work for no-pay for months in order to repay the costs of their H-series visas, and room and board. Still there are more opportunities in the U.S than Mexico, and this has produced an increase in illegal immigration. According to data produced by the Pew Hispanic Centre, eight percent of all babies born in the United States in 2008 were from illegal parents.

The lure of success and economic freedom is a constant magnet for immigrants. Illegal immigration has been a major problem for the United States, and every so often the laws have had to be changed or amended. Starting with the 1986 Immigration Reform and Control Act (IRCA) signed by President Reagan, amnesty was granted to 3 million immigrants already in the United States. The 1990 Immigration Act, signed by President George H. W. Bush modified and expanded the 1965 act; it significantly increased the total immigration limit to 700,000 and increased visas by 40 %. Family reunification was retained as the main immigration criteria, with significant increases in employment-related immigration.

President William Clinton signed The Illegal Immigration Reform and Immigrant Responsibility Act of 1996, which states that immigrants unlawfully present in the United States for 180 days but less than 365 days must remain outside the United States for three years unless they obtain a pardon. If they are in the United States for 365 days or more, they must stay outside the United States for ten years unless they obtain a waiver. If they return to the United States without the pardon, they may not apply for a waiver for a period of ten years. But over the years, it seems that this law has not been effectively enforced.

Increasingly the debate is centered on illegal immigration. The border between Mexico and the U.S is so porous that thousands enter the United States from mostly Mexico and other South American countries. In addition, the 2001 attacks which involved 20 foreign born terrorists, also exposed the weaknesses of the immigration system. The economic recession of 2008 and continued low employment rates, has made any discussion about immigration more difficult.

More and more the political parties drift further apart on the issue and in the meantime the problem gets bigger as the number of illegal immigrants continues to grow. From a political stance the Democrats have always benefitted from an increase in immigration. It is said that Hispanic voters influenced the outcome and election of Barack

Obama in 2010, and "may have saved the Senate for Democrats". Fact or not this is a problem for the Republicans. Many members of the GOP do not recognize the threat of a growing Hispanic population. On the other hand the Obama administration is prepared to do everything to increase Democrats' popularity among Hispanics.

In a move to make further inroads in the Latino community the administration proposes to give amnesty to some 11 million illegal immigrants. Several bills and executive orders have been used to implement this strategy. On April 24. 2013, Attorney General Holder on C-Span said:

> *"Creating a pathway to earn citizenship for the 11 million unauthorized immigrants in this country, is absolutely essential. This is a matter of civil and human rights."*

The Dream Act was first introduced in 2001 in a bi-partisan bill by Dick Durbin (D-Sen-Il) and Orin Hatch (R-Sen-Ut). The original Bill proposed:

"Conditional permanent residency to certain immigrants of good moral character who graduate from U.S. high schools, arrived in the United States as minors, and lived in the country continuously for at least five years prior to the bill's enactment. If they were to complete two years in the military or two years at a four-year institution of higher learning, they would obtain temporary residency for a six-year period. Within the six-year period, they may qualify for permanent residency if they have "acquired a degree from an institution of higher education in the United States or [have] completed at least 2 years, in good standing, in a program for a bachelor's degree or higher degree in the United States" or have "served in the armed services for at least 2 years and, if discharged, [have] received an honourable discharge."[10]

Some states have enacted their own Dream Act legislation. In 2012 President Obama declared that his administration would stop deporting young illegal aliens who match certain criteria previously proposed under the DREAM ACT. The debate continues and proponents of the Act argue that the economic benefits outweigh the costs. Opponents argue that the Act encourages illegal immigration, and that in fact jeopardises the status of legal applicants. But often ignored are the economic realities of implementing the ACT. The independent Congressional Budget Office estimated the 2010 version of the Act would reduce (federal) direct deficits by about $1.4 billion over the 2011-2020 period and increase federal government revenues by $2.3 billion over the next 10 years. The same report also notes that the Act "would *increase* projected deficits by more than $5 billion in at least one of the four consecutive 10-year periods starting in 2021."[11]

Obama's perceived amnesty has caused a humanitarian crisis. Believing that they would be given U.S. citizenship, thousands of unaccompanied children are crossing the borders. These children and some pregnant women, mostly from Central America, are paying criminals to get them across the Texas border. Because of the sheer number resulting from this latest influx of illegal immigrants, these refugees are being shipped across the country and housed under terrible conditions.

There are also the consequences of the Mexican-American War of 1846, which resulted in the U.S., occupation of New Mexico and California, the invasion of Northeastern and Northwest Mexico. American forces conducted a blockade, and took control of several garrisons on the Pacific coast further south in Baja California. As a result under the Treaty of Guadalupe hidalgo, Mexico accepted the loss of Texas and declared the Rio Grande as the border with the United States. There are many Hispanics of Mexican origin who believe that they could recapture these territorial losses through the ballot box. Even if this hypothesis is not true, we cannot ignore that through immigrants sending money back to their families in Mexico, illegal immigration can be regarded as one of Mexico's biggest export.

While the debate continues, solutions are not being found. The United States policy of reunification does play a huge part in future legislation. How can any administration deal with the 11 million illegal immigrants already in the country? Is deportation on a massive scale the answer? – Obviously not.

The Democrats prefer a complete amnesty, because they believe that in the long run it will guarantee them the Hispanic votes for ever. The Republicans worry about the economic costs, and security. The political implications are enormous for both parties.

The political climate in Washington is so toxic, that congressional inaction on immigration is frustrating State officials. As a result many states are enacting their own laws. Keenly aware of the rising political power of Latinos, state legislation is not homogeneous and depending on which party is in power the legislation is either restrictive or progressive in nature. Some of the new laws relax restrictions on undocumented immigrants, while others restrict social welfare dollars to legal, rather than illegal immigrants.

Some states require employers to use the E-verify system, which compares information from employee's Employment Eligibility Verification Form I-9 to data from U.S. government records. A match allows the employee to work in the United States. A mismatch alerts the employer who must resolve the problem within eight days. A number of states have passed laws that allow illegals to obtain drivers' licenses; others offer in-state tuition for children of undocumented immigrants. Some states have new laws that protect the victims of human trafficking.

The issue of security also looms very large in the debate and suggested solutions to the problem are very hard to arrive at. The hodgepodge of state legislation proves that immigration in the United States is badly in need of reform. But the will to do so is inexistent due to political ideology, and budgetary concerns.

Many politicians recognize the urgency of the situation. While some may have suggestions, the ideas are so diverse that a compromise seems to be illusive. Many potential presidential candidates have come up with their preferred solutions, but the chasm among GOP politicians is still very wide. Former Florida Governor Jeb Bush for instance says that about illegal immigration: *"Yes they broke the law, but it's not a felony .It's an act of love"*. Others believe that illegals should be treated as criminals and they should be deported. Senator Marco Rubio who co-sponsored a Bill with seven other senators from both parties now opposes the Bill.

The Bill would have given a path to citizenship to some of the estimated 11 million undocumented immigrants living in the U.S. He now favours a piece meal approach as preferred by the majority of Republicans in the House. The situation is insane, and reform is not likely to come soon. The Republican Party must come to grips with the reality of the status quo. They will lose the White House in 2016 and perhaps for ever lose the Latino vote. Bill O'Reilly of Fox News has some great ideas that the Republicans should look at very seriously. In one of his daily memos on April 09, 2014, he suggested the following:

- Those who cross the border illegally or overstay their visas should pay a price.
- Because the government has been guilty of not enforcing the laws to stop illegals from crossing the border, it must bear some responsibility.
- All illegal immigrants must register with the Federal government within six months. Failure to do so will considered a felony.
- Compassion must be shown, but illegal immigrants must pay a fine and apply for citizenship without any guarantee of preferential treatment.
- Immigrants must learn English, given the right to work, but no welfare.
- Borders must be upgraded to make it extremely difficult to cross and should be verified by Congress.
- Criminals must be charged and deported immediately.
- Once the new rules are put in place, no other illegal will ever be put on the citizenship track.

These ideas seem to be very fair and they would go a long way towards finding a compromise and resolving one of the biggest issues in U.S. politics. But, this would be too simple in a divided Congress. The President threats to sign new executive orders to get his immigration proposal forward will further damage the already toxic political environment prior to the 2014 mid-term elections.

If ever the immigration issue is resolved, to consolidate their standing in the immigrant community, the GOP should take a page from the Hon. Minister Jason Kenney of Canada and come to grips with the fact that many immigrants are more conservative than liberal. Hispanic social and religious values are more aligned with conservative values. Many Hispanic Evangelicals and Roman Catholic strongly oppose gay marriage and abortion. To achieve future success the GOP must reverse the voting trends of Hispanics who in 2012 voted 27% for Romney and 71% for Obama. A comprehensive, just and fair reform of the immigration policies will go a long way to bring the Latino vote to the Republicans.

As stated earlier security is a huge problem and the possibility of terrorists using the tunnels built by drug cartels to enter the U.S can also become a problem for Canada. So is the threat of terrorists entering the United States from Canada as was the case with Ahmed Ressam, who was caught in Port Angeles, Washington, in December 1999 with explosives and detonators in his trunk intended to blow the Los Angeles Airport.

In conclusion, because of the lengths of their borders both Canada and the United States have a vested interest in working together to control immigration. The economic future of both countries depend on a growing population, while diversity and compassion should be taken into account, existing laws must be enforced to protect the security and economic wellbeing of both countries. Those who want to relax or change the laws to suit their political leanings and guarantee their political future may be short sighted and in the long run contributing to the demise of their culture, and prosperity.

CHAPTER 10

THE MEDIA, HOLLYWOOD AND THE LIBERAL ELITE

There is no doubt that the media has a great influence on political outcomes. The use of the word media encompasses: newspapers, magazines, television, radio, the internet and all social media outlets. Both the right and the left would like to have a major share of exposure. But often the reality is that the left has gained much of the ground and in recent past has greatly influenced election results in both Canada and the United States. Today public opinion is greatly shaped through the use of social media, and increasingly by Hollywood and 'A' List celebrities.

Although Canada, in 2014 has a conservative government it does not mean that the media does not attempt to tilt the balance towards the liberals. In the U.S. it is clear that the media tilts to the left. Too often the main stream media harbours the sentiment that liberals are intellectuals and have compassion, whereas conservatives are angry, extreme morons. In this chapter we shall examine media concentration, and the role played by the main stream media to influence political views on both sides of the border. Furthermore we shall scrutinize how the media reports on events that result in the acceptance or rejection of major government policies, exposing the major influence the media has in our daily lives.

In 2001, Professor David Taras argued in his book that the Canadian media was in the midst of a cataclysmic change. The main culprit seemed to have been Conrad Black and his media empire building. He wrote:

> *"Some would argue that Black's strangle hold is especially disturbing because Black is an ardent and passionate political warrior. He has strong right-wing opinions, tends to hire journalists who share his views, and knows that newspapers are formidable political weapons. With such overwhelming power clutched in Black's fist, diversity is being threatened."*[1]

Today conservative media concentration is far from the truth. In fact in Canada just like the United States, and many industrialised countries, the media has aggressively tilted to the left. The bias towards liberal reporting is only counteracted by talk radio and some cable TV. Even then, the news is filtered to give a liberal rose coloured slant.

When the Canadian Broadcasting Corporation (CBC) was created it was to promote two strategic objectives: the first was to counter an increasing U.S. culture coming from the air across the border. The second was more about national unification to bridge the gap between regions and more importantly the division between French and English Canada. A vision, perhaps noble in design, has turned into a much reviled institution rife with elite and pompous news and programs. Taras says it best:

> *"The great irony perhaps is that the CBC, which has been viewed with such suspicion by politicians of literally every stripe, has come to be seen as a symbol of government bureaucracy and officialdom."*[2]

Ownership of the television sector, including speciality and pay-tv, is now in the hands of the big-4, namely Rogers, Shaw (Corus), Bell and Quebecor. Each of these corporations also holds a number of newspapers, magazines and internet operations. As if concentration was not bad enough, the public is bombarded by 24-hour news, mostly sourced from the same outlets. Many if not all foreign news, including U.S developments are sourced from the same outlets including Reuters, the Associated Press, the BBC, ABC, NBC, CBS, MSNBC or CNN; all of them providing a liberal point view. While at the same time sources like Fox News, Sky TV are shunned because they provide a conservative point of view, more often than not more balanced in nature and content.

Through regulations set up by the CRTC, Sun News Network is not allowed to be widely distributed like other networks. In 2014, Al-Jazeera applied to have its Arab-language channel released from controls put in place to prevent the spread of hate speech. In their application the network argued:

> *"that rather than ensuring a balance between freedom of expression on the one hand and guarding against the harms of abusive comment on the other, the condition goes too far in stifling free speech while working against the goal of developing a diversity of editorial voices."*[3]

Since all news outlets have a bias; right or left, it remains to be seen who the CRTC favours in its decision to allow widespread public access to news by Sun Network or Al-Jazeera Arabic.

Talk radio which is mostly dominated by right-leaning personalities has taken a prominent place in the media industry. In Canada Charles Adler is the voice of the over thirties. His new show on Quebecor's Sun Television provides a new platform, which allows his views to be vetted by political and journalistic guests who appear on his shows. In effect Charles Adler has become the antidote to the Canadian liberal media.

Another talk show who had a great influence on conservative views was Dave Rutherford who operated from Calgary's QR 770, another Corus outlet. Incidentally, upon his retirement in 2013, he was replaced by a former Liberal MLA Dave Taylor, who together with Angela Kokott is now the source of news in Calgary.

Unfortunately for the public, the so-called main stream media more often than not is devoid of investigative reporting. In fact as Howard Kurtz of Media Buzz wrote:

> *"there is a cancer eating away at the news business – the cancer of boredom, superficiality and irrelevance – and radical surgery is needed."*[4]

This cancer not only affects the U.S, but it also has a significant influence on Canadian media, who have followed in the same path. The effect can be clearly seen in the way that anything 'Harper' is portrayed. Before his election as prime minister, Stephen Harper was often portrayed as a heartless, taciturn, right-wing freak with a hidden agenda. As with the description of Joe Clark's lost luggage on an official trip, Harper's wardrobe and his visible paunch at a NAFTA meeting made headlines. Now as a successful prime minister he is scrutinized and often criticized for his conservative policies and foreign policy stance.

Harper is often criticized for taking Canada away from its conciliatory and neutral stance on foreign affairs. On his recent historic tour to Israel, the headline in the *National Post* was: *"Harper heckled as PM warns of 'new strain' of anti-Semitism in Israeli parliament speech"*. It was no surprise that one of the two hecklers was Ahmad Tibi the Deputy Speaker of the Knesset and former adviser to Yasser Arafat. Tibi is one of twelve Arab-Israeli members of the Knesset. The media chose a negative headline instead of giving credit to the PM for his historic visit and speech. To those who believe that Canada has lost its position as an 'honest broker', the report of heckling must have been music to their ears.

During Harper's visit, Ivison the reporter for The *National Post* looked for missteps and ulterior motives. Instead of reporting about the relationship between Israel and Canada, Ivison and other members of the press tried to ambush the PM about his position on Palestine. While in Ramallah, he commented: "When I'm in Israel, I'm asked to single out Israel. When I'm in Palestinian Authority, I'm asked to single out Israel, and in half the other places around the world, you ask me to single out Israel,"

The Economist magazine wrote that: "the rationale for the trip and for the policy that underlies it causes puzzlement in Canada." No the visit does not puzzle all Canadians; it annoys liberal thinkers and those who deny any Palestinian responsibility for the stalemate towards a peaceful solution. What was missing, or given little ink in the reports, was the amount of Canadian dollars that Harper gave to the Palestinian Authority and Jordan.

Whether one likes Harper or not, the fact remains that peace in the Middle-East will never be achieved as long as the Arab world refuses to acknowledge the existence of Israel, as a sovereign state and part of a two state solution.

The lack of accountability in reporting is not confined to Canada and the United States as exemplified by the following Swedish case:

> *"A young Somali journalist in Sweden named Amun Abdullahi got herself in trouble with the politically correct elite by reporting the truth about the radicalization of young Somalis in Rinkeby (a culturally enriched suburb of Stockholm), where they were recruited for jihad by the Islamic terrorist group Al-Shabab.*
>
> *The treatment meted out to Ms. Abdullahi made her decide to move back to Somalia. She acknowledges that Mogadishu is a dangerous place, but she considers Sweden more dangerous, because "here you cannot tell the truth."*
>
> *A few months later criticisms emerged from an entirely different front.*
> *From her own colleagues on one of Sweden's most influential political radio shows, "Konflikt"*
> *Here Ekot's and thereby Amun's research was dismissed as mere "hearsay" and "rumors".*
> *Behind it stood Randi Mossige-Norheim, who has been awarded the Swedish "Grand Journalism Award" among many others. It's simply normal to ask "did it really happen?"*[5]

In the United States the situation is even worse, as the main stream media now virtually operates as the Obama propaganda machine. Since

Obama's arrival on the political scene there has been a concerted effort to ignore his weaknesses and portray all his policies and actions as being not only strengths but also brilliance. It started at MSNBC when Chris Matthews commented on Obama's 2008 campaign speech and said:

> *"I have to tell you, you know, it's part of reporting this case, this election, the feeling most people get when they hear Barack Obama's speech. My, I felt this thrill going up my leg. I mean, I don't have that too often".*[6]

From then on, the way that news is being reported on MSNBC is mostly based on interpretation of the Obama administration with a liberal eye.

The two wars in Iraq and Afghanistan have taken a toll on American's patience. When Obama was elected, he promised 'hope and change', yet after over 5 years in office very little has changed. In fact whatever changes were made have often been for the worse. However, the main stream media continues to either ignore the failings of the administration or echo the mantra that Bush was responsible for all the ills of the nation. There is no doubt that Bush was responsible for many bad policies, but to continue to assign blame to his administration five years after his departure, is not only disingenuous, but demonstrates strong partisanship in the media. As a result the majority of the public gets the wrong information and the trend towards socialism continues to grow.

As the economy stalls and unemployment grows, the main stream media ignores or does not report the facts. For example if the number of people who have stopped to look for a job is taken into consideration, the reported rate of 7% unemployment would really be closer to 13%, yet the press continues to say that the rate is falling. There is very little report about increasing crime within the black community, as well as the growing unemployment rate among young blacks. But the race issue is constantly being brought forward to excuse the failures of the Obama administration.

The most egregious reporting has been about the implementation of Obamacare. While the majority of Americans were against the proposed health act, the liberal media portrayed it as a significant improvement for Americans. Upon implementation, the whole system has been fraught with massive problems, ranging from system problems to economic disaster. The media refuses to report that millions may lose their insurance and that the administration and the President were involved in a bold face lie when they promised that "you could keep you insurance if you like it".

Dr. Danielle Martin, a Toronto physician enthusiastically defended the reputation of Canada's Medicare system during some tense exchanges in the U.S. Congress. She was invited to testify by the committee chairman, Independent Vermont Sen. Bernie Sanders, a self-described socialist who would like to see the U.S. adopt a single-payer system like the one in Canada.

Ignoring the fact that many Canadians feel that their system is broken and in need of reform. The Canadian media chose instead to report how Dr. Danielle Martin is being courted by political parties at the municipal, provincial and federal level, as a result of her testimony before the U.S. Senate sub-committee.

While there may still be some balance in reporting by some of the main stream media, MSNBC with a cadre of political pundits has become the equivalent of the "Tass Agency" of the old Soviet Union. Many, if not all of their hosts, not only believe in liberalism but spew misinformation and do not rely on facts for their statements. Too often they have had to apologize for their comments. So much so that an 'apology' by MSNBC's opinion hosts is no longer really what it is meant to be.

The other phenomenon which shapes political discourse today is the Internet. The old barriers which separated newspapers, radio, television and magazines have all fallen. The online medium now provides the news 24 hours a day. In haste to respond to the need for immediate reporting, we gave up perspective, and accuracy. As traditional reporting loses its role of gatekeeper and investigator, sensationalism increasingly and more often takes precedent to the truth, reducing the quality of our news.

The younger generation finds its news in cyber-space; a source dominated by the likes of Facebook and Twitter. Regrettably, too often this form of communication is rife with conspiracy theories, rumors, provided by bloggers who publish opinions, without factual backup. As old media struggles to meet the demands of a fast paced world, true discussions are lost. Christopher Waddell states: "All of this rapid and ongoing change suggests a continued fracturing of mass discussion about political issues and public policies into piecemeal debates among smaller groups concerned about their own issues, receiving political messages tailored specifically for them and relying on the narrowly targeted media designed with their interest in mind."

Hollywood

The entertainment industry is openly involved in American politics. Many actors and other members of the industry are now engaged not only in fund raising, but in vicarious policy making. Let us be clear, everyone has right to his/her opinion and can decide to support any cause they so choose. However, given their increase in stature and influence in a fickle world of celebrity worship, some entertainers have increased access to the media and their bully pulpit. The problem is that in most cases, much of their supporting statements for liberal policies are devoid of substance and facts. Another incursion in politics is the production of TV series with a political bent – *House of Cards* and the *West Wing* for example. In 2013 there were plans to produce a bio-pic of Hillary Clinton. After the Republicans protested that it was propaganda for a Clinton bid for the White House the proposed production was cancelled. However, in 2014 there will be a new series called '*Madam Secretary*', obviously portraying a female Secretary of State dealing with world issues – any resemblance to Hillary Clinton will presumably be purely coincidental.

Actors and movie producers have taken the time to create movies with a liberal bent. This is not new; during the war similar approaches were used to promote the military. But today the film industry is very much involved with the current administration. Not only do they raise enormous amounts of money for the Democrats but they also participate in the tacit support of liberal policies. The irony is that most of these new government acolytes are part of new liberal elite. They have access to millions of dollars and do not have an ordinary life. They travel by private jets, and yet criticize the use of oil. They make millions and yet complain about income inequality.

The hypocrisy is rampant among the celebrity 'A' List. With loud, sometimes violent, opposition they are constantly harping against the Alberta Oil Sands and the expansion of the Keystone XL pipeline. In January 2013, songwriter Neil Young, started the 'Honour the Treaties Tour' to raise $75,000 for the Athabasca Chipewyan First Nation's legal defence fund. During the tour he compared the Alberta Oil Sands to Hiroshima, and ignored the fact that the development of the oil sands contributes to the economy of Canada. Young failed to address the real issues and ignored the facts. Michael Den Tandt of the *National Post* has an interesting set of questions that Young cannot and will not answer:

> *"If the oils sands are shuttered and Fort McMurray, Alta., becomes a ghost town, what then? How does he provide for revenue to replace what is lost? Will it come, say, from income tax hikes? Or by seizing the assets of the wealthiest? Perhaps the shortfall could be made up via carbon tax? Or a surcharge on gas guzzling SUVs and pickup trucks?"*[7]

In Calgary while entertaining his supporters, Young's five tour busses were kept idling outside, spewing CO^2 in the air to keep them warm. But more importantly this is a man who writes and performs songs with some of the most racist lyrics. For example in *Pocahontas:* he wrote:

> *"I wish I was a trapper/I would give thousand pelts/To sleep with Pocahontas/And find out how she felt."*

Or recalling a sex romp 'with a little Indian', he said:

> *The first time was not really great. At least I didn't get any diseases. So it was good."*[8]

That's Liberal hypocrisy at its worst.

Following in the footsteps of celebrities like James Cameron and Neil Young, who criticize the Oil Sands of Alberta, we can now add Archbishop Desmond Tutu, who devoid of facts said:

> *"The fact that this filth is being created now, when the link between carbon emissions and global warming is so obvious, reflects negligence and greed,"*[9]

The Nobel Laureate who has left his home of South Africa for a better life in America has added environmental activist to his title. Instead of lecturing Canadians on economic and resource development, he should perhaps concentrate on the continuing plight of his fellow countrymen who still toil in the gold and diamond mines of South Africa.

The late night shows, now substitute for news as most do not read newspapers or watch the news or even listen to the radio. Most people watch U.S. late night shows with the likes of Jay Leno, Jimmy Fallon, Jon Stewart, David Letterman, Bill Maher, and Stephen Colbert, all of whom are hardened progressives. Canada has its own liberal presenters with CBC's Rick Mercer and George Stroumboulopoulos; the latter has his own show on CNN during the summer months

For many of the viewing public these shows provide them with what they believe is the news. These types of comedy/variety shows are very popular and these hosts have under the guise of political satire created a new channel for liberal policies. The worse of them, Bill Maher has on some occasions transgressed the limits of satire through personal attacks. He even use the c*** word to describe Governor Sara Palin. Donald Trump has temporarily dropped a law suit against Maher for saying:

> *"that he would pay $5 million if Trump could prove that he was not the son of Trump's mother and an orangutan, riffing on Trump's offer to donate a large sum of money to charity if President Obama would release his college records."*

This is an example of another late night joke that was not really done so much in jest, but instead tried to make a political point. Presumably there are no bounds anymore where TV ratings are concerned. Words have consequences, and late night shows are now shaping political discourse to the detriment of facts and truth.

The Liberal Elite

Over the past two decades, liberals and their friends in the media have built an aura around themselves. In their minds all conservatives are morons, while all liberals are intellectuals. Furthermore conservatives are extreme and angry, liberals are moderates and compassionate.. This evaluation of their self is demonstrated in articles, movies and more importantly in political analysis.

During the Bush years, the elected President was always being portrayed as an incompetent, with less intellect than his liberal opponents. He was ridiculed on Saturday Night Live, because it was easy to mock his accent and what they viewed as his inability to articulate his ideas, based on their assertion of what was right for them.

Obama on the other hand is viewed as an articulate and great orator, notwithstanding that he said that there were 57 states and while talking about the military he referred to the corps personnel as the *'corpse men'.*

The biggest issue with the liberal elite is their notion that they have solutions to all the world problems. Many entertainers have good intentions, but more often than not their positions are devoid of substance and unsubstantiated facts. As an example, Bono of U2 fame has campaigned for the debt write-off for African countries. While noble in its proposal, the fact remains that most of the money lent to African countries did not go towards the programs for which they were destined; but instead went to Swiss bank accounts held by dictators and despots who ruled these poor countries. Then again, Bono may be entitled to criticize, as he donated $10 million of his own money to help eradicate AIDS in Africa, In fairness, he also heaped praised on George Bush for his support for the same cause.

Other magnates like Warren Buffet and millionaire stars, support tax increases to support Obama's mantra of income inequality. The liberal elite always promote the expansion and prosperity of the middle class, however every time they raise taxes as a remedy, it is the middle class that gets affected the most. Under a progressive tax system, millionaires can afford tax increases, but the middle class is always squeezed between the 'one percenters' and the very poor. The middle class always ends up paying more as a percentage of their earnings and therefore rarely see growth in their real income.

With the constant debate about global warming and climate change, the liberal elite have chosen to fight for the well – being of mother earth. They support policies like a carbon tax, the increase use of bicycles instead of cars while they drive gas guzzling SUVs, promote light bulbs containing mercury requiring a hazmat cleanup, and costs ten times more than incandescent traditional bulbs.

The liberal elite have often embraced many good causes, like the eradication of malaria and the search for remedies for diabetes, Parkinson and other ills. However, while embracing causes they should take some common sense approach to their actions, before embracing government supported legislations and taxes that can harm instead of help. The media should start vetting themselves and provide fact based instead of partisan information to the public. Many times the people they choose to help too often end up with the wrong end of the stick.

The liberal elite have a track record of making statements that have not been fully vetted. Some of the movers and shakers in Hollywood use their influence without understanding the consequences of their actions. Some of them even believe that to deal with their celebrity is equivalent to going to war. Many times the media is so engrossed in covering these people that they ignore the real news. Today's infatuation with the celebrity culture has blurred the role of the media. The public still seeks the truth; unfortunately political bias and frivolity in the media has usurped the search for news legitimacy.

CHAPTER 11

MORALITY, NORMS, VALUES AND POLITICS

In the last presidential election the United States became embroiled in a national discourse about values, morality and sexual mores. While it has been of a lesser importance in Canadian politics, it seems that the influence of the debate south of the border is starting to have an effect here too, and social conservatives are beginning to flex their muscles again to get their views in the public domain.

While this is not a discussion about the rights or wrongs of social issues, it is important to examine the context used by both sides of the argument. We have liberals and social conservatives at each other's throat debating issues on contraception, homosexuality, same-sex marriage, the start of human life, abortions, polygamous marriage and of course the role of religion in politics. The level of the debate in United States may differ from Canada's due to our different political systems but the issues are the same.

The Liberal Point of View

The liberal position on today's social issues has its roots in the sexual revolution of the sixties, and the growth and influence of the feminist movement. Through well-crafted activism, and driven by secular humanists several liberal factions have been able to sway elections and enact new policies which have resulted in the rift in today's society.

On abortion much of the debate in the U.S. is centered on the United States Supreme Court's decision in *Roe v. Wade*, which ruled that the right of privacy under the 14th Amendment would extend to a woman's decision to have an abortion. It further affirmed that a person has a right to abortion until 'viability' which was further defined as:

> *"the interim point at which the fetus becomes ... potentially able to live outside the mother's womb, albeit with artificial aid"*[1]

The interim point was placed at 28 weeks, and allowed States to ban abortion after the 28 week period. Forty-one states now have laws that ban post-viability abortion. However, the battle as to when do human life starts rages on.

The issue of contraception took center stage during the 2012 Presidential elections, when an Obama supporter Sandra Fluke, a women's rights activist inserted herself into the debate by giving a speech to Congressional Democrats on contraception mandates. She put forward that Georgetown University, which she attended, should be compelled to provide contraceptive drugs covered under the Patient Protection and Affordable Care Act. She objected to the Conscience Clause exception which applied to church organizations, and maintained that Georgetown University. Religious schools and other religious institutions should not be exempt from the Act, as it would cause financial, emotional and medical burdens due to the lack of contraception. The Obama campaign seized on this issue and proclaimed itself as the protector of women's health rights.

There are a number of government funded groups who provide services to women, who continuously push for the right for abortion and contraception. Among these groups is Planned Parenthood, who has been caught (by hidden cameras) in giving advice to pregnant women who may have passed the 'viability' term.

The case of Dr. Kermit Gosnell the abortionist, who was found guilty of murdering three babies born alive to poor minority women, brings to the fore the question of late term abortions. In this gruesome case, Gosnell severed the spinal cord of the new born with a pair of scissors to cause 'fetal demise'. Controversial as this maybe, leftist and feminist organizations continue, if not overtly, to support late term abortions.

While condemning the accused Gosnell, Eric Ferrero, Planned Parenthood Federation of America Vice President for Communications in an apparent statement blaming Pro-life Americans said:

> *"The jury has punished Kermit Gosnell for his appalling crimes. This verdict will ensure that no woman is victimized by Kermit Gosnell ever again.*
>
> *"This case has made clear that we must have and enforce laws that protect access to safe and legal abortion, and we must reject misguided laws that would limit women's options and force them to seek treatment from criminals like Kermit Gosnell."*[2]

What is sad and divisive are comments made by abortionists:

> *1. "They [the women] are never allowed to look at the ultrasound because we knew that if they so much as heard the heartbeat, they wouldn't want to have an abortion."* **–Dr. Randall, former abortionist**
>
> *2. "Even now I feel a little peculiar about it, because as a physician I was trained to conserve life, and here I am destroying it."* - **Dr. Benjamin Kalish, abortionist"** [3]

The issue of abortion is one that is not going away soon. While abortions may be considered acceptable in cases of rape, and when the life of the mother is a stake, it is still immoral to allow late term abortions, especially after 28 weeks. With modern medical technology and advances many babies born even before the 28 week term are alive and well today.

Contrary to many States legislation which allows abortion up to 24 weeks, on June 18, 2013, The House of Representative passed a Bill restricting abortion to the first 20 weeks after conception. Prior to its passage, the left's discussion to the proposed Bill was very typical. On the June 15, 2013 *Melissa Harris-Perry* show on MSNBC, guest host Ari Melber opined:

> *"Republican obsession with controlling your uterus." … coming up next, gird your loins. Republican lawmakers are coming, and they're coming for reproductive rights fast and furious … So don't let the talk of a more women-friendly party fool you, and don't believe them when they say that jobs and the economy are clearly the main thing they're focused on. This is the mainstream Republican mission now, with the backing of the House Speaker and a slew of governors who could be serious presidential candidates in 2016. So, as we said, make no mistake and gird your loins, this is what Republicans are about."*[4]

In the meantime the Bill will go nowhere as the Democrat Controlled Senate will ignore it and President Obama has already threatened to veto it.

The Criminal Law Amendment 1968–69 legalized abortion in Canada as long as a committee of doctors deemed that it was necessary for the mental and physical well-being of the mother. The 1969 law introduced by the Pierre Trudeau government was subsequently struck down by the Supreme Court of Canada in the case of *R. v. Morgentaler*, who has been called ' the man who divided Canada'. Since this legal decision, Canada has had no law governing abortion. The decision has been left to the woman and her doctor. As reported by Jonathan Kay:

> *"Osgoode Hall Law School professor Shelley Gavigan declared categorically that 'the unborn child and the pregnant mother speak with one voice – and that voice is hers.' " Later on, Liberal MP Carolyn Bennett put up a slide entitled "role of an elected official," and declared that politicians have "no right" to oppose abortion – because "that is the responsibility of women."*[5]

The other aspect of changing social mores is the issue of same sex marriages. This issue is not about marriages alone, but about the treatment of Lesbians, Gays, Bisexuals and Transgenders (LBGT). The left has embraced this cause despite the divisiveness that it still causes in society.

LBGT's are human beings, and their rights should be respected. What is controversial is the continued push for the relationship between same-sex people to be called marriage. Although recognized in many countries, in the United States there are still some States which do not recognize same-sex marriage. The problem would go away, if same-sex relationships would be recognized legally as a 'civil union' between two people of the same-sex with all the legal rights afforded to heterosexuals' relationships.

However the liberals have found a very successful way to impose their views on society by using the media, and especially Hollywood to expose us to LGBT relationships. There are numerous movies, sitcoms, and other TV programs who regularly promote these relationships. In fact there are very few shows which do not contain a homosexual or any other form of relationship. It seems that every script must contain at least one homosexual scene to make the plot more 'artistic'. Homosexual content in films and TV (e.g. *Modern Family*) very often are awarded for creativity and artistic direction. Hollywood and its members are a major source of funding for the Liberal policies and political parties, with their participation in electoral campaigns increasing as time goes by.

Elections have consequences. The left was emboldened by Clinton's victory over George H. Bush. He quickly reversed the Mexico Doctrine which denied foreign aid and funding to groups who promoted or provided abortions. But he backed down on his promise to lift the ban on lesbians and gays to serve in the U.S. military. However, in 1993 Clinton signed the commonly known policy of "Don't ask, don't tell" (DADT):

> *"The "don't ask" part of the DADT policy specified that superiors should not initiate investigation of a service member's orientation without witnessing disallowed behaviors, though credible evidence of homosexual behavior could be used to initiate an investigation. Unauthorized investiga-*

> *tions and harassment of suspected servicemen and women led to an expansion of the policy to "don't ask, don't tell, don't pursue, don't harass"* [6]

At first President Obama, for political expediency, supported 'civil unions', and opposed the Defense of Marriage Act (DOMA), which did not allow federal benefits to same-sex couples legally married in their states. Later he worked to repeal (DADT) in December 2010, and after a federal appeals court decision DADT was finally ended in September 2011. In the end Obama must be viewed as a supporter of gay rights, and in his 2013 inaugural speech, he further emboldened the LBGT movement when he said:

> *"Our journey is not complete until our gay brothers and sisters are treated like anyone else under the law – for if we are truly created equal, then surely the love we commit to one another must be equal as well."* [7]

In June 2013, the Supreme Court of the United States repealed part of DOMA, but section 2, which allows states to still not recognize gay marriages of couples wed in other states still stands. As a result California Sen. Dianne Feinstein (D) and New York Rep. Jerry Nadler (D) reintroduced their Respect for Marriage Act, which seeks to repeal DOMA entirely. The battle is not over, since Californians who voted against gay marriage are going to court to ensure that their votes still count in a democracy.

As predicted by opponents of same-sex marriage, there comes the next wrangle in the definition of relationships. Promoted as a path to world peace, activists are now proposing poly-amorous relationships, meaning relationships between numerous partners, for example man-woman-man, or woman-man-woman or any combination of multiple partners of either sex. In 2010, two academics: Cacilda Jetha and Christopher Ryan put forward the thesis, based on a study of the bonobo or pigmy chimpanzee that promiscuity led to non-violence. Therefore the academics contend that poly-amorous relationships would lead to world peace. This is a new indoctrination from the left. As Barbara Kay wrote in The *National Post*:

> *"This conflation of the right to marriage with sexual desire – even promiscuous desire – is not, as we see, an entirely grassroots phenomenon; rather it is top-down activism rooted in theories generated in ivory towers."* [8]

Already the supporters of this type of relationship are labelling opponents as 'closed-minded'. The Law Commission of Canada has already stated that they saw "no reason in principle' to limit registered partnerships to two people. Once again it seems that the majority is being subjected to the views of a minority who believe that society should not only change to accept their beliefs, but if society does not do so it will smack of bigotry.

To make matters worse, we find that a 'gay lobby' exists within the Vatican. It has been known for centuries that gays existed within the prelate, and now according to a recent meeting of the Latin American and Caribbean Confederation of Religious Men and Women, Pope Francis revealed a file given to him by his predecessor, Benedict XVI. In a speech on June the 6, 2013 he said:

> *"The reform of the Roman Curia is something that almost all Cardinals asked for in the Congregations preceding the Conclave. I also asked for it,"...*
>
> *"I cannot promote the reform myself, these matters of administration ... I am very disorganized; I have never been good at this. But the cardinals of the Commission will move it forward,"* [9]

To further liberal issues, activists on the left have pursued an attack on religion. In their view every policy should be devoid of any religious influences, and liberals prefer a complete separation of church and state. In a recent case in Quebec, Mr. Alain Simoneau objected to a 20-second prayer and religious symbols at Saguenay City Hall. However the Quebec Court of Appeal ruled that the prayer and crucifix did not infringe on a person's religious freedom.

The disdain for religion is often directed at traditional Christian beliefs, ignoring other religions in the debate. The secularist position is prevalent in many countries including the United States. Secular activists goals include wanting to eliminate the word Christmas and any artifact or display, like a nativity scene, to be allowed in a public place. Further as to demanding that Merry Xmas not be used in schools or public institutions, and should be substituted for Happy Holidays because the old traditional greetings may offend other religions.

The Conservative Point of View

The conservative movement in Canada is considered to be more 'progressive' than the conservatives in the United States. Social conservatives who believe that the government has a role to play where issues of morality, such as abortion and gay rights are concerned are growing on both sides of the border. But as we defined and discussed in Chapter I, the conservative movement is fragmented, and on the issues of morality it is even more so. Social conservatives believe that matters of sexuality, abortion, the definition of family and gay rights are now grounds for government intervention and therefore political motivation. '*Laissez-faire*' conservatives and libertarians on the other hand take a more liberal approach on these issues, and thus believe that governments should not interfere in the private lives of citizens.

William F. Buckley Jr. was greatly influential in shaping the modern day Republican Party. He believed that conservatism should embrace a moderate ideology acceptable to both traditionalist conservatives and also libertarians. But it was the success of the Reagan and Bush era that emboldened 'social conservatives', Reagan's campaign which broadened the base of the party by bringing in the so-called Reagan Democrats, created a party which embraced both the fiscal and social conservatives. As many supporters like televangelists Oral Roberts and Jerry Falwell joined the GOP they brought in a new emphasis on social issues and religion.

The ability to mobilize local conservatives and organize social movements gave social conservatives within the GOP the ability to influence the Republican Leadership. Successive electoral wins for Reagan and George H. Bush resulted in many policies, and Supreme Court appointments which helped the social conservative cause. Even during the Clinton presidency he was unable to lift the ban on gays and lesbians in the armed forces due to the opposition by social conservatives in Congress. Furthermore his tryst with Monica Lewinsky provided more ammunition for conservatives to promote family values, a key position for social conservatives. The growing number of one parent family is not only a burden on society but also causes many economic and psychological problems. Even Hillary Clinton has concerns about the lack of father influence in today's society, as she wrote:

> *"The disappearance of fathers from children's daily lives, because of out-of-wedlock births and divorce, has another, less tangible consequences."* [10]

The decision by the Hawaii Supreme Court that the state's ban on same-sex marriage was unconstitutional, although later overturned; it gave social conservatives another cause to motivate them. As a result the Republican Congress passed and in 1996 Clinton signed the Defense of Marriage Act (DOMA) which started the conflict about gay rights, because it could be reversed by legislature or could be overturned by the courts. In fact today many states have passed legislation making same-sex marriages legal, but it is still controversial.

George W. Bush came into power with strong support from social conservatives and he immediately proceeded to eliminate funding for organizations that provide abortions abroad. His administration also took strong positions with regards to euthanasia, stem cell research and contraceptives. The efforts of The Food and Drug Administration for Plan B contraceptives to be approved were blocked. The use of stem cell research was restricted to research on existing lines of cells but research using new sources of stem cells was denied. He also appointed strict constructionist judges, John Roberts and Samuel Alito to the United States Supreme Court and proceeded to uphold the partial-birth abortion ban.

While social conservatives have a strong political position in the United States, it cannot be said that it is the same in Canada. On this side of the border it has always been that Canadians were more liberals that their neighbours to the south. Social conservatives in Canada are generally viewed as 'extremists', especially by the media. Nevertheless the battle grounds are the same, but the results have been divergent.

The conflict has its origin in the 1967 Omnibus Bill which proposed, among other amendments, to decriminalize homosexuality and to allow the setting up of therapeutic abortion committees in hospitals. Supported largely by elitist groups such as the Canadian Bar Association, the Canadian Medical Association, and the United Church and of course the liberal media lead by the *Globe and Mail* newspaper. Because the Progressive Conservatives (PC) decided to allow a free vote by its members, it was easy for the Trudeau government to impose party discipline and passed the bill.

The passing of the bill has led to a situation whereby Canada does not have any law or regulations approving abortions or the rights of fetuses. Most PC members who are pro-lifers oppose abortion on the basis of their personal conscience, and usually do not want to impose their views on others. But over the years and changing leadership, more specifically under the Mulroney government, some conservatives made their views more public and activist groups started to emerge among conservatives. The Evangelical Fellowship of Canada (EFC) who were mostly social conservatives were joined by the mostly Roman-Catholic group REAL Women (Realistic, Equal, Active for Life) and the Canadian Council of Catholic Bishops (CCCB), the involvement of the CCCB caused a rift among Catholics who were pro-life on one hand and those who were pro-choice, on the other.

In January 1988 the Supreme Court of Canada struck down the abortion law as being unconstitutional under the Charter of Rights and Freedom. Justice Brian Dickson wrote:

> *"Forcing a woman, by threat of criminal sanction, to carry a fetus to term unless she meets certain criteria unrelated to her own priorities and aspirations, is a profound interference with a woman's body and thus a violation of her security of the person"*[11] .

As a result, the Mulroney government attempted to address the issue of abortion three times. The first in May 1988 took the approach that early term abortions would be subject to fewer restrictions that late term ones. To this bill was added the amendments for the right of the fetus and the woman's right to choose. The bill failed. In July 1988, they brought back a bill without the amendments. This too failed.

Then in 1989, in the *Daigle* case the courts ruled that *'a man has no legal right to veto a woman's decision to have an abortion'* and that *'a fetus had no legal status under the existing law.'* Chantal Daigle proceeded to have an abortion and later stated that she regretted having it.

Once again in the face of the courts decisions, Mulroney attempted to change the law. This time in a compromise under Bill C-43 abortion would be criminalized:

> *"unless the abortion is induced by or under the direction of a medical practitioner who is of the opinion that, if the abortion were not induced, the health or life of the female would likely be threatened"*[12].

Newly released cabinet minutes obtained by the Canadian Press under the Access to Information Act show the tensions that existed within the Mulroney cabinet between those who were against abortion and wanted a 10 year jail sentence for those who performed the procedure, and those lead by Barbara McDougall, the only woman sitting on the cabinet's priorities and planning committee, who wanted more latitude for the prochoice movement. With party discipline in place the House passed the Bill, but was defeated in the Senate because two PC senators voted against it.

Gay rights, which had not been at the forefront like abortion, emerged as an issue for social conservatives in 1993. In 1992 Justice Minister Kim Campbell lifted the ban on gays in the military. Later that same year, in a political move to remove the issue of gay rights from the political agenda, she introduced an amendment to the Canada Human Rights Code which said that sexual orientation could not be used by private employers to discriminate against employees.

The 1993 federal elections saw the virtual disappearance of the Progressive Conservatives from the political scene. The Joe Clark conservatives who had long espoused a more progressive position on gay rights, and social issues were replaced by the Reform Party and later by the Canadian Alliance.

The evolution of social conservatism under Preston Manning is not as clear cut as one would think, since Manning was more of a populist rather than a social conservative. Remember that in 1996, Manning expelled two MPs. – Bob Ringma and Dave Chatters for defending 'the right' of business owners to employ gays only at 'the back of the shop'. It was more the Progressive Conservatives under Joe Clark who differentiated themselves from the Reform Party which really made social conservatives move to the Reform Party. The shift from abortion to gay rights became the most important issue for the party and it allowed social conservatives to become more acceptable. So much so that by the time that the Reform Party morphed into the Canadian Alliance, it became easier for the leader – Stockwell Day to be openly social conservative.

When the Canadian Alliance and the Progressive Conservatives finally merged under the banner of the Conservative Party of Canada, it became clear that social conservatives had found a place where their concerns are now accepted as normal politics. Stephen Harper the leader of the new party, does not have close ties with social conservatives he seems to be more of a *laissez-faire* conservative on social issues. And yet under his leadership social conservatives have found a more permanent place in Canadian politics. Over the years he has been able to keep all factions of the party in tune on social matters. In 2005 in a debate over Bill C-38, he argued that:

> *"Marriage is a fundamental distinct institution, but that same-sex couples can have equivalent rights and benefits and should be recognized and protected."*[13]

Despite the media's continued portrayal of Prime Minister Harper as a 'controlling freak', their premise that he has a 'secret agenda' no longer sticks as the trend seems to be more towards moderation rather than radicalism. Social conservatives have been accepted within the Conservative Party of Canada; while they are not dominant within the party they are certainly more prominent. This transformation is better explained by James Farney who concludes:

> *"What these changes represent is the disappearance of norms, held by both populists and conservatives, that placed social issues outside of partisan politics. Canadian conservatives now see social issues as 'normal' political issues to be decided by the party as a whole, given the electoral ramifications of any particular position."* [14]

Today society is faced with a multitude of choices, but the questions are: Is society being indoctrinated to accept new mores and morals that differ from traditional values? The family unit is being undermined by a change in society's values. Although same-sex marriage is more acceptable, does it mean that we must abandon our beliefs to accommodate alternative lifestyles to the detriment of traditional values? Even Hillary Clinton who is in no uncertain terms a progressive wrote:

> *"The real problem for families today is the many challenges they face in raising their children according to the values they hold."*[15]

She is right. However what kind of a village does she wants us to live in? What are the values she proposes? Are they traditional values like a mother/father family unit, a same-sex family or even a poly-amorous family?

The debate on abortion continues as it becomes more focused on the real issue – 'what are the pre-born'. With more reports of abortions by doctors like Gosnell, it is quite clear that this act is an egregious violation against those who cannot defend themselves.

No wonder that recently the pro-life movement in Canada has started a new campaign to bring the issue to the fore. Three Conservative MPs, B.C. Mark Warawa, supported by Albertans Brent Rathgeber and Leon Benoit, were recently muzzled by the Prime Minister for trying to bring forward a non-binding motion to condemn sex-selective abortion. We know that the Prime Minister is very reluctant to re-open the abortion issue. However, on campuses and in front of MPs offices, there have been a growing number of demonstrations by pro-life groups. Recently in Calgary, Stephanie Gray, executive director of Canadian Centre for Bioethical Reform, started a summer campaign containing graphic anti-abortion pictures, targeting the Prime Minister and other MPs.

What makes the debate about social issues so divisive is the language used to describe the issues. Should we talk about ***'pro-life'*** without speaking about ***'pro-death'***? On gay rights why is it impossible to talk about the issue without inserting the words 'bigots', ***'homophobes'*** into the conversation? Social conservatives cannot express their point of view without being vilified or demagogue. Why not accept the term ***'civil union'*** with all legal rights, instead of imposing the word ***'marriage'*** for same-sex unions?

A politician cannot refuse to attend a gay pride parade without being ostracized or threatened at the ballot box. Or worse still a politician who attends a 'March for Jesus' is deemed unfit for leadership, despite not supporting the views of the organizers. As result interim Alberta Premier Hancock said:

> *"It's something we can do in an inclusive society to demonstrate that everybody belongs in this province, and they have a right to be who they are."*[16]

The Premier is absolutely right; however we shouldn't be inclusive and accept people from both sides of the issue. What about the freedom of association? We are all part of diversity, and the thought s and opinions of everybody should be accepted – within limits.

On the other side of the debate, LBGT groups are now building new 'gayberhoods' based on the Castro District of San Francisco. Many gays and transsexual are choosing to live in special communities, so that they can be the neighbour next door instead of the gay neighbour next door. Having complained about being ostracized by the main stream isn't the creation of 'gayttos' segregation in reverse?

Wouldn't it be nice if we could follow the ideas of Dr. Ron Paul, who was a candidate for the Republican Presidential nomination in 2012? He is a well-known libertarian who addressed the Manning Networking Conference in Ottawa, and as reported by the *National Post* Dr. Paul explained:

> *"I don't see people in groups. I don't see rights as designated like women's rights or gay rights or minority rights... Everybody has an individual right to their life and they should be treated equally under the law ... This is not because government says so ... My belief is that it's a natural God-given right to your life and your liberty."* [17]

Social issues are about values and liberties; values that we learn or acquire through life experiences. In the greater scheme of things we should '*live and let live*'. Justin Trudeau is an example of a politician who is unwelcoming to pro-life candidates in his party, and plays games to gain votes to the detriment of those who hold traditional values.

There is nothing wrong with traditional values; others with different views are welcomed but they should not impose their views on the majority. This would be the tyranny of the minority.

CHAPTER 12

SAY NO MORE...

Some forty years ago, when Canada and the United States were different countries, prejudice and discrimination were common place. As a result of the U. S civil rights movement and the changing demographic of Canada the protection of minorities became an important initiative.

Both the *Canadian Charter of Rights and Freedoms, and the United States Constitution, as amended,* guarantee a number of rights and freedoms. While the language may be different; both countries provide mechanisms for these rights to be interpreted, supplemented, and implemented by a large body of constitutional law.

The *Canadian Charter of Rights* provides that:
Everyone has the following fundamental freedoms[1]:

- (*a*) freedom of conscience and religion;
- (*b*) freedom of thought, belief, opinion and expression, including freedom of the press and other media of communication;
- (*c*) freedom of peaceful assembly; and
- (*d*) freedom of association.

The first ten amendments of *United States Constitution* are known under the collective name of the *Bill of Rights*. The First Amendment provides that:

- Congress shall make no law respecting an establishment of religion, or prohibiting the free exercise thereof; or abridging the freedom of speech, or of the press; or the right of the people peaceably to assemble, and to petition the Government for a redress of grievances [2]
- The First Amendment prohibits the making of any law respecting an establishment of religion, impeding the free exercise of religion, abridging the freedom of speech, infringing on the freedom of the press, interfering with the right to peaceably assemble or prohibiting the petitioning for a government redress of grievances[3]

These rights are fundamental to a free and democratic society. Human rights were intended to eliminate discrimination against minorities including blacks, Jews, women, gays and other groups who had been the target of bigotry. Unfortunately, over the years, these rights have been interpreted, by some, to mean something else. The U.S courts, the Canadian Human Rights Commission (HRC), and other provincial HRCs have passed judgement in some cases that may have had a negative and confusing impact on the original intent of these constitutional rights. Increasingly political correctness and a growing number of lawsuits which have challenged these rights have resulted in a situation where citizens are afraid to speak up and express their opinions, for fear of legal incriminations. The Left, better than the Right, has used and misused these rights to muzzle people they disagree with, and in many cases have virtually prevented debate on many important issues. We shall explore the impact and potential harmful results of challenges to these fundamental rights.

The right to stifle debate

Canada has come a long way; we are a multicultural country, where rights are protected. We have seen a female Prime Minister, openly gay politicians, a Muslim Mayor, and Aboriginals have voting rights. However, the rights of freedom should be applied uniformly. Today the country has taken another turn, where more often than not, the Left has taken steps to stifle free speech. Increasingly it seems that the only people who have a right to free speech must belong to a leftist group. The parsing of words is constantly being used to deny free expression. Political correctness is so prevalent that kids, for example, are no longer allowed to play 'cowboy and Indians'. The name of sports teams must be changed because they offend one group or another. The use of social media has increased the incidence of offensive discourse. Everybody seems to be offended in one way or another, but the left more so than anybody else.

In Canada the HRCs have taken an activist position, and today they have taken upon themselves to monitor political discourse, impose fines on people for expressing politically incorrect opinions, and imposing bans on the publication of certain views. As a result of some of the decisions made by the HRC, members of the public are beginning to question the role of these commissions. They operate under a list of procedures treated mostly as suggestions rather than rules. Unlike a court of law, in the past hearings were held in secret. As Levant wrote:

> *"There is an old legal maxim that says justice must not only be done, it must be* seen *to be done. Canada's HRCs have set Canada back in regard to both objectives. Their lawless practices have not only undermined centuries-old principles of due process and natural justice, they have eroded public confidence in the rule of law."*[4]

Three well known Canadians have battled what has become a huge bureaucracy, and what can be termed the 'language police'; and much of what we shall discuss has already been challenged by Ezra Levant, Mark Steyn and John Carpay.

It is unfortunate that the establishment of HRCs, which started as a noble idea has now turned into a bureaucracy that given their broad and uncontrolled powers is now resulting in stifling meaningful debate. More importantly we shall see through several examples, that the findings and decisions of HRCs benefit certain factions to the detriment of the majority. The 'thought police' are driven mostly by the Left, and too often HRCs have sided with the view that today 'everyone has the right not to be offended', and therefore their rights may have been infringed. So stupid are some of the cases taken up by the HRCs that their existence and decisions rise to the level of the absurd, with outcomes straight from a story by Franz Kafka.

Ezra Levant, a Sun News TV host, was the publisher of the *Western Standard* magazine. He was dragged before the Alberta Human Rights Commission (AHRC) for publishing cartoons of the prophet Mohammed that had generated controversy and news around the globe. The cartoons themselves were the news story, and they had already been published in Denmark. Later, Calgary Muslim leader Syed Soharwardy withdrew his AHRC complaint and he said:

> *"Over the two years that we have gone through the process, I understand that most Canadians see this as an issue of freedom of speech, that that principle is sacred and holy in our society ... I believe Canadian society is mature enough not to absorb the messages that the cartoons sent. Only a very small fraction of Canadian media decided to publish those cartoons."*[5]

In another case, *Maclean's* magazine was hauled in front of the BC Human Rights Tribunal for publishing an excerpt from Mark Steyn's bestselling book : *America Alone: The End of the World as We Know It*. The article "The Future Belongs to Islam" was widely debated by readers of the magazine. Six months after the publication Mohamed Elmasry, president of the Canadian Islamic Congress (CIC) filed three human rights complaints against the magazine. During the trial Elmasry's lawyer called Khurrum Awan to give evidence against *Maclean's*, instead of Elmasry. Furthermore, in a clear case of conflict of interest, the commission lawyer examining Awan had hired Awan in his law firm. *Maclean's* eventually won the case in the BCHRT, but had to waste time and money to defend a case which had already been dismissed by both the federal and Ontario HR commissions.

The latest decision by the Alberta HRC, is the case of Ladislav Mihaly, an immigrant from Czechoslovakia (as it then was), who in 1999 sought accreditation from the Association of Professional Engineers, Geologists and Geophysicists of Alberta (APEGGA). In order to be accredited by APEGGA he needed to pass four exams in addition to the standard National Professional Practice Exam (NPPE), Mihaly failed the NPPE examinations three times. In 2008, Mr. Mihaly appealed to the AHRC on the basis that he was being discriminated because of where he came from. In another one of their Kafkaesque HRC's decisions, tribunal chairman Moosa Jiwaji ordered the following:

> *"Not only must APEGGA pay $10,000 in damages to Mr. Mihaly, he ordered, it must within three months "establish a committee ... to specifically explore and investigate options to appropriately and individually assess [his] qualifications ... with a view to correcting any perceived academic deficiencies." Mr. Jiwaji suggests offering Mr. Mihaly "exemptions" from the NPPE or "the Fundamentals of Engineering exam" – hey, they're only fundamentals – perhaps "combined with the implementation of a different method of assessment." APEGGA is furthermore to "match Mr. Mihaly with a mentor," provide "networking" opportunities and help him improve his English"*[6].

As a long-time proponent of better foreign qualification evaluation for immigrants, I find this decision not only absurd but detrimental to foreign professionals seeking legitimate recognition for their hard earned qualifications. Moreover, are we to accept qualifications at face value and perhaps endanger Canadians because we should not have a proper, rigorous system of assessment?

The problem with Canada's HRC is that when they were created the intentions were good. They were supposed to provide victims of discrimination with an inexpensive means to fight back against bigotry. However over the years they have morphed into an institution which dealt with human rights to one dealing mainly with freedom of speech.

Complaints are sometimes frivolous, because complainants are protected from malicious prosecution. HRC commissioners have limited legal training, and the system lacks the intellectual, institutional expertise and does not have the same procedural safeguards of the legal system. Over the years decisions made by these commissions have been so controversial, and come under attack. More specifically, Section 13(1) of the *Canadian Human Rights Act* which stated that it is discriminatory to communicate by phone or Internet any material "that is likely to expose a person or persons to hatred or contempt." A former Liberal MP Keith Martin proposed a bill to repeal the section. He said:

> *"rogue commissions where a small number of people [are] determining what Canadians can and can't say." Martin also asserted that some of history's most important ideas "were originally deemed to be sacrilegious and certainly in opposition to conventional wisdom. Who's to say that a commission cannot rule those ideas out of order and penalize people for saying or thinking them?"*[7]

The contentious Section 13(1) was finally repealed on June 26, 2013.

Gagged Campuses

John Carpay is the President of the Justice centre for Constitutional Freedoms; over the years he has fought many legal battles to ensure the rights of free speech in Canada. His battles are focused on the right of free speech on campuses. Too often today speakers, especially those on the right, are attacked or even banned from speaking on Canadian campuses. Carpay represented seven University of Calgary students who were censored for setting up their graphic anti-abortion display on campus. The University refused to explain whether the campus security had the right to censor the peaceful expression of opinion on campus. Subsequently the Crown Prosecutors' Office stayed the charges prior to trial.

Another incident at Mount Royal University in Calgary saw Nicholas McLeod who was peacefully distributing pro-life literature on campus, being physically stopped by several security guards, who threw him to the ground, handcuffed him, and confined him to a small room for several hours, with his hands still cuffed behind his back. As Carpay informed the public, on this occasion:

> *"The MRU security guards apparently believed – incorrectly – that they had the authority to determine which ideas can and cannot be disseminated on campus."*[8]

There are many incidents on campuses which have forced University presidents to take action, unfortunately they usually side with the mob, which results into censorship and curtail free speech. Carpay wrote:

> *"Pandering to mobs undermines universities as a crucible for the development of ideas. Whenever a university cancels an event of a minority group because the majority (or another vocal minority) threatens to protest, those making the threats are rewarded. This quickly produces a spiral of more threats and more censorship. Bullies are emboldened, and those who wish to peacefully express their views are wrongly silenced in the very place where dissent is essential to maintain the vibrancy of our society's intellectual life."*[9]

The mob on campuses is usually left-wing organizations who believe that they alone have a right to free speech. While some universities do not give in to the demands of the mob, unfortunately many instances of universities capitulating to the mob exist. To name a few: The University of Waterloo condoned the silencing of *National Post* columnist Christie Blatchford (2010) and MP Stephen Woodworth (2013), who had been invited to speak on campus. In both cases U-Waterloo campus security stood by and watched while loud and unruly protesters effectively forced the speaking engagements to be cancelled.

In March of 2013, the Ryerson Students' Union denied certification to the Ryerson Association for Equality (RAE). The student group's constitution said its goal was to "create a progressive and constructive voice and lend representation to any and all Ryerson students concerned with the issues of men and boys." RAE was allegedly affiliated with two external organizations (*A Voice for Men*; and *the Canadian Association for Equality*), which the RSU deemed "hate groups"

In March 2010, subsequent to an unusual letter by University of Ottawa academic vice-president François Houle to Ann Coulter which stated:

> *"I hereby encourage you to educate yourself, if need be, as to what is acceptable in Canada and to do so before your planned visit here. Promoting hatred against any identifiable group would not only be considered inappropriate, but could in fact lead to criminal charges."*[10]

When the University of Ottawa refused to provide adequate security to uphold free expression rights in the face of an unruly mob, Coulter's speaking event was cancelled.

There seems to be a growing trend in our universities for protests against conservative speakers. Muslim groups on campuses have taken upon themselves to protest against any speaker who has a different view of the Palestinian/Israeli conundrum. The Muslim Student Association (MSA) has supported student protest in Quebec, and Ontario. In 2007, the MSA was identified by the New York Police as 'an incubator for radicalism'.[11]

In their pledge of allegiance, MSA members declare that "Jihad is my spirit" and that "I will die to establish Islam."

In 2010, a group of Muslim students at the University of California Irvine, planned a protest during a speech by Michael Oren, the Israeli ambassador. Eleven students were charged with misdemeanor charges of conspiring to disrupt a meeting and disrupting a meeting. Subsequently, anti-Israel demonstrations were held by the UC Irvine Black Student Union and the Muslim Student Union.

In 2014, Prof. Paul Grayson of York University denied a request by a non-identified student to be exempted from attending classes with female classmates, requesting to take the class via the internet. The Professor's decision was overturned by the university, creating a debate about gender and religious rights. Prof. David Seljak of the University of Waterloo asserts that under the Charter of rights both religious and gender rights are guaranteed. The issue is the clash between secularism and religion. Women's rights have long been recognized by the law; should we as Canadians disregard the values that we have come to cherish and accommodate aversion by one group against another?

Throughout history there are numerous incidents of peaceful students' protest. Today's issue is not who protests, but rather who has the right to protest. Freedom of speech and expression is a Canadian right and privilege and should be upheld as long as there is no violence.

We should be reminded that The Supreme Court of Canada has described freedom of expression as:

> *"little less vital to man's mind and spirit than breathing is to his physical existence … it is difficult to imagine a guaranteed right more important to a democratic society … Freedom of expression "serves to protect the right of the minority to express its view, however unpopular," in the face of "the majoritarian view of what is true or right."*

The law needs to be applied without any bias or prejudice. Too often one group is favoured to the detriment of another, harming the right to freedom of speech.

The use of words and Political Correctness

Under attack by liberal thinkers, the ordinary citizen has to be careful about the use of certain words. Political correctness is now entrenched in our daily lives. Freedom of speech is viewed differently, it is now more common to be viewed as 'watch what you say' just in case it might offend somebody or some group. Let us examine some of the effect of such a change in society.

The word ***'bully'*** is now synonymous to describe almost anybody you have a conflict with, even a person you disagree with. While bullying in the correct sense of the word has always been a problem, more recently it has become more pronounced among young people using the social media, there needs to be more care in assigning it to most situations without proper context.

Bullying is a problem. The incidence of teen suicide in society is now an epidemic. Society and legislators have been striving to identify the problem and demanding strong reactions to bullying. Bullying should not be condoned in anyway; In fact laws should go as far as making bullying which causes death to be a criminal offense – murder in the second degree, would be a proper charge.

However, the use of the word bully in every dispute to portray one's opponent is not freedom of speech. 'Bully', today is too often used to demean one's opponent. If you do not like the leader of your political party, as in the case of Alberta; the word 'bully' should not be used in the place of assertive. Unions who are negotiating contracts should not identify the employer as a ''bully' just because they cannot get their way. Moreover, words lose their meaning, and power when over-used. If everybody is a racist, then nobody is a racist. If everyone is a bully, then nobody is a bully.

In regard to a recent rant, a Calgary councillor, was chastised for comments made on Twitter. Councillor Sean Chu, frustrated by the idea and information provided for additional bike lanes tweeted the following: "This is nothing but bullshit. 7ST increased to 1160 cyclists per day? What was she on? The Emperor continuously getting new clothes. Winter?"

One cannot condone the salty language, and the allegation that the administrator could be doing drugs. Councillor Chu should definitely tone down his rhetoric but still make his dissatisfaction known. The usual response from his leftist colleague Councillor Brian Pincott was that Chu's remarks about the administrator was tantamount to guess what? – Bullying. To question the intent of a civil servant is not 'bullying', it is the job of a councillor to do so on behalf of the public. How he does it may be questionable, but to stop him from doing it would be against free speech.

Facebook's chief operating officer, Sheryl Sandberg, with Girl Scouts USA CEO Maria Chávez have recently launched a campaign against the word **'bossy'**. In their opinion the word is debilitating to young girls, because it discourages girls from leading. Should we ban the use of a word because in the opinion of some it might have a different connotation based on gender? Or should we rather encourage opportunity as Margie Warrell wrote:

> *"We want both our sons and daughters to know that their voice matters, that they are immensely capable, and that if they hold an ambition that deeply inspires them, then it's because they have everything it takes inside them to achieve it. Will that sometimes take being bossy? You bet."*[12]

Better still, as Jemima Lewis wrote in the D*aily Telegraph*:

"Instead of banning it, Sandberg and her gang – none of whom, one suspects, could have smashed through the glass ceiling without a strong bossy streak – ought to reclaim it."[13]

Microaggression is a term increasingly used on university campuses to define acts of insensitivity against minorities. In many cases those acts are perceived, because the accused are not even aware they may be causing harm. Two recent examples comes to mind:

- A professor at the University of California LA, was accused of 'microaggression' for correcting spelling and grammar in his minority students' dissertations.
- Brian Farnan, vice-president, internal, of the Students' Society of McGill University (SSMU), was pressured by other SSMU executives into apologizing for distributing a satirical You Tube video that poked fun at U.S. President Obama The gif showed U.S. president Barack Obama walking away from a press conference and kicking down a door. Farnan's actions were subjected to numerous enquiries and debates. Mc Gill University has a web site which encourages complaints about microaggression complaints, which is defined as "sexism, het-

> eropatriarchy, transphobia, classism, racism, ableism." University campuses have become the incubators of social outrage, which in many cases do not distinguish between pranks and real outrage, and prevent freedom of speech.

Political correctness is creeping into everyday life. People question the use of certain words and expression because they could offend. Doctors are now hesitant to use the word 'fat' when discussing obesity. Broadcasters are banned from playing certain songs on the airwaves, because the lyrics contain certain words that may offend. However, rappers and their highly suggestive and denigrating lyrics get all the exposure that broadcaster can provide them.

Schools have banned playgrounds games because they may endanger kids. Ball games have been stopped for fear of injury. Competitiveness is gradually being removed from sports. For politically correct reasons in certain junior leagues, kids are no longer allowed to stack up the score, for fear of humiliating the opposition. In some competition everyone gets a medal because there should be no 'losers'.

During the 2014 Sochi Olympics, there was a worldwide uproar against Russia's law prohibiting speech that promotes alternative lifestyles to children. Mainstream media consistently referred to it as Russia's 'anti-gay' law even though it placed no restrictions on homosexual behaviours or lifestyle. In response to this 'anti-gay' law, activists in some cities raised a rainbow flag on the municipal flagpole at city hall (usually without prior permission). As a result activists in several cities decided to fly the pride flag. In Calgary the Mayor ordered the flag to be flown for the duration of the games. However, one day the cord holding the flag was cut; the immediate reaction from the Mayor was that it was a 'hate crime' instead of an act of vandalism.

Political correctness is now the new excuse for a nanny state. Governments at all levels are interfering in our daily lives to legislate what we can and cannot do. What and how we should eat, and of course how we should think and speak.

Outing is the disclosure of a LBGT person's sexual orientation without that person's consent. This practice has been used for a long time, but became more public in the eighties when Taylor Branch, the famed author and historian, wrote that 'outage' would become a political tactic in which the closeted would find themselves trapped in a crossfire.

Outing may be found to be a libelous, but in recent years it has become more acceptable in the gay community. Michelangelo Signorile, a supporter of gay rights, justifies the practice of outing public officials to influence the debate of gays in society. Former U.S. Congressman Barney Frank supports the practice of outing against a person who actively campaigns against LBGT rights. He also explained on a Bill Maher HBO show that:

> *"I think there's a right to privacy. But the right to privacy should not be a right to hypocrisy. And people who want to demonize other people shouldn't then be able to go home and close the door and do it themselves."*[14]

Frank is right, but as more and more celebrities and others voluntarily 'come out' as gay, why is it that there is still so much talk when a celebrity or sport personality proclaims that he/she is gay. Gays are recognized for their achievements in many spheres, business, political and the sports arenas. Martina Navratilova, Greg Louganis, Mark Tewksbury and several other gay athletes have been eulogized for their athletic feats. Why is it still news when another athlete among many declares that he/she is gay? Is it a matter of flaunting it, or is it to impose a way of life on others?

Politicians can no longer ignore participation in Gay Pride Parades for fear of being called bigots. While there are many gay politicians, do we need a media circus to announce one's sexuality? In that case what of politicians who are gay but do not make it public? There are those who would like to see inclusion without transparency in politics. Chloe Atkins and Associate Professor at the University of Calgary stated:

> *"The increasing desire for transparency in government means the threat to candidates' and politicians' privacy has*

> *grown ... Potential candidates may well opt out to run because they fret about the exposure of personal confidences.”*[15]

In her view she believes that transparency may prevent good candidates to come forward. She also believes that there should be set funds for politicians to spend as they please. Does that mean that citizens should elect people who have no regard for tax payers’ money? Does she also believe that nepotism is OK , while conflict of interest should be discarded in the name of diversity?

If we profess equality, maybe we should be more transparent, and then perhaps there will no longer be any need for public and separate manifestations and thus create one single society, where nobody is ostracized for their beliefs.

Diversity, is the other buzz word being used to vilify those not agreeing with liberal ideas. For example, any change like affirmative action or preferential treatment for one group or another are automatically branded as bigotry. Diversity has become an industry in itself. Corporations now have VPs of diversity.

Canada boasts one of the most diverse populations in the G8. We are proud of the Canadian society which encompasses mixed languages, cultures and religions. However, in the name of diversity we cannot ignore our history and multiculturalism which does not embrace Canadian values should not be the norm. Discrimination in any form should not be tolerated, but to use diversity to promote an agenda which favors one group above another is in itself discrimination. Too often, politicians use the word diversity to promote their views above the views of others, and most of all to vilify their opponents’ different point view.

Another aspect of the use of diversity is the increasing debate about reference to any name of sports team and other activity which make reference to Native Indians. The famed football team the Washington Redskins have been asked to change their name; so have the Atlanta Braves. In Canada, The Kiwanis Music Festival is changing its name to the Calgary Performing Arts Festival. The name “Kiwanis” was coined from the Ojibwe language expression derived from the word *giiwanizi* meaning to "fool around". What about the Calgary Stampede, Calgarians wear cowboy and Indian clothes for the festivities; would this attire be considered racist? Is this trend really about diversity, or is it an attempt to, eradicate the recognition of the First Nations in our lives?

The danger of misusing diversity to reach an end to political means may result in dangerous situations that may be extremely difficult to reverse. In England, for example, the recognition of diversity has created conditions where certain factions are allowed to spew their hatred of each other.

In a March 15, 2014 investigative program by Nour-Eddine Zorgui of the BBC entitled: *Freedom to Broadcast hate*, he disclosed the following:

In the midst of sectarian war in both Syria and Iraq, Shia and Sunni TV and broadcasting stations are operating in the United States and the United Kingdom to incite hatred of each other.

- In California Ahl El Bait TV USA is operated by Founder and Presenter Hassan Allah Yari to offend Sunnis.
- Safa TV is funded by Kuwaiti Khalid Al Osaymi
- In a quiet town outside of London in Buckinghamshire, UK a former church was converted in to a mosque and is the operating centre for a 24 hr. Shia TV studio Fadak TV UK. The Founder and Presenter is Yasser Al-Habib who is sponsored by the Khodam Al-Mahdi Organisation, a UK registered charity. Fadak TV is reported to be funded from funds from Iraq.
- Founder and key presenter Sheikh Abu Al-Muntasir Al Balushi broadcasts from Wesal Farsi UK which is a Sunni channel in London which calls for an uprising against the regime in Iran.

While we see many Muslim protesters against virtually everything, we do not see many protesters against Islam. Freedom of expression is now a one way street. As explained by Mark Steyn the free world has taken the view that:

> *"the West is free to mock and belittle its Judeo-Christian inheritance, and, likewise, the Muslim world is free to mock and belittle the West's Judeo-Christian inheritance."*[16]

In 2005 Anne Owers, her majesty's chief inspector of prisons, banned the flying of the Union Jack, because the cross of St George which is part of the flag was used by the Crusaders, and therefore it could be seen as offensive to Muslims.

Where do we stop to accommodate, instead of allowing the freedom of expression?

Initially, the *United States Constitution's* First Amendment applied only to laws enacted by Congress, and many of its provisions were interpreted more narrowly than they are today. The application of the law has resulted in many cases where we have seen instances where the freedom of speech and freedom of religion have been challenged.

In the United States, it is becoming very difficult for Christians to express themselves freely without being called bigots. Traditional Christian values are under attack from Muslim activists and atheists alike. It seems that these groups are offended at the drop of a hat by anything religious. The display of crosses and any symbol of Judeo-Christianity are viewed as offensive. The use of Christmas in any greetings is constantly coming under attack. Increasingly demands are made to drop the word "Christmas" for "Holidays". Schools, of all places, are teaching kids to greet each other with "Happy Holidays" for fear of offending students of other faiths.

It is becoming more difficult for Christians to express their faith and beliefs for fear of being attacked by the liberal media or atheist groups. The recent case of reality show star Phil Robertson is a perfect example of overreaction to somebody's personal beliefs.

In 2013, Phil Robertson of *Duck Dynasty* fame had an interview with *GQ* magazine, when asked a question about his faith he made the following comments:

> *"Start with homosexual behavior and just morph out from there. Bestiality, sleeping around with this woman and that woman and that woman and those men" he says. Then he paraphrases Corinthians: "Don't be deceived. Neither the adulterers, the idolaters, the male prostitutes, the homosexual offenders, the greedy, the drunkards, the slanderers, the swindlers–they won't inherit the kingdom of God. Don't deceive yourself. It's not right."*[17]

But he also said:

> *"We never, ever judge someone on who's going to heaven, hell. That's the Almighty's job. We must love 'em, give 'em the good news about Jesus – whether they are homosexuals, drunks, terrorists. We let God sort 'em out later, you see what I'm saying ...*
>
> *"I would never treat anyone with disrespect because they are different from me. We are all created by the Almighty and like Him, I love all of humanity. We would all be better off if we loved God and loved each other."*

Immediately, after publication of the interview, there was an outrage from GLADD, which, on Dec 18, 2013 prompted A&E's Dan Silberman, Sr. Vice President Publicity to issue the following statement:

> *"His personal views in no way reflect those of A&E 2014 networks, who have always been strong supporters and champions of the LGBT community. The Network has placed Phil under hiatus from filming indefinitely."*[18]

The furor about Robertson's comments exposed the wide social and political rifts in the United States. Conservatives argued that Robertson was being attacked because of his personal and Christian beliefs. In reinstating Robertson A&E released the following statement:

> *"While Phil's comments made in the interview reflect his personal views based on his own beliefs, and his own per-*

> *sonal journey, he and his family have publicly stated they regret the 'coarse language' he used and the misinterpretation of his core belief based solely on the article," A&E executives said in a statement. "But* 'Duck Dynasty' *is not a show about one man's views. It resonates with a large audience because it is a show about family … a family that America has come to love."*[19]

The opposition to Christian beliefs is not restricted to North America; in the U.K. it seems that Prime Minister David Cameron is being rebuked for reaffirming his faith. In an article for *The Church Times* he wrote:

> *"I believe we should be more confident about our status as a Christian country, more ambitious about expanding the role of faith-based organisations, and, frankly, more evangelical about a faith that compels us to get out there and make a difference to people's lives."*[20]

Instantly, he was demonized by fifty-five public figures, who accused the British prime minister of fostering "alienation" and promoting sectarianism and division in the country by actively emphasizing Christianity. In contrast, presumably the 'Gang of 55' would condone the alleged confiscation of Easter eggs by 'Muslim morality squads' in Birmingham. No reference to secularism or religion there!

The United Kingdom has always been a Christian country, notwithstanding its long history of partition between the Anglican and Roman Catholic churches. In fact, unless we want to deny it, a clear reminder should be the Union Jack, which is made up of the St. George's Cross, the St. Andrew 's Cross, and the St. Patrick's Cross.

In another case, Mozilla CEO Brendan Eich had to step down. In a blog, Mitchell Baker Mozilla Foundation Chairperson wrote:

> *"Mozilla prides itself on being held to a different standard and, this past week, we didn't live up to it. We know why people are hurt and angry, and they are right: it's because we haven't stayed true to ourselves. We didn't act like you'd*

expect Mozilla to act. We didn't move fast enough to engage with people once the controversy started. We're sorry. We must do better. Brendan Eich has chosen to step down from his role as CEO. He's made this decision for Mozilla and our community. Mozilla believes both in equality and freedom of speech. Equality is necessary for meaningful speech. And you need free speech to fight for equality. Figuring out how to stand for both at the same time can be hard."[21]

Reality is Mr. Eich did not just resigned, he had to since he was 'outed' by gay groups because in 2008, he made a $1,000 donation to the campaign to pass California's Proposition 8, a constitutional amendment that outlawed same-sex marriages. The company professes to believe in freedom of speech and yet somebody who expresses his beliefs in the form of a donation must be ostracized. This is a form of totalitarianism that permeates today's society. Just like those who oppose 'climate change' as a proven science are called 'deniers' as if they refused to believe in the holocaust. The left has substituted 'boycott' for 'bullying', therefore it must be OK. Fortunately there are still some people with a more open mind. Andrew Sullivan a gay blogger for The Dish wrote:

"If this is the gay rights movement today – Hounding our opponents with a fanaticism more like the religious right than anyone else – then count me out ... If we are about intimidating the free speech of others, we are no better than the anti-gay bullies who came before us."

Every one of us harbours certain unexpressed prejudices. However, in a world increasingly dominated by Social media can we afford to have our every word scrutinized? What used to be private is now public. Should we always be looking over our shoulders for the nearest recording device, or must we accept that we now live in an era controlled by squealers, and snitches? Is Orwell's 1984 here?

The left continuously purports themselves as the defenders of women's rights. Yet, when the Council on American-Islamic Relations (CAIR) demanded that the invitation and the conferring of an honorary degree to Ayaan Hirsi Ali are rescinded because of her wrong thoughts and evil words. President Fredrick Lawrence of Brandeis University promptly acquiesced. The real issue is that she had dared to criticize Islam and Muslim behavior. Which Lawrence characterised as "certain of her past statements," which he said were inconsistent with the university's "core values."

Reacting to the demands of the Left sometimes creates a problem for all of us. We should look at the facts, and the context in which certain words are uttered before reaching conclusions. The use of hyperboles to define situations and label antagonists cannot help to create a better society. Too often the Left believes that freedom of speech should only be used by them, while the right, which is always viewed as extreme, should not be allowed to express their views and opinions.

We fought two World Wars, and lost much blood and treasure in Afghanistan and Iraq defending this very right of freedom. As François-Marie Arouet better known under his pseudonym of Voltaire said:

> *"I do not agree with what you have to say, but I'll defend to the death your right to say it".*[22]

The concept of 'freedom of speech' is so misused that increasingly we run the danger of seeing that the silent majority is being muzzled by the vocal minority. A society that continuously redefines which ideas can or cannot be debated is doomed to stagnate and eventually perish.

CHAPTER 13

HARPER'S CANADA

Stephen Harper won a federal election in 2006, and formed the first Canadian Conservative government in 13 years. In 2008 he returned with another minority government to guide the country through one of the worst global recessions. In 2011, Harper finally secured a majority government which has allowed his government to focus on the economy. Having to work with a minority government twice, it is obvious that Harper could not make drastic changes, but given his majority win in 2011, he could have done some things better.

In 2015, the Harper government will have to face a federal election, and it is time to analyze his successes as well as his failings. While most of the policies implemented during his government's tenure have been focussed on the economy, there are other policies that have been implemented to make Canada a better place.

The Economy

Faced with the upheaval of a world recession, Canada is lucky to have had a Prime Minister who is an economist, instead of being a lawyer like most of his predecessors. During the 2008-09 recessions Canada generally outperformed the Group of Seven (G7) industrialized economies through the implementation of some bold economic policies. However, not all of these policies were strictly conservative in nature, because of being in a minority government situation. His government strategy has been to keep taxes low, eliminate the deficit, and put into place trade policies that will benefit Canada in the long run.

The appointment of Jim Flaherty as Finance Minister (2006–2104) has served the country very well. Despite the fact that he had to create a deficit due to the recession, he must also be credited for bringing it back under control and leaving us with a surplus prior to his untimely death. Flaherty was considered as one of the financial leaders of the G8, The only tarnish on an otherwise illustrious tenure as Finance Minister must be his decision and the way that the Unit Trust structure was eliminated and the other one being his final musing on the promised income splitting policy. Even his strongest critic has to acknowledge that Flaherty was pretty successful. Andrew Coyne wrote:

> *"Not only is the government's fiscal position strong, with a debt to-GDP ratio that is the envy of the developed world, but so is the economy: by all of the usual indicators – unemployment, inflation, real incomes – it has rarely been in as good shape. If you are the kind who blames Finance ministers for recessions, you are obliged also to credit them for recoveries"* [1]

As a result of the Harper/Flaherty team, unlike the rhetoric of liberals who profess to look after the middle class, the Harper government has actually helped the working and middle classes during hard times.

- In the 2006 budget, the Conservative government kept an election promise to cut the GST from 7% to 6%. Those opposed to this change, had inferred that the retailers would increase prices to compensate, which happened in some cases. It was also stated that some provinces may raise their sales tax, but it did not happen – at the end of the day the consumer was the beneficiary of the tax cut.
- The most controversial and perhaps damaging decision was the government's change of position on the Income Trust Tax

policy. Having promised not to change the policy, the Finance Minister did just that and shut down the sector. As a result it costs investors close to $35 billion in value and destroyed tens of thousands of seniors' life savings.

- The 2007 budget saw no tax cuts, but a tax credit for children under 18 was announced. In a mini-budget in October of 2007, further tax cuts were proposed; including $14 billion in corporate tax to make the Canadian corporate tax rate the lowest in the G7, a further reduction in the GST to 5%, an increase in the basic personal tax exemption to $10,100 per year.
- While the 2008 budget saw no significant tax cuts, the Conservative government implemented one of the best savings program ever seen in Canada. The Tax Free Savings (TFSA) account which allowed every Canadian over 18 to invest in a special account a sum of $5,000 per year. While investments were not tax deductible, as with the RRSP, the new TFSA had no tax on withdrawal or capital gains. Gas tax rebate fund for cities was made permanent and $10.2 billion was directed to the repayment of the national debt.
- The 2009 budget saw the looming recession dominate the economic decisions. As a result a $33.7 billion deficit was forecasted for 2009-10. To mitigate the ravages of an economic downturn the government proceeded with a stimulus package which included the following: $12 billion for infrastructure, $8 billion for social housing, $1.5 billion for job training, and $2.7 billion for the auto industry. In addition a new home renovation tax credit of up to $1,350, and some $20 billion for individuals and $2 billion for businesses in tax credits were announced
- The 2010 budget was somewhat of a sleeper. In a still sluggish economy the focus continued to be job creation with $12.7 billion to create jobs, infrastructure stimulus and new skills program. $4.2 billion to support industries and create the "Econ-

omy of Tomorrow". There was also $3.2 billion in income tax relief and minor tweaking of unemployment benefits.

- The budgets between 2011 and 2013 were virtually staying the course types. No significant policy changes were made, but the focus was to stay the course on eliminating the deficit by 2015 before the next election. The initiatives from these budgets were to be delivered over a period of time ranging from one to five years. They were:
- The Guarantee Income Supplement for seniors who rely on Old Age Security was increased, but eligibility for OAS will gradually rise from 65 to 67 years old. There were tax credits for family caregivers, children's art programs as well as student loan forgiveness for doctors and nurses who were prepared to re-locate to rural areas. The EI premiums tax was increased from 1.78% to 1.83%. Then came some cuts dear to the conservative base, namely funding for the Canadian Broadcasting Corporation, The National Film Board and Telefilm Canada were reduced by 10%. The civil service would be reduced by 4.8% through attrition and layoffs.
- The focus on jobs continued with the creation of a new Canada Job Grant to train workers and $241 million over five years for First Nations skills training. Gas tax funding for cities to increase two percent each year, and a New 10-year, $14.4 billion infrastructure fund to start in 2014. Tariffs were eliminated for most imported sports goods, kids' clothing. Funding of $1 billion over 5 years for aerospace industry and research, and $119 million over five years to transition homeless off the streets were created. The refund for veterans' funerals and burials doubled to $7,376. For small business, the EI credit for new hires was extended; as was the tax credit for adoption-related expenses.
- Two significant trial balloons were included in the 2013 budget which could have significant impact in future years they were

snitch line and rewards to catch international tax cheats and the proposal for sick leave to be placed on the table in public sector labour talks

- Faced with an election in 2015, the 2014 budget was just 'boring' with no significant policies for the immediate year but promises to be delivered in future years. On target for the elimination of the deficit in 2015 it is likely that Canadians can expect many goodies prior to the elections. To save $7.4 billion over six years the government plans new rules for upcoming collective bargaining talks for federal workers. $500 million for strategic research for the Canadian auto sector. $305 million to extend broadband internet in rural and northern areas. Overall program expenditures for 2014/15 will be lower than the previous year – the first time this has happened since 1995. No tax increase but another $500 added to the yearly TFSA allowable contribution.
- The plan by new Finance Minister Joe Oliver to cut EI premiums, thus axing 15% of payroll taxes for small business, will save small businesses some $550 million over two years. This is a welcoming tax cut that we hope will make it easier to create jobs.

Most of the above policies are good and help the middle-class. However what has been missing from this Conservative government is a serious look at corporate subsidies. The recent $250 million to the Automobile Innovation Fund, in addition to $400-million more to the venture capital business fly in the face of conservative free market principles. Subsidies to any industry come at a cost to another industry. In a sense it is favouritism and the government should curtail its policy of subsidies and use it only in harsh economic times. Corporate welfare is a waste of taxpayers' dollars and Harper should practice what he preached, when in 2004 he told the Toronto Board of Trade: "In the past 30 years, too many corporations have been drawn into the trap by the available plethora of government loans, grants and subsidies ... government should concentrate on creating a favourable tax environment, rather than try to pick winners and losers."

Chrysler, who has yet to repay $1.2 Billion of the $2.9 Billion bailout of the GM/Chrysler bailout, has backed out of a request for a new $400 million subsidy. To explain the company's position, in an op-ed for the *Globe and Mail* Chrysler's chairman Sergio Marchionne wrote. "in light of the federal government's and the Ontario government's past practices of providing support, ... Chrysler Canada approached the governments to assess their level of interest in the investment."

The inference is that since governments are readily prepared to give money to the auto industries we may as well ask and see what happens, even if we do not need the money. Chrysler's brazen approach to corporate welfare provides a perfect example of why corporate subsidies should be curtailed.

A preferred alternative would be to grant tax credits or even tax exemption for a limited time.

Supporting Families and Communities

Conservative values have always included families and communities, and the results show that remarkably, two of every five Canadians in the bottom income group in 1990 are now in the top 40% of income earners by 2009.

Harper has not shirked from helping the middle class and he has supported a Universal Child Care benefit rather than a national child care plan. In a series of policies his government has provided millions to create a child-care policy that took into consideration stay-at – home parents, unlike Liberal policies which was an agreement with the provinces. Canada is a country where protectionism is rife. In a series of policies which attempt to protect the consumer, the government has implemented policies that increased competition in the market place, including the telecommunication, air services and financial industries. One of the most significant policies has been the abolition of the Canadian Wheat Board monopoly.

The next positive step taken by Harper has been the reform of the Dairy Supply Management, a 60 year old regime which has no place in a globalized economy. The current system which favours mostly Quebec farmers, costs Canadian consumers $2.3-billion a year in excess product prices. With negotiations on a new trade deal with the EU, the time has come for the abolition of another millstone around the necks of Canadian consumers and farmers alike.

Trying to increase competition in the wireless market, the government sold another $5.27 billion of broadband spectrum. Problem is that no foreign company bought any part of the sale. The majority purchase was by the big three, Telus, Bell and Rogers. Even with Quebec's Videotron entering the market, the industry is still an oligopoly. The government must change it views on foreign ownership and remove a regulatory regime that continues to impose absurd conditions on the market.

The purview of the Canadian Radio-television and Telecommunications Commission (CRTC) needs to be reviewed. This body which regulates broadcasting in Canada needs a serious dose of reality. One of the criteria for the CRTC is to protect Canadian content, People want the freedom to choose their TV channels, thus it should allow Sun News Network, and other independent channels to operate under the same rules as any other outlet. Conrad Black stated:

> *"If the CRTC sensibly applies the criteria it is supposed and expected to uphold, it will support both talented independents such as Moses Znaimer, and those seeking to put Canada's finest, and often internationally recognized content in front of the whole country"*

More recently the government has started to look at cross-border price discrimination, which has Canadians paying higher prices than their American neighbours, even when the dollar is at par.

The Gun Registry

In 1995 the Liberal government implemented the Gun Registry program at a cost estimated to be over $1 billion. This policy was strongly opposed by the Conservatives and while not succeeding in abolishing the program, they eliminated within the scope of the registry long guns such as rifles and shotguns.

There are an estimated 200,000 firearm owners who have been saved from criminal sanctions by a string of amnesties granted by the Harper government. However, the Conservatives left in place the criminal code provisions that make criminals out of law-abiding firearm owners. In fact, according to the Canadian National Firearms Association it seems that the police have been using information from the long-gun registry that was supposed to be destroyed in accordance with an Act of Parliament.

While the Registry is still in operation in Quebec, in the rest of Canada there are still some lingering problems. The government brought back the gun license fee. Under the law, gun owners must renew their licenses on their birthday. But due to glitches in the RCMP web portal many Canadians could become criminals, as explained by Matt Gurney in the *National Post*:

> *"If my licence doesn't get renewed, that means I will go, at the stroke of midnight in the near future, from a lawful firearms owner to a criminal who illegally possesses firearms I'm not licenced to own."*[2]

In effect the long gun registry has not really been abolished, and for the sake of increased revenue many Canadians may still become criminals under the law.

The Firearms Act which replaced the previous Gun Registry law is still fraught with regulations which give the justice minister power to ban anything through orders in council. As in High River, after the flood of 2013, the RCMP confiscated guns and reclassified non-restricted sporting firearms, which have been commonly available in Canada for over a decade – without incident. This legislation allows for the violation of property rights and criminalizes owners and compels them to surrender their firearms for destruction without compensation. Hopefully the

Conservative government's passage of Bill C-42, the *Common Sense Firearms Licensing Act*, will prevent gun owners from becoming criminals by default.

Foreign Policy

For years Canada, under successive Liberal governments, has espoused a 'soft approach' towards foreign policy. Despite many objections from certain quarters who either believe that there is no such thing as a Conservative foreign policy or that the current government is too quick to move away from past Canadian position on world affairs, Harper has adopted a more assertive position on major foreign policies.

First his position towards the United Nations has been more reticent over the years. As the U.N becomes more irrelevant, the Harper government has taken positions which are more independent of the organization than has been the case by previous Canadian governments. Unlike many factions on the United Nations, who increasingly display an anti-Semite position, Harper's stance and support for Israel has been demonstrated very clearly during his visit to Israel and by the subsequent comments made by Foreign Minister John Baird. This government stands firm on an Israeli State as part of a two state solution. In contrast with the Obama administration and the European Union, the Harper government has taken a stronger stance on the Iranian nuclear debate. On Syria, while the government provided aid to refugees, it has also been very critical of the Assad government's slaughter of his citizens.

In the face of increasing religious persecutions and attacks on Christians around the world, Harper established the Office of Religious Freedom within the Department of Foreign Affairs and International Trade. The appointment of Dr. Andrew Bennett as the first Ambassador to the Office signals that the Canadian government is committed to the promotion of religious freedom and beliefs around the world. The Prime Minister said:

> *"Around the world, violations of religious freedom are widespread and they are increasing, … Dr. Bennett is a man of*

> *principle and deep convictions and he will encourage the protection of religious minorities around the world so all can practice their faith without fear of violence and repression."*[3]

Recognizing the importance of the Artic, Prime Minister Harper has made a commitment to ensure that Canadian sovereignty is not violated. He said:

> *"In defending our nation's sovereignty, nothing is as fundamental as protecting Canada's territorial integrity; our borders, our airspace and our waters ... More and more, as global commerce routes chart a path to Canada's North and as the oil, gas and minerals of this frontier become more valuable, northern resource development will grow ever more critical to our country."*[4]

The serious situation in Ukraine is a perfect example of Harper's approach to foreign policy. While the world watched and made vague pronouncements about the Russian invasion of the Crimean peninsula, Harper sent his foreign Minister to Ukraine to show support for the Ukrainian people. He was also the first world leader to suggest the expulsion of Russia from the G8. Of course the opposition found only one problem with the government's reaction, that they were not invited to go to Ukraine as part of the delegation. On March 22, 2014 Harper was the first leader of the G7 to visit Kyiv in solidarity with the Ukrainian people, while the United Nations continued to dither.

There are many in Canada, including four former Prime Ministers, who are not supportive of Harper's foreign policy. In the past Jean Chretien, Paul Martin, Joe Clark and Kim Campbell have been critical of Harper. In most cases they infer that Harper's policies diminish Canadian influence on the international scene. Their position is based on the Canadian role of 'honest broker'. What all of them miss, is that in the past Canadian foreign policies , except for Mulroney's in some cases, have been to follow the rest of the world, mainly as put forward by the U.N. The result has been that many international conflicts have resulted in more problems than solutions, The U.N. today is filled with member countries ruled by despots from around the world, and any participation with the U.N. means that Canada has to work with countries like Zimbabwe, Libya and Syria. To be an honest broker means that you have to negotiate with people who are honest and willing to make the necessary compromises. Today the world is different. Russia and China have replaced much of the influence that England, the United States, France, Germany and Canada had on major issues. Many of the appointments on U.N committees are so bogus that there is no reason for Canada to take part in the continuous farce that sees countries that have the worse human rights, serve on committees dealing with that particular issue.

Canada has long been a champion of the U.N. However it has also been far too indulgent of it. So much so that today we gain absolutely no respect from U.N's committees. Recently it was reported that: the UN high commissioner for human rights, Navi Pillay (a Tamil South African from Durban and notorious anti-western racist), still saw fit to criticize the absence of human rights in Quebec, lumping Canada in with Syria, Mali, Eritrea and North Korea.

When Mr. Harper decided not to attend the Commonwealth Conference in Sri Lanka, he was criticized by the Canadian liberal detractors, but even *The Economist* magazine believes that the Commonwealth needs to be reformed or allowed to die. It states:

> *"Yet bringing reform to and toughness to the Commonwealth requires leadership, which it lacks. Britain, Australia and Canada would like to provide this, but cannot. Whenever they seek to improve the club – which they largely pay for – they mainly succeed in uniting its poorer members in resentful opposition to their perceived post-colonial condescension."*[5]

Most criticism of Harper's foreign policies, are scholars, diplomats and other interest groups that sees the Conservative government curtail their funding and move in a direction more in tune with today's problems rather than stay with the policies of old. They are out of tune and out of date.

International Trade

Harper is following in the footsteps of Brian Mulroney who was responsible for the trade agreements with the U.S and later extended to include Mexico. The survival of Canada as an economic force lies in international trade. Canada relies far too much on its trade with the United States which accounts for close to 85% of our exports. NAFTA is a good agreement for Canada, however with Obama in the White house and a Senate controlled by Democrats, the partnership seems to be stagnating. Obama is too close to the unions and is a protectionist at heart. He truly believes in a 'buy American' approach to trade, which threatens to become a recurring feature in all public works spending bills, with major implications for jobs and investment in Canada.

The Obama administration is not a friend of Canada when it comes to trade, as exemplified by the lack of cooperation in the case of the Keystone XL pipeline. Furthermore , at one stage Obama even considered not inviting Canada to be part of the Trans-Pacific Partnership (TPP) a proposal to create a free trade zone in the Pacific, which would include the U.S., Australia, Brunei, Chile, Malaysia, New Zealand, Peru, Singapore and Vietnam. Ultimately, President Barack Obama invited Canada and Mexico to attend the 16th round of TPP talks.

With friends like Obama, who needs enemies? It is therefore very astute for Harper to seek other trade partners. His negotiations with the European Union make perfect sense. Under the Comprehensive Economic Partnership Agreement (CETA), many Canadian industries will benefit from reduced tariffs on European consumer goods, investment and technology transfer from the EU. Small – and medium-sized Canadian companies will now have opportunities to subcontract to larger Canadian and European firms that are operating across the Atlantic, and globally. While the initial negotiations between the U.S and Canada were subject to much debate and sometimes a lack of general support, recent polls suggest that 80% of Canadians support the CETA deal. Andrew Coyne puts it best:

> *"This is creative statecraft, a leadership role for Canada that would not have been possible had we entered into a full-blown customs union with the U.S., as some had once advised. It is a notable achievement for the government, and for Stephen Harper personally. May it point the way to others like it."*[6]

Furthermore, as a result of the invasion of Crimea by Russia, and the sudden rift between the EU and Russia, the Canadian/EU deal makes more sense. Europe could be looking at Canada as a new major supplier of oil and gas as Russia flexes its muscles and retaliate for economic sanctions by increasing its prices or even cutting supply to the rest of Western Europe. The sooner the deal is ratified the better.

After a few smaller trade agreements with a number of smaller economic players, such as Panama, Jordan, Colombia, Honduras, Peru and the European Free Trade Association (Iceland, Liechtenstein, Norway and Switzerland), Harper is seeking further ties with Asia. Despite the perennial objection of the usual suspects like Trade Unions, Harper is negotiating a free-trade deal with South Korea. This deal would open the South Korean markets for agricultural products. Critics claim that the deal may costs Canadian jobs, and that the market will be flooded with Korean made cars like Kia and Hyundai. However the Trade Department believes that the deal will have a limited impact on the auto industry since 85% of autos manufactured in Canada are for export.

The deal will bring tariffs down and in the long run benefit both countries. According to estimates by the Canadian Press the key facts of the deal are:

- South Korea GDP: $1.1 trillion. Canada GDP: $1.8-trillion. Canada-South Korea merchandise trade in 2012: $10.1-billion.
- Average South Korea tariffs on Canadian goods: 13.3%.
- Average Canadian tariffs on South Korean goods: 4.3%.

- Tariff lines to be eliminated by South Korea once deal fully implemented: 98.2%.
- Tariff lines to be eliminated by Canada once deal fully implemented: 97.8%.
- Tariff lines to be eliminated by South Korea on first day of implementation: 81.9%.
- Tariff lines to be eliminated by Canada on first day of implementation: 76.4%.

International trade agreements are beneficial to Canada, unfortunately what is still missing is a more open door policy. It is one thing to deny mergers or takeovers by foreign companies when it involves security, but what is missing is a more open policy which does not use 'protectionism' to stop routine takeovers by friendly nations' corporations.

In pursuing these trade deals, Prime Minister Harper has positioned himself and the Conservatives as the only party that can manage the country's economy; consequently placing Harper as strong economic manager.

The Military

Canada and the rest of the world responded to the terrorist attack of September 11, 2001 by invading Afghanistan. Canada's contribution cannot be measured just in terms of fire power but we must acknowledge the loss of blood and treasure in defeating the forces of terrorism. Now that Canada has withdrawn from Afghanistan after the longest mission lasting 12 years, we should reflect on how the Harper government responded to this enormous challenge.

Both the Liberal and Conservative governments supported the war in Afghanistan to defend the values and way of life of all free people in the civilized world. The outcome of this war will still be debated for years as all allied forces leave Afghanistan. Will the efforts of our braves be for nought as the Taliban come back to reclaim the territory?

With military budgets being cut, there is a growing fear that our veterans are not being given the support required to re-integrate in society. Suicides among our returning troops are rising. The government must step-up and provide the soldiers and their families with comfort and financial help in true conservative fashion. A first step would be dramatically cutting unnecessary administrative costs within the public service and transfer the savings towards veteran support. A Conservative government should be first to increase support for the military.

Law and Order

With a tough-on-crime philosophy the Harper government enacted a number of policies to impose tougher sentences for violent crimes and drug related offences. A car-theft policy was introduced to minimize and halt organized crime in the car and parts theft, chop shops and stolen property trafficking. In 2009, the government introduced a new anti-gang legislation that would make gang-killing a first degree murder offense. It has also introduced an anti-bullying law to addresses the growing problems associated with bullying on the internet. The Youth Criminal Act (2012) amended the rules for detention prior to sentencing (also called pre-trial detention) to make it easier to detain certain young people and eliminate the presumption in favour of releasing a young person provided under the YCJA of 2003. Despite the attempt by the government to strengthen the laws, there have been several cases where the justice system has challenged these changes and it is becoming quite apparent that there now exist a dissention between the legislative and the judicial branches in Canada.

As a result of increasing sexual offences against children, the government's proposed new legislation may go a long way towards punishment that fits the crime. The new law will create a publicly accessible data base of high-risk child offenders. Sentences for multiple crimes against children will be served consecutively. For too long in Canada sex offenders have been released too early. These laws are required and the Conservative government is right in passing this new law as Justice Minister Peter MacKay said:

> *"Each day, sadly in Canada, there are far too many children who become victims of sexual assault. These crimes cause unimaginable devastation in the lives of children, in the lives of their loved ones."*[7]

As a result of our legal system victims of crime too often are forgotten. In a bold, but still not satisfactory enough for both sides of the issue, once again the Harper Conservative government has put forward legislation that will give additional rights to victims of crime. Some of this proposed legislation will cause dissent, but at least we now have a new Victims Bill of Rights. As Minister Peter Mackay puts it:

"We believe the justice system must put the rights of victims ahead of the rights of criminals. That's why Canada's Conservatives promised to rebalance the scales of Canadian justice with a Victims Bill of Rights"; including the:

- **Right to information**: Victims will have access to information about the justice system, victim services, and specific information about their case.
- **Right to protection**: Victims will have their security and privacy protected during the criminal justice process.
- **Right to participation:** Victims will be able to present a victim impact statement and have their views considered at various stages of the criminal justice process.
- **Right to restitution:** Victims can ask the court to consider restitution when there are easy-to-calculate financial losses.

Reconciliation

Righteously, Harper made great efforts to make up for some of the ills that have plagued the country for many years. His government has apologized for the actions of past governments which have created some of the divides in Canada.

The horrific treatment of Canada's aboriginal children in the 1870's is certainly a black mark for Canada. In recognizing the wrongs created by a policy of assimilation, based on the assumption that aboriginal cultures and spiritual beliefs were inferior and unequal, he said:

> *"on behalf of the government of Canada and all Canadians, I stand before you, in this chamber so central to our life as a country, to apologize to aboriginal peoples for Canada's role in the Indian residential schools system."*[8]

He also apologized for the Chinese head tax imposed on Chinese immigrants between 1885 and 1923.In so doing he also offered symbolic payments to living head tax payers and living spouses of deceased payers, as wells as funding community projects.

Perhaps the most significant olive branch extended by the Harper government was his attempt to settle the perennial debate about the Québécois nationhood which as explained in Chapter 4 is at the center of one of Canada's great divide. On November 27, 2006, Harper tabled a parliamentary motion that read: "That this House recognize that the Québécois form a nation within a united Canada." Or in French: *"Que cette Chambre reconnaisse que les Québécoises et les Québécois forment une nation au sein d'un Canada uni."*

Of course much of these apologies were motivated by politics, but at least Harper did try to pour water on the fires of discord. One would think that these attempts for reconciliation would be well received, and satisfy. However, there are still those holding resentment.

Training and the Workforce

In Canada there is an ongoing debate about the lack of a qualified workforce. It is true that in some regions of Canada, mainly the West, there are many jobs that go unfilled. The problem has many folds. First, people do not really want to move across the country to get a job. Second, some jobs are not filled because Canadians do not want to do them, either because they are low paying jobs or they are in less glamorous industries. Third, the structure of the economy has changed many jobs in the manufacturing and even in the technology industries, and they are being moved abroad. Fourth, in Canada there is a protectionist view regarding the recognition of foreign qualifications.

Young Canadians suffer disproportionately from unemployment – about one in five is without work. Employment trends are weakest for Aboriginal Canadians. The Harper government has addressed this problem through several policies, mostly through the Economic Action Plan. Several initiatives were put into place to promote training and the acquisition of skills for the workforce, including the provision of Apprentice loans, the expansion of vocational training programs, and the promotion of students to enroll in technology, engineering, and science and mathematics courses in order to fill the jobs of the future. In addition, according to a government statement:

> *"By working in partnership with employers, immigrant-serving organizations and professional associations, NACC's Alternative Pathways for Newcomers project will help internationally trained workers choose a career path that suits their skills and experience.*
>
> *Specifically, NACC will make information on alternative careers available to skilled newcomers, develop a website where they can access information online and create regional information centres where individuals and community organizations can access and share information, so they can put their talents to use in communities across Canada more quickly."*[9]

But even proposals can run into problems, more specifically when the federal and provincial governments cannot agree. The contentious Canada Job Grant program has ran into many obstacles. The initial proposal had several caveats imposed by the federal government. In a compromise, Federal Employment Minister Jason Kenney agreed to allow more flexibility in the source of funding for the programs. If the agreement comes into force the provinces and the territories will be able to use the funds as they see fit, and will not have to match Ottawa's contribution to the program. Alberta became the first province to sign the agreement, it is hoped that other provinces will follow for the sake of our economy.

There is also the question of education on reserves which need to be resolved as soon as possible. There are too many aboriginal children who are falling through the cracks and are unable to get jobs. We believe that the government should take the proposals of Shawn Atleo for better education on reserves. In a letter to the government he listed the following conditions: 1. First Nations control of education; 2. Assurance of stable and adequate funding; 3. Recognition of the importance of First Nations language and culture; 4. "Jointly determined" oversight of First Nations education rather than unilateral federal oversight; and 5. Ongoing meaningful engagement between First Nations and Ottawa on education matters. However, who knows what will happen now that Atleo has resigned as AFN Chief and there exist dissention among the other chiefs.

A key theme of the Conservative platform has been Connecting Canadians with available jobs – from aging citizens to new immigrants and those with disabilities – while addressing the skills shortage via upgraded training programs. Will the Harper government succeed, or will the part concerning immigration become a problem. We shall address the immigration issue in another chapter.

Parliamentary Reforms

The Conservative majority in parliament was mainly achieved because of the accountability problems of the previous Liberal government. The Conservative government promised transparency and accountability. While they have tried to live up to these promises, in the main they may have failed, but not entirely as we shall see.

In 2006, Harper created the Federal accountability Act, and with it the Parliamentary Budget Officer (PBO). The Act states: "The parliamentary budget officer should, be given "free and timely access to any financial or economic data in the possession of the department that are required for the performance of his or her mandate."

Problem is that the (PBO) Kevin Page is so good at his job that he became a political liability for the government. His reports on the government's Defense budget, specifically concerning the purchase of F-35 airplanes have been damaging.

Since the days of the Reform Party, Senate reform has been a major focus for the Conservatives. In a move to make changes to the Senate the PM appointed some Senators who would support his proposed reforms of the Upper House. Subsequently, in a disclosure, which has become a scandal on the Hill, Senators Pamela Wallin, Patrick Brazeau and Mike Duffy are under investigation for abusing their expense claims for travelling, and secondary residence. While these three conservative Senators have been at the center of the investigation, other Liberal Senators have also abused the system. While Justin Trudeau, the liberal leader decided to expel all Liberal Senators from his caucus, it can be said that Harper may have been guilty in appointing three Senators who may have had dubious conservative credentials. Dan Leger in his new book, *Duffy: Stardom to Senate to Scandal,* reveals Duffy had desperately wanted a Senate seat for years (presumably representing any Party). Leger said:

> *"He [Duffy] was sending love letters" to each leader, looking for an appointment. "This Senate stuff – I thought it was a joke until I really had a chance to talk to folks from the Mulroney years, the Chretien years, the Martin years..."*[10]

Unfortunately, among Harper's appointments were three Senators who created more problems, rather than provide him with the support he needed for reform. He obviously did not learn a lesson from the defection of former Conservative leadership candidates, Belinda Stronach and Scott Brison. However, the PM may be tainted by this scandal, but it may also provide him with the ammunition to make the necessary Senate reform required and demanded by many Canadians.

In a controversial decision the Supreme Court stopped the appointment of Justice Marc Nadon to its ranks. This act of "judicial activism," may please Quebec, but may also have a ripple effect in the rest of the country. Prior to the appointment, Harper had sought advice from former Supreme Court judges Ian Binnie and Louise Charron, as well as the constitutional scholar Peter Hogg, all of whom vouched for Nadon's eligibility. The Supreme Court Act provides that at least three judges of the Supreme Court shall be appointed from among the judges of the Quebec superior courts or the Quebec bar. In their (6/1) majority decision, the Supreme Court found that Justice Nadon did not fulfill both of these criteria and therefore he was ineligible. This new dispute between the Prime Minister and the Supreme Court may also delay or even scuttle any debate about Senate reform, which will be very unfortunate for the whole country.

The newly introduced *Fair Elections Act*, promoted the creation of a registry for so-called 'robocalls', as well as impose stiff penalties for anyone found guilty of impersonating a political party or an officer of Elections Canada. It further limited the size of bequests to political parties, while increasing the limits of both contributions and spending. It also will allow the parties to create a list of who voted and who did not vote. The new Act provided that from now on, Elections Canada will run elections and a newly independent Commissioner of Elections will be the one to investigate potential breaches of the act. That means that the Chief Electoral Officer will lose his power of investigation.

As a result of irregularities during the 2011 elections a report was commissioned. The Neufeld audit estimated that 'irregularities' occurred on 165,000 separate instances or 500 administrative mistakes per riding. In his report he identified administrative problems, but no fraud. But now the author of the report Mr. Harry Neufeld believes that Bill C-23 should be abandoned because it may benefit the Conservative party.

What critics believe may be controversial, is how the Bill curtails some of the communication powers of the Chief of Elections Canada and the ban on 'vouching'. Currently voters who do not have identification showing their current address can get another voter to vouch for them. The government contends that this process leads to voter fraud.

In the larger scheme, why somebody with no identification be allowed to vote? Or better still, should it not be the responsibility of every Canadian adult to have up-to-date identification? What should the government do? Wait for fraud to happen before changing the law? The changes are not entirely perfect, but at least it attempts to make some improvements. With several changes made to the Act to rectify some of the complaints and concerns, the government was successful in passing this badly needed piece of legislation.

The best omission in *Fair Elections Act* is any talk about 'proportional representation'. This electoral reform is always put forward by losers, who would want to get rid of the 'first past the post' system. They maintain that there are too many votes that get wasted because people voted for a candidate other that the one elected. Canada should not even consider proportional representation, because if we look at Italy as an example where the system exists, we can see that so many different political factions are elected that they cannot have a government which lasts more than a few months. As a result Italy is turning into a banana republic and an economic basket case. Do we want this situation for Canada?

Public Sector and Trade Unions

If there is one area that Harper may have been deficient, it must be the size of the public sector and the relationship with trade unions. While just 16% of private sector workers belong to unions, the public sector union membership stands over 70%.

According to a study by Ian Lee, a professor at Carleton University's Sprott School of Business, the size of the public sector under Harper has grown he states:

> *"A big surge came with the election of the Conservatives in 2006 and peaked in 2010-2011 at 375,500 employees – including 283,400 in the core public service and agencies and another 92,100 in the military and RCMP."*[11]

While the government promises cuts, it certainly teeters on reforms to the public sector and trade union laws. Most studies show that public sector unions have benefits and salaries that are 12% higher than private sector employees. Pension plans are so large and in some cases unfunded that they can create bankruptcy for local governments as seen in Detroit. The Rand formula under which trade unions operate is badly in need of reform in the 21st century. A Treasury Board report which shows that 25.000 jobs have been cut from the civil service since 2010 bodes well for future public sector reform. The federal government must lead and embrace structural reforms of the public sector and promote changes to labour laws to prevent bankruptcies and promote growth.

Canadian made policies does not usually have a major impact on the international scene, it is important that any government implements and sets an agenda that would seek to place its citizens' security and well-being first and foremost. The Harper government largely succeeded in sheltering Canadians during the economic downturn and did provide stronger leadership on foreign policies never demonstrated under a Liberal government.

Although PM Stephen Harper has been portrayed as an autocratic "control-freak type" leader, some conservatives believe that he could have done much more. However, the same critics forget or ignore the autocratic abuses of the Trudeau and Chretien years. In the next Chapter we demonstrate how Harper's policies, choice and style varies from the leftist Obama who has led the United States from the leader of free market to a socialist entitled society.

CHAPTER 14

THE STATE OF THE UNION

The policies adopted by the United States, not only affects the citizens of America but in the grander scheme of things they affect the whole world. Since trade with the U.S accounts for 85% of Canada's export, any slowdown in the U.S economy greatly affects Canada. Likewise foreign policies have a major effect on the status of world peace In light of these facts it is important to examine the past policies of the Obama administration and its current and future effect on the world at large. Obama was elected with the aura of a saviour and the mantra of hope and change.

Obama inherited an economy in freefall. George W. Bush and his predecessors can be blamed for the housing and financial industry debacles and the cost of two wars. But after six years of his administration, Obama can no longer blame his inability to improve the economy on the George Bush era.

After six full years of the Obama administration, the world is not safer, and the President is still campaigning. Much of his foreign policy is in disarray and the economy is still sputtering with high unemployment and an anaemic economic growth. It is important to discuss the effect of the Obama presidency which has been further to the left than most presidents before him.

President Obama reminds me of some of the students, mostly from Africa and the West Indies, with whom I attended college in England. These students may have had legitimate reasons to dislike British rule and colonialism, and many also harboured anti-Semite sentiments. Just like them, Obama gives the impression that he strongly believes that he has to right the wrongs of the past. There is nothing evil or intentional about his policies and actions. Obama, like Jane Fonda and other leftists, believes that past U.S policies are at the root of the world's problems.

Coming into office after making so many promises during his presidential campaign, Obama found himself in a position to have to please a vast array of supporters. He has constantly used wedge issues such as the 'war on women' and 'income inequality' as foils to beat up on his political opponents and cater to his left base. Furthermore, overburdened by a premature Nobel Peace Prize, he believes that he has to live up to these great expectations. As a result we have seen a President in constant campaign mode, making decisions heavily based on political ideology and driving the U.S. to the point where a majority of citizens believe that Obama is a failed leader.

It is the view that his presidency and policies will have a negative impact both at home and abroad, and we shall demonstrate how his leftist policies just like those of former President Jimmy Carter is going to leave Americans and the rest of the world with a bitter taste in the mouth long after he leaves office.

Failures of "Hope and Change"

Candidate Obama arrived on the scene at a time when America was tired of two wars and was reeling from a stubborn recession. 'Hope and Change' his campaign slogan comes from his book 'The Audacity of Hope'. With a great personality and oratory skills not seen since Ronald Reagan, Obama tapped into the psyche of a young generation who did not read newspapers or followed the news. He was branded to be the next great Democrat since John F. Kennedy. His campaign promises included:

- to get 30 million Americans insured in a better national healthcare system,
- a foreign policy that would change the world's view of an Imperial America,
- a push to reduce the effects of climate change and reduce global poverty,
- dreams of achieving a Middle East peace

He created an unchallengeable media platform that resonated across America and the world. How anyone could challenge his intentions and goals for a better world – the liberals had found their Messiah.

However bold and well intentioned his promises were, there existed a major flaw which was completely ignored by all as the media only exhibited his qualities and none of his weaknesses. For all his charm, Obama had a short federal Senate career (2005–2008); he had no substantial legislative achievement to speak of. In fact very little was known about Obama. He was director of Chicago's Developing Communities Project. He attended Harvard Law School and was editor and president of *Harvard Law Review*. He taught constitutional law at the University of Chicago Law School for twelve years. He was a member of the Illinois Senate for seven years. He had never held any executive position or managed a major organization; in fact his leadership skills had never been tested.

The weight of expectations, coupled with a lack of experience has resulted in a lack of good domestic strategy and a timid approach to foreign policy. His policies have been ideological and with an eye always focussed on his legacy as President, he has ignored the results of his decisions and continued on a dogged path that, in many ways may result in a dismantling of the American Dream.

Economic Failures

Two wars and the collapse of the banking system had a huge effect on the economy. The George W. Bush administration must bear responsibility for part of this crisis. President Obama still blames Bush for the longest recession since the Depression, failing to acknowledge that his policies, and leftist ideological philosophies have done nothing to improve the situation.

To say that things are improving would be disingenuous because the economy was so far down that it has nowhere else but to go up. However growth is forecasted to be in the low single digits for 2014. The unemployment rate is still around 7%, but if the number of workers who have stopped looking for work is included, the real number would be closer to 13%.

With the implementation of Obamacare, according to the Congressional Budget Office (CBO), they estimate that the ACA will cause a reduction of roughly 1% in aggregate labor compensation over the 2017–2024 period, compared with what it would have been otherwise; a reduction of $70B in loss wages coming from low wage earners. The design of subsidies in the ACA discourages people from working, by 2024 it is projected that there may be a 2–2.5 million job loss. In addition, more part time instead of full-time jobs will be created to avoid the ACA as many businesses may reduce their work force to 49 from 50. For all his bluster of job creation, Obama may in fact create more unemployment through the ACA.

The financial crisis of 2008 which Obama inherited, gave him a perfect canvas to paint a new socialist economy for the United States. The Obama administration directed most of its economic policies based on the heavy involvement of the government. Starting with the *American Recovery and Reinvestment Act of 2009 (ARRA* a huge stimulus of $831 billion between 2009 and 2019. In the first term he was blessed with a majority in both the House and the Senate, and he used it to further Keynesian policies and pass the Affordable Care Act.

Mired in ideology, the President talked repeatedly about creating jobs and yet was unable to have a coherent policy to achieve that goal. Additional spending was not needed if the President only had the wherewithal to allow the tax free repatriation of billions of dollars held by

American corporations willing to create jobs. Furthermore, his administration believes that corporations who move their residence abroad to avoid paying federal corporate taxes are 'unpatriotic'. Obama fails to understand that unlike tax evasion, tax avoidance is still legal, and that it is punitive tax regulations that causes corporations to seek refuge in other countries. More companies are resorting to corporate inversion as a strategy for tax avoidance. Through this strategy the U.S. parent company gives up its U.S. residency by acquiring or merging with a foreign corporation. Ideologues and interventionist governments promote instead of reducing tax avoidance, and the Obama administration is no different. What is required is corporate tax reform which will lower one of the highest rates of corporate tax in the world.

A reluctance to cut expenditure and yet increase funding to green projects like Solyndra which never came to fruition, accompanied by new social programs that added to the deficit, the United States debt currently stands above seventeen trillion dollars.

Bad Medicine

In his first term he was blessed with a majority in both the House and the Senate, and he used it to further Keynesian policies and pass the Affordable Care Act in a completely partisan manner. Despite an overwhelming opposition to the ACA, Obama's desire to be the President who would provide the United States with a national healthcare forced him to make so many unilateral changes to the law, that the initial legislation does not look anything like the one that was passed by the Democrat majority.

The original idea was to provide healthcare coverage for the 49 million (2010) or so Americans, who according to the Census Bureau, did not have insurance coverage. But as the implementation of the ACA came online, the real flaws and major problems that were not identified when the law was passed surfaced – including an estimate that the ACA will provide for 16 million uninsured Americans, but may now leave some 31 million Americans uninsured.

The first problem was the complete collapse of the $300 million website used for registration. Six days into the launch the government acknowledged that they had to fix the design and software problems that prevented customers from applying online for coverage, they blamed the problem on an unexpected surge in traffic. But experts said that the site had been built on faulty and sloppy software foundations. Marred by several serious issues, it had to be shut down, revamped and rebuilt.

The second problem was the low number of people enrolling. By the 31st of March 2014 deadline approximately only 7 million had enrolled. Of these enrollees, it is not known how many have actually paid their premiums. A majority of citizens were signing up for Medicaid; if that trend continues federal and state governments could be in serious financial trouble. Currently the federal government spends some $265 billion per year on Medicaid, and combined with Social security and Medicare they already account for 48% of federal spending, and in three years those three programs will account for over 50% of federal expenditures.

In addition, Medicaid reimburses doctors very little. And because of the red tape and paper work required many doctors either limit or even refuse to take Medicaid patients. In fact only 69% of physicians accept Medicaid patients. As a result the wait times for Medicaid patient is doubled compared to privately insured patients. By increasing the number of citizens on Medicaid, and doing nothing to increase the number of doctors, Obamacare will make it worse and wait times may increase just like Canada.

The success of Obamacare rest largely on the number of young people enrolled in the program. Their number is crucial to offset costs from older enrollees and prevent an increase in premium rates. So far the so-called 'invincibles' have not signed in the numbers required to subsidize cheaper plans for the old and the sick. It may be that young Americans are waiting for the last minute to enroll and perhaps even choose to pay the penalty rather than pay the high premiums. .

But the biggest issue for Obamacare may be the broken promises and the lies used by the President and his supporting cast in both the House and Senate to implement the law. Many people are finding that they cannot keep their doctor or their insurance, as promised. The President had said that premiums would fall by as much as $2,500 per family; but according to a report by Forbes, and based on a Manhattan Institute analysis of the HHS numbers, Obamacare will actually jack up underlying insurance rates for young men by an average of 97 to 99%, and for young women by an average of 55 to 62%. As for states, the worst off is North Carolina, which is expected to see individual-market rates triple for women, and quadruple for men.

As for the administration's claim that the ACA would cost around $900 billion over 10 years and that it would not add 'one dime to our deficit'; reports project different numbers. A May 2013 Congressional Budget Office report puts the real price tag around $1.8 trillion. On Feb. 26, 2013 the Government Accountability Office, projected Obamacare will increase the long-term federal deficit by $6.2 trillion. An Investor Business Daily Analysis reported the Affordable Care Act could actually add $18 billion in red ink.

The CBO estimates that "as a result of the ACA, between 6 million and 7 million fewer people will have employment-based Insurance coverage each year from 2016 through 2024 than would be the case in the absence of ACA."

In August of 2014, Ezekiel Emanuel, one of the architects of Obamacare, stated that within 10 years 80% of employer provided insurance will disappear. In fact S&P Capital I.Q, estimates that the number will be closer to 90%. For many employers the costs of providing employee insurance will be so great that they will decide to opt out of the program and place their workers on to the government backed program; thus increasing government involvement and costs. Obama promised that Americans could keep their insurance – if they liked it. Alas it was another promise easily broken by the President.

Amidst, the continuing reports of higher premiums, high deductibles, and the inability to get the doctor or hospital those patients want or used to have, many stories of hardship are being reported. Yet once again in a display of pure partisanship, during a Senate floor speech Wednesday Feb 26, 2014, Senate Majority Leader Harry Reid declared

> *"There's plenty of horror stories being told. All of them are untrue. But in those tales turned out to be just that. Tales. Stories made up from whole cloth. Lies distorted by Republicans to grab headlines or make political advertisements."*[1]

Not surprisingly, a day later Sen. Reid denied that he ever made the comment. The continued partisan support of the ACA by the Democrats, despite the less than stellar enrollee numbers, is a clear demonstration of the continued partisan environment under Obama.

Appeasement

Obama was an early opponent of President Bush's 2003 war in Iraq, even before he was elected to the U.S. Senate. Therefore it is not surprising that he would be an apologist and appeaser as President – but at what costs?

Once elected, the President embarked on his 'American Apology Tour'; going around the world and apologizing for America's misdeeds. He would throw criticisms at past U.S foreign policies and proclaimed that he would change the situation. He promised that America will no longer act unilaterally, and will not interfere in other countries internal affairs, refrain from feeding anti – Muslim sentiments. His major speech at the United Nations earned the praise of dictators like Fidel Castro, Muammar Qaddafi and Hugo Chavez. All the while he was turning his back away from Eastern Europe allies Poland, Czech Republic. His Cairo speech 'A new Beginning' called for mutual understanding between the United States and the Muslim world. Obama naively believed that he would be willing to "extend a hand" to those "who cling to power through corruption and deceit" if they "are willing to unclench" their fists[2], and in so doing resolve all the problems of the Middle East. The appointment of Hilary Clinton and John Kerry as successive Secretary of State did not help either. In fact little did the world know how wrong all three were going to be.

The expectations of the Arab Spring, which many believed was going to bring democracy to North Africa and the Middle East quickly fizzled when the new regimes did not display more empathy towards the West but in fact aligned themselves with extremists. Tunisia, Libya and then Egypt fell into the hands of disorganized governments who did not have control on terrorist elements within their borders. Egypt once an ally of the United States fell into the hands of the Muslim Brotherhood. Libya became so uncontrollable that the American Embassy was attacked and saw the death of four Americans. Syria saw the brutal Assad regime slaughter hundreds of thousands of his own people. Iran pursued its race towards becoming the next nuclear power. These incidents and their implications merit a more detailed discussion.

Benghazi

A civil war and a NATO led intervention saw the fall of the Gaddafi regime; on October 20, 2011 the Libyan Dictator was captured and executed by rebel forces. The new Libyan National Transitional Council, being a government in transition did not have a great amount of control of what was happening within its borders. Although they tried to disarm the rebels, terrorist forces were operating in certain parts of the country.

On September 11 2012, an armed group of approximately 150 men attacked the American Mission, and a CIA Annex in Benghazi killing the U.S. Ambassador Christopher Stevens, Foreign Service Officer Sean Smith, and security officers Tyrone Woods and Glen Doherty and wounded a number of others. This attack and killing of an American Ambassador and personnel which is still being investigated by Congress may well be one of the worse foreign policy moments for the Obama administration.

Transcribed from the Fox News Reporting: "**Death and Deceit in Benghazi**" by Bret Baier the following is a chronology of the incident and the administration's reactions.

After the civil war, Benghazi continued to be a hot bed of local skirmishes, between Libyans. Spring of 2012 attacks on western personnel

started and a request for more security is requested.
June 5, 6 an IED exploded. CS asked to keep two security officers, the request is denied.
June 11 the British embassy is attacked and the British are pulled out.
June 25, CS informs Washington of increasing problems and it needed security
Innocence of Bin Laden the screen play is scheduled in S. California and portrays Mohamed as a gay child molester. On July 2 *Innocence of Muslims* is uploaded to You Tube
July 6. Charlene Lamb said no extension of security request is required.
Aug 8. CS says that there are targeted attacks. Security chief leaves Libya.
At the Convention Democrats tout their success for the death of Gaddafi.
Sept 8 Egyptian TV airs portion of the video, and protest ensues
Sept 11. Police officer takes picture of the embassy in Egypt being stormed .Greg
Hicks said the video was a non-event in Libya.
At 4 pm Clinton is advised. Consider every option to get as much support as possible. Annex is told to stand down that no help was coming.
5pm in DC. Security team was in Tripoli with no planes. Drone armed with cameras flies over embassy.
Annex is attacked. Foreign Emergency Support Team was not deployed.
Ansar al-Sharia claims attack. Tripoli team had to stay at airport because there was no transport
5 hours after attack authorization is given to prepare to deploy to Tripoli. But do not deploy
10.00 pm DC Clinton speaks to President. Clinton links attack to video
Sept 12 Beth Jones, Sheryl Mills Vic Noonan send e-mail 'I spoke to the Libyan ambassador and … I told him that the group that conducted the attacks, Ansar-al-Sharia, is affiliated with Islamic terrorist"
Sept 12 President links the video to attack.
Sept 13 Sec. Clinton links video to attack again
Sept. 14 At the arrival of the bodies, Clinton states again that the video is the cause.

The Lars Larson Show Oct 23 2012. The father of Tyrone Woods said that Clinton told him" She mentioned that thing about, we're going to have that person arrested and prosecuted, that did the video"
The maker of the video is arrested for violating his probation is still in jail today.
Sept 16. On *Face the Nation* The president of Libya's National Congress dismisses the notion of a spontaneous attack and states that it was a planned attack
At the same time United Nations Ambassador Susan Rice goes on five Sunday shows and stated that the attack was the result of the video. And in so doing insults the Libyan president
On September 25 at the U.N. President Obama re-iterates that the video was the reason for the attack

On Aug 06, 2013, Erin Burnett of CNN hosted **"The truth about Benghazi"** and reported:

Libyan guards said that more than 50 bearded men with Afghan style turbans with rocket propel grenades were assaulting the embassy
Sept 11 – 5.00 pm President told the embassy is under attack.
6.00 pm urgent Pentagon meetings. Forces in Spain, Croatia and North Carolina are asked to get ready.
Special ops in Tripoli ordered not to go Benghazi, but to stay and help in Tripoli
Warnings: British Red Cross and UN closed Benghazi outposts
Two prior attacks on the US Benghazi mission
Detailed warnings in 4,000 classified cables
3 days after the attack CNN's Arwa Damon found the Ambassador's diary.
Sept 16. Secretary, Susan Rice, Rice says: "...it was a spontaneous not a premeditated response to what had transpired in Cairo. In Cairo as you know, a few hours earlier there was a violent protest. It was undertaken in reaction to this very offensive video that was disseminated ... "
Arwa Damon, Senior International Correspondent, spoke to some people who may have been involved. Ali Harzi is the only one arrested in

Turkey but released for lack of evidence. Ahmed Abu Khattala, met in a coffee shop for 2 hours, and in an interview he does not deny he was there.
Congressional investigations revealed that those who testified have denied any knowledge of a video being the trigger for the attacks. Michael Morell, former CIA Deputy Director acknowledged that the 'video reference, was not attributed to his analysts. Retired Brigadier General Robert Lovell–USAF testified that there never was a connection between the attacks and a video.

After months of enquiries and unanswered question about Benghazi, on April 18, 2014 an e-mail obtained by Judicial Watch as a result of a lawsuit became the 'smoking gun' that Republicans were looking for. This e-mail, issued at 8.09 pm Sept 14, 2012 and written by Benjamin Rhodes Asst. to President and Deputy National Security Adviser for Strategic Communications, titled – RE: PREP CALL for Susan (U.S. Ambassador to the United Nations) stated:

> *"To underscore that these protests are rooted in an internet video, and not a broader failure of policy."*[3]

This e-mail was sent to David Plouffe, Dan Pfeiffer, Jay Carney and Jennifer Palmieri all senior members of the President's staff. To continue to plead ignorance would be a farce. At the time, nobody seemed to know where Sec. Clinton and the President were on that fateful night. It took over 600 days, before HRC revealed on a book tour, that the President was in the White house and that she was on the 7th floor of the State Building. By contrast during the raid and killing of bin Laden, official photos showed senior members of staff, the President and Sec. Clinton, siting in the situation room watching the events unfold. It is inconceivable that while an Ambassador and four Americans are under attack and being killed, nobody at the highest level of command would inform the President or the Secretary of State.

The release of the e-mail caused even the main stream media to question the tardy release of the information. ABC News correspondent Jonathan

Karl was very insistent in questioning WH press secretary Jay Carney when he asked:

> *"Why were you holding back this information? Why was this email not turned over to the Congress? Why it was not released when you released all the other emails? This is directly relevant. Why did you hold it back? Why did it take a court case for you to release this?"*[4]

With answers still not forthcoming from either the White House or the State Department, finally in May 2014 House Leader John Boehner called for the appointment of a special House committee to investigate Benghazi. Are we going to get the answers? Who objected to make reference to terror groups is still a mystery. But were all the facts obfuscated because of the impending Presidential elections? If so could it be compared to the Iran/Contra affair? Or even Watergate?

So far the only good news is the arrest, 642 days after the incident, of the attack's mastermind – Ahmed Abu Khattala,

Syria

Following in the footsteps of her boss, President Obama, at the start of the Syrian civil war Sec, Clinton said that Bashar al-Assad was a reformer and a different leader. Then responding to questions whether the U.S should intervene as they did in Libya she said:

> *"What's been happening there the last few weeks is deeply concerning, but there's a difference between calling out aircraft and indiscriminately strafing and bombing your own cities," Clinton said, referring to Qaddafi's attacks on the Libyan people, "than police actions which, frankly, have exceeded the use of force that any of us would want to see."*[5]

Later and with reports that Assad forces had used chemical weapons, the President in August 2012 said:

> *"I have, at this point, not ordered military engagement in the situation. But the point that you made about chemical and*

biological weapons is critical. That's an issue that doesn't just concern Syria; it concerns our close allies in the region, including Israel. It concerns us. We cannot have a situation where chemical or biological weapons are falling into the hands of the wrong people.

We have been very clear to the Assad regime, but also to other players on the ground, that a red line for us is we start seeing a whole bunch of chemical weapons moving around or being utilized. That would change my calculus. That would change my equation."[6]

The conflict continues and with thousands of dead Syrians and millions of refugees, the President's 'red line' turned into 'pink' then disappeared as he appointed John Kerry as his new Secretary. If Sec. Clinton had been ambiguous on the Syrian issue, Kerry was even worse when he took part in negotiations with Russia, China and European partners. In September 2013, an agreement is reached under UN Resolution 2118 which provides for a timeline for the destruction of Syria's chemical weapons. On October 31, 2013 The Organisation for the Prohibition of Chemical Weapons (OPCW) announced that it had met the deadline for destroying all declared equipment and facilities related to chemical weapons production. The United States and other European countries agreed to destroy the chemical weapons. But by January 30, 2014 only about four percent of the priority chemicals had been removed. Supported by Russia Assad blames security issues, and demands more security equipment. In the midst of another report about the use of chemicals in Syria, on April 24, 2014, while in Tokyo the President boasted:

"Eighty-seven percent of Syria's chemical weapons have already been removed, that is a consequence of U.S. leadership. The fact that we didn't have to fire a missile to get that accomplished is not a failure to uphold international norms, it's a success."[7]

The President may claim success but the war goes on. Chemical weapons as define by the agreement under Resolution 2118 are not being used; but people continue to die as chlorine gas is being used by the regime. Once again the 'red line' has been crossed and yet only Russia is the winner as Putin gets a foothold in the Mediterranean with access to a Syrian harbour for his navy.

The making of a War President

In 2007 and during his campaigns to become the Democrat nominee and then President of the United States, Barack Obama consistently opposed the 2002 Iraq War Resolution. In 2014 in a complete turn of events he believes that the resolution that he opposed gives him a legal basis for airstrikes in Syria. His level of hypocrisy never seizes to amaze.

The President's reluctance and inability to negotiate a residual force with the Iraqi government left a vacuum in the region. The result has been the expansion of a terrorist force even more dangerous than Al Qaeda. The terrorists have been able to organize themselves into a virtual state called The Islamic State in Iraq and Syria (ISIS) or as Obama prefers to call them The Islamic State of Iraq and the Levant.(ISIL). Whatever you call it this terrorist group is well funded by selling resources on the open market from captured oil and gas fields and ransom money from European countries that are too willing to pay instead of fight. Despite being advised of the dangers posed by ISIS in 2013, Obama waited a year before developing a strategy to do anything.

The world was shocked when ISIS beheaded two American journalists, Steve Sotloff and James Foley. The President dilly dallied for close to a month and even stated that he did not have a strategy, while he had the time to play golf. On September 10, 2014, in the midst of dwindling poll numbers (58 % disapproval) Obama finally responded to the ISIS threat. In another crafted speech to the nation he announced that he will take action to degrade and destroy ISIS. Once again leading from behind, the now 'war President' touts a coalition of the willing to fight the terrorists in Iraq, Syria and anywhere else. His lack of engagement got a tepid response from nineteen Arab States and only a few NATO members and Australia show any initial commitment. He may have a 'plan' but no real strategy as the world searches for concrete solutions to a problem that if radical Islam has its way will be with us for years to come. Once the 'coalition of the unwilling' was announced the President proceeded to let the world know about his strategy. Instead of telling the world what he was prepared to do, he explained 'what he was not going to do'. The world seeks leadership, and a feckless Obama is once again not the one to provide it.

To the President's credit on September 22, 2014 a coalition force of U.S and a number of Arab countries launched air strikes on Syria. After refusing to get involved in Syria for almost a year, Obama ordered the air strikes on Khorasan militants preparing an 'imminent' attack on the U.S. In his address to the United Nations on September 24, 2014, the President justified the air strikes and stated that it was the start of a long campaign to 'destroy ISIS'. Seeking more support from other countries he once again re-iterated that there will be 'no U.S. boots on the ground' a strategy that is not widely supported by military experts. Just using air strikes will not decimate ISIS or any terrorist group. They will hide and only infrastructure will be destroyed. An international force or Arab forces supported by Western expertise will be needed to combat the terrorists on the ground. The bigger issues are, will members of the international coalition put 'boots on the ground' to finish the enemy? Why is Turkey, a member of NATO sitting on the fence? Is it because of the Turkish disdain for the Kurds or the President's inability to galvanize allies against a common enemy? Once again Obama through his rhetoric shows that when it comes to war, he has his head firmly buried in the sand. This is a President reluctant to go to war seemingly at any costs. His aggrandised speeches are never followed by actions and leading from behind leaves his allies perplexed and hesitant to support his strategies. The world will be fighting this war against ISIS years after his Presidency has elapsed.

Iran

Since the Carter days, Iran has been a geopolitical thorn. The hostage taking in 1979 was just the start of a long and protracted war of words between the Ayatollahs' regime and the Western world. The Iranian government has made no bones about its intention to destroy Israel, and in its goals to do so they have pursued an open search to make a nuclear bomb. Despite the United Nations six resolutions to address Iran's nuclear program, they have continued to enrich uranium. On November 20, 2013 an interim agreement was arrived at between Iran and the P5+1. The agreement contained:

- Pauses construction of the Arak heavy water reactor
- Neutralizes Iran's stockpile of uranium
- Suspends enrichment above 5% for 6 months.
- Iran agrees to not add centrifuges to its existing cascades, but leaves intact more than 18,000 centrifuges that will continue to operate.
- Allows daily IAEA inspections at Fardow and Natanz
- They do not have to destroy already enriched uranium. and means that they can start the process very within a matter of months..
- Iran will be given relief from sanctions to the tune of US $7 billion.

On CBS – *Face the Nation.* Kerry said of the agreement:

> *"It's not based on trust. It's based on verification. It's based on your ability to know what is happening. So you don't have to trust the people you're dealing with; you have to have a mechanism put in place whereby you know exactly what you're getting and you know exactly what they're doing. And we believe we are at the beginning of putting that in place with Iran."*[8]

While the President proclaims it's 'an important first step', others in his own party have a different opinion. U.S. Sen. Robert Menendez (D-NJ), Chairman of the Senate Foreign Relations Committee, said:

> *"This agreement did not proportionately reduce Iran's nuclear program for the relief it is receiving. Given Iran's history*

> *of duplicity, it will demand ongoing, on the ground verification ... Until Iran has verifiably terminated its illicit nuclear program, we should vigorously enforce existing sanction."*[9]

The initial agreement freezes but does not reverse Iran's nuclear program. With 19,000 centrifuges (2013) in place, Iran could restart its program within 3 months, Independent sources report that the deal is only a postponement and it pushes back Iran's program by only 6 weeks. In his 2014 State of the Union address the President vows to veto any new and additional Congressional sanctions that may be imposed during the talks. When the 30th of June 2014 deadline elapsed, the President agreed to another extension to the negotiation. In the meantime Iran gets to keep the money and continue its nuclear program. Another 'red line' turned 'pink'.

Ukraine

The "Obama Doctrine", which the President believes should only be achieved through diplomatic negotiations, has taken a turn for the worse. His foreign policy which has been based on getting approval from Russia and China has backfired miserably. Vladimir Putin, a former KGB operative, has read the President brilliantly and has used his tactics to push Ukraine to the brink of a civil war as well as put himself in apposition to rebuild the old Soviet Union boundaries.

In 2008, Russia invaded South Ossetia-Georgia. The world did not respond forcefully to this first move by then Prime Minister Vladimir Putin. George Bush had talks but the situation was never resolved to Georgia's satisfaction. Putin is using the same pretext (to protect the ethnic population) used by Hitler, who started in Austria, then Czechoslovakia, and proceeded to invade Poland which triggered World War II. A day after the Sochi Olympics Russian forces used the dissent within Ukraine to takeover Crimea. The result is that Russia has gained a major strategic access to the Black Sea. He may be eyeing further incursion in East Ukraine. To expand his imperial ambition one can speculate – what's next? Could Estonia, Latvia, and Belarus be next?

President Obama appointed Hillary Clinton who gave Russia a 'reset button' to normalize relationships between Russia and the United States. In the ever increasing Middle East conflicts the President chose to use Russia as an intermediary/partner in negotiations to stop Syria's use of chemicals and to get a transitory agreement to stop Iran's uranium enrichment. In both cases the U.S. has finished with egg on its face. Syria continues to use chemicals to kill its citizens. Iran is most likely to restart enriching uranium and get closer to building a nuclear bomb. All the while Putin has gained more influence in the Middle East, a region that the Soviet Union had lost completely.

In 2012, when discussing U.S. plans for an anti-missile shield, the world should have taken the (off-mic) conversation between Presidents Dmitry Medvedev and Obama more seriously, the exchange went like this:

> *"President Obama: On all these issues, but particularly missile defense, this, this can be solved but it's important for him to give me space.*
>
> *President Medvedev: Yeah, I understand. I understand your message about space. Space for you ...*
>
> *President Obama: This is my last election. After my election I have more flexibility.*
>
> *President Medvedev: I understand. I will transmit this information to Vladimir."*[10]

During the 2012 Presidential debates Mitt Romney's comments about Russia being 'the greatest geopolitical threat' were dismissed by the President and laughed at by the media. He was quoting from his book '*No Apology*' when he wrote:

> *"Reactionaries have seized their opportunity to take Russia backward even while rebuilding Russian military power. We are now obliged to be wary and vigilant once more, because by mid-century, our grandchildren may well view Russia with the same concern that we and our parents once did."*[11]

The invasion of Crimea and the Russian threat to the region is the result of President Obama's foreign policy as implemented by an inadequate Secretary of State. In addition there is the inability and reluctance of Europeans to come to grips with a very serious situation because of their dependence on Russia for energy. The downing of a civilian airline by pro-Russian terrorists is a direct result of a weak foreign policy towards Russia. Obama has left himself with no options but only economic sanctions. Putin has found the flexibility given to him by President Obama and the world may not be laughing anymore as the emboldened Putin privately stated that he could invade Riga, Vilnius, Tallinn, Warsaw and Bucharest in two weeks.

Israel

The relationship between Israel and the United States has never been as strained as it is under the Obama presidency. Statements made in public or in private leaves no doubt about the President and his Secretary of State's policy towards Israel. In an accidentally broadcast conversation between then France's President Nicolas Sarkozy and the President at a G20 meeting, the following transpired:

> *"I cannot bear Netanyahu, he's a liar," Sarkozy told Obama. You're fed up with him, but I have to deal with him even more often than you, Obama replied, according to the French interpreter."*[12]

The failed attempt by Sec. Kerry to reach a peace deal between Israel and the Palestinians has made matters worse. Sec. Kerry who is responsible for the failures in Syria, Iran, Ukraine and now Israel is so frustrated by his inability to negotiate anything and perhaps sees the possibility of a Nobel Peace prize disappear in a puff of smoke, made one of the most undiplomatic comments in a conversation to the Trilateral Commission. On April 25, 2014, on a tape obtained by Josh Rogin of *The Daily Beast*, Kerry is overheard saying:

> *"A two-state solution will be clearly underscored as the only real alternative. Because a unitary state winds up either be-*

> *ing an apartheid state with second-class citizens–or it ends up being a state that destroys the capacity of Israel to be a Jewish state. Once you put that frame in your mind, that reality, which is the bottom line, you understand how imperative it is to get to the two-state solution, which both leaders, even yesterday, said they remain deeply committed to."*[13]

This comment immediately provided fodder for Hanan Ashrawi of the Palestinian Legislative Council who said:

> *"We think it (apartheid) exists already in the occupied territories, in Palestine, and within Israel there's a very intricate system of discrimination that already exist."*

Emboldened by Sec. Kerry's statements, Hamas kidnapped and killed three young Jewish men. In retaliation some Jews killed a young Palestinian. These events were the trigger for Hamas, a proxy for Iran, to launch thousands of rockets into Israel. The latest conflict turned into an all-out war, with casualties and death on both sides. Once again Sec. Kerry interjected himself into negotiating a deal, after Hamas rejected a ceasefire proposed by Egypt. Once again Sec. Kerry showed his lack of understanding for the Mid-East conflict as he negotiated with Qatar and Turkey, both supporters of Hamas, while neglecting to invite Jordan, Egypt or Saudi Arabia to take part in the negotiations. He also failed to rebuke the United Nations who returned rockets to Hamas, when they were found in two buildings under the jurisdiction of the U.N.

The total lack of leadership from the White House makes it more difficult to find a solution to the conflict. Constantly issuing statements about 'Israel's right to defend itself' without clearly stating that Hamas bears most of the responsibility for breaking all the negotiated ceasefires, cannot and will not solve any problems. The United Sates and the Western world better face the facts; the world is dealing with terrorists who are sworn to the destruction of Israel, and ultimately the West.

What is often forgotten is that Israel is the only democracy in the Middle East. One in five citizens is a Palestinian and Muslim. Arabs are elected members of Knesset, have seats on the Supreme Court and Universities with affirmative action policies.

With the exception of the use of drones and the killing of Osama bin Laden, this President's foreign policies have been an abject failure. His reluctance to acknowledge acts of terrorism, and refusal to use words like 'islamists', 'terrorists' or 'jihadists' have blurred the focus on the real enemy. When Major Nidal Hasan, a self-proclaimed 'soldier of Allah', killed 13 soldiers and injured more than 30 during a November 2009 shooting rampage, the events were classified by the Department of Defense as 'workplace violence". The administration changed the term 'war on terror' to 'man made catastrophe contingency'. In 2001, Sec. Clinton refused to classify Nigerian jihadist-islamist organization Boko Haram as a terrorist organization.

Not all Muslims are terrorists, but in this new war all global theological terrorists are radical Islamists. Why not call them for what they are?

Guantanamo

Knowing full well that closing Guantanamo is not supported by the majority of Americans, including some Democrats, Obama believes that releasing captured terrorists will fulfill his empty promise of closure. If there are no more prisoners, Guantanamo's existence becomes a moot subject.

In a desperate move to salvage his dwindling popularity before the 2014 mid-term elections, President Obama made one of the worst decisions of his tenure. Having made the stupid promise of closing the prison in Guantanamo, his administration, under the excuse of fulfilling a noble American tradition of 'not leaving a man behind', negotiated with the Taliban in an exchange of prisoners. With an executive order and not informing Congress, the President signed on the release of five of the most dangerous Taliban leaders in exchange for Sgt. Bowe Bergdahl, who had allegedly been kidnapped in 2009.This departure from most governments position of 'not negotiating with terrorists', may well endanger Westerners as terrorists see an opening in kidnapping as a means for the release of their captured and jailed comrades.

Pandering to his far-left base and ignoring the real threats to world peace, including attacks on Christians and Western culture around the world, the President failed to enforce compliance with either the U.S or even UN sanctions on numerous occasions. His release of the five Talibans, who even Amnesty International believes to be war criminals, goes beyond comprehension. The way the President released the Talibans is perhaps illegal and unconstitutional, it will be for Congress to decide whether his actions are impeachable. As a result of Obama's narcissistic decisions based purely on his political agenda, we now live in a far less secured world.

The War on Women

One of Obama's wedge issues in his bid to transform America is the so-called war on women. There is no doubt that there are inequities in any system. Historically, women have taken jobs in sectors that provide a lower wage. Men usually earn a higher income in their chosen field . Women have chosen careers that allow them more free time for their families, while men have chosen careers that demand that they spend more time at work. Depending how one use statistics a number of disparities may exists, but the President's constant assertion that women make only 0.77 cents on the dollar is incorrect. The Bureau of Labor Statistics show that women who do not get married have virtually no wage gap, they earn 0.96 cents for every dollar a man makes. There is a strong case, however for equal pay for equal work. We also see more women executives in the board Room, although the proportion is still small compared to male executives.

The irony is that equal pay for women does not exist in the White House, who employs a larger share of workers at the lower scale. Republicans have more female staff in higher staff positions. There are four Republican Governors: Jan Brewer, Susana Martinez, Mary Fallin, and Nikki Haley compared to one Democrat – Maggie Hassan.

The President may continue to 'huff and puff' on his continued campaign trail but this is pure propaganda of social science.

Income Inequality

President Obama through his policies has made no bones about his desire for wealth redistribution. He sincerely, but erroneously believes that the issue of 'income inequality' is a good political strategy. This may be true, but reality is that governments are the culprit in the creation of income inequality.

Socialist policies which provide all sorts of programs that have no term limit produce a culture of entitlement which permeates the society. Attacks on the rich and recurring legislation for minimum wage increases create a wage in society but do not produce badly needed positive economic outcomes.

First, let us take the minimum wage rhetoric. To raise the minimum wage in many circumstances increase the costs of doing business so much that the resultant effect is the layoff of some workers. The other side of the coin is, if costs goes up they are passed down to the consumer. For every increase in minimum wage there is a loser somewhere.

The President may not have openly supported the 'Occupy Wall Street' movement, but Nancy Pelosi did on his behalf. This movement which produced more chaos, crime and disruptions achieved nothing. It created a dislike for the so-called 'one-percenters'. But what we ignore is that the Obama administration has poured millions of dollars to prop-up the one-percenters, (bankers). The Quantitative Easing (QE) policy has also contributed to the so-called income inequality.

When short term interest rates are close to zero, central banks can no longer buy short-term government bonds to lower interest rates to stimulate the economy. As a result, the alternative is QE, a policy that sees the central bank purchase specific amounts of financial assets from commercial banks. The Fed through its quantitative-easing efforts has more than quadrupled its balance sheet to over US $4.2trillion. The effect is to increase the value of the assets, lower their yield and increase the monetary base. Since money is cheap the rich for example, can borrow and invest in the stock market, the values go up and the rich get richer. Despite an increase in the monetary base, if due to a lack of confidence there is no business reinvestment, the result is no job creation and low economic growth.

But the real truth about inequality stems from social programs. On January 8, 1964 President Johnson declared the war on poverty. Yet, fifty years later the situation is no better. Clinton said: "Welfare should be a second chance not a way of life." Unfortunately for many it has become a way of life, there is abuse and lack of control in the system, to bring things in perspective. The following statistics from the U.S. Census Bureau and Sentier Research LLC show a very grim picture:

Since Obama took Office Sentier Research shows:

- Median Household Income down $55,958 to $51,404 (2013)
- Poverty has increased by 6.7m to record 46.5m
- Labor force dropped from 65.7% to 62.8%
- Median Household income: Then $55,939 Now $52,163

U.S Census Bureau reports:
Poverty Rate Then: 13.2% – Now 15%. or 46.9 million
Food Stamps: Then 32 million. Now: 47.4 million. According to FNS USDA Gov.

But perhaps worse are the unintended consequences of the Supplementary Nutrition Assistance Program (SNAP), and the Food Stamp program. The government spends some $78B a year on Food Stamps. But a Recipients Poll says 57% taking Advantage, 36% truly in need. In New York activists campaign to get people to sign up for food stamps. SNAP is the new name. Get rid of stamps and use a 'debit' EBT SNAP card. The Obama administration has made qualifying much easier. In 1996 food stamps were issued for 3 months, every 3 years, the exception was if you were working 20 hours/workweek or enrolled in a workfare or training program Obama abolished the restrictions. Furthermore, there now is an Agriculture Department program to get Spanish speaking Americans to sign up. USDA removed the advertising. In North Carolina 17% are on food stamps. The efforts are to break down what was known as mountain pride. In Ashe County which use to be a hardworking community who refused to take stamps, they were approached by government to get them to take stamps. The idea was to use stamps to by seeds for planting instead of food. The person who put this idea in place was given the 2011 Hunger Champions Award.

For all the Obama rhetoric about inequality, his polices has done little for the African American community which makes up 13% of population, of which 23% are food stamp recipients, 19% of disability recipients, 20% of Medicaid recipients. The rest of America does not fare better, in fact there is very little improvement in the economy and the unemployment rate is still high. Poverty in America seems to have taken root, and the Obama government is creating a culture of dependency and entitlement in a country which was once the envy of the world.

The most egregious argument about income inequality is the attack on rich Republicans like John McCain and Mitt Romney, while there are no reports on rich Democrats like Al Gore, John Kerry or the Clintons. It is fascinating to see liberals push for income inequality with policies like tax the rich and redistribution of wealth. They rarely push for programs that give a hand up, but always put forward programs that give a hand out. Of course, these programs are always accompanied by tax increases to fund them.

Transparent as Mud

When Obama came to office, he promised to have the most transparent White House and administration. Unfortunately, during his tenure many situations have been far from being transparent, the largest being the Benghazi scandal, where this administration has certainly be anything but transparent.

Fast & Furious

In the aftermath of a 'gunwalking' program started under the Bush administration to track the sale of firearms, the Obama administration started a new program called 'Fast and Furious' in 2009. The strategy was to identify and eliminate entire arms trafficking networks rather than low-level buyers. By June 2010, suspects had purchased guns at a cost of over US$1 million at Phoenix-area gun shops. Many of the guns were being used by cartel members in Mexico. On December 14, 2010, U.S. Border Patrol agent Brian Terry was shot and killed by what was later traced as gun obtained from a Phoenix store involved in the program. In 2011 the program was closed but of the 2,000 or so guns sold only some 660 have been recovered, the rest remains in the hands of criminals.

On May 3, 2011 Attorney General Eric Holder testified to the House Judiciary Committee that he did not know who approved Fast and Furious. A statement that will be questioned when documents showed that the Attorney General's office had been sent briefings on Fast and Furious as early as July 2010. The House Oversight and Government Reform Committee voted to hold AG Holder in contempt, for refusing to disclose internal Justice Department documents in response to a subpoena, 17 Democrats voted 'yes' while many in their ranks walked off the floor.

Veterans Scandal

In what seems to be a never ending series of scandals and cover ups in the Obama administration, we can add the Veterans Affairs (VA) Scandal. A whistle-blower alleged that some 40 veterans had died while waiting up to 21 months for care at a VA hospital in Phoenix. Arizona, In addition, it is also purported that wait-time data were manipulated to show efficiency in dealing with the patients in order to earn bonuses. After weeks of investigations the VA Inspector General released a report stating that the wait-times at the Phoenix VA hospital was 115 days and not the 14 days wait-time goal. The report also found 'systemic' misconduct throughout the VA. Ultimately the whole scandal saw the President accept the resignation of Veterans Affairs Secretary Eric Shinseki.

Internal Revenue Service

In 2013, it was revealed that the Internal Revenue Service (IRS) had been involved in the investigation of right-leaning political organizations based on their names and affiliations. The controversy has triggered several investigations, including an FBI investigation ordered by

AG Holder. Although liberal groups and the Occupy movement were included in the investigation, the majority of scrutinized organizations were either 'Tea Party' or conservative groups.

The IRS is so feared that both the left and the right expressed their outrage at such an overreach by the IRS. Senator Claire McCaskill (D-MO) told CBS:

> *"I'm mad. It is un-American, it is wrong, and we have to make sure that this gets fixed ... We should not only fire the head of the IRS, which has occurred, but we've got to go down the line and find every single person who had anything to do with this and make sure that they are removed from the IRS and the word goes out that this is unacceptable. It is un-American, it is wrong, and it cannot occur again."*[14]

Michael Macleod-Ball of the American Civil Liberties Union (ACLU) expressed his disapproval to *Forbes* magazine:

> *"Even the appearance of playing partisan politics with the tax code is about as constitutionally troubling as it gets ... With the recent push to grant federal agencies broad new powers to mandate donor disclosure for advocacy groups on both the left and the right, there must be clear checks in place to prevent this from ever happening again."*[15]

In 2013, a Congressional Investigation was started to look into the role of the IRS. Lois Lerner the director in charge of tax exempt department became the center of attention when she refused to testify and invoked her 'fifth amendment'. As a result The US House of Representatives, including 6 Democrats, voted to hold Ms. Lerner in contempt of Congress for refusing to testify about alleged IRS targeting of tea party organizations seeking tax exempt status. The House, including 26 Democrats, also approved a measure asking Attorney General Eric Holder to appoint a special prosecutor to investigate the IRS case.

However, it is unlikely that the Department of Justice, under AG Holder, will investigate the IRS scandal since it is likely that they have been involved in targeting conservative groups. Congress could have given Ms. Lerner immunity and she could have revealed what she knew. So far the whole scandal remains unresolved. Yet the IRS has been given additional powers to enforce certain parts of the Affordable Care Act go figure!

A year after the House Ways and Means Committee's request for Ms. Lerner's e-mails, on Friday June 13th 2014, it was revealed that all her e-mails from 2009 to 2011 had been *(magically)* lost due to a computer crash. Only e-mails to and from IRS employees were available. But no e-mails between outside groups and organizations, the White House, the Justice and Treasury Departments and Democrat offices could be found. It was also reported that the hard drives had been destroyed. Ironically, this comes from a department which demands that businesses and citizens keep documents for at least seven years, under severe threats of penalties, yet the IRS could not keep its own data for two years.

Spying on Citizens and Friendly Leaders

In 2001, U.S. President Bush started the National Security Agency's terrorist surveillance program. Criticized by the left as an attempt to silence his foes in 2007 the program was allegedly suspended and returned supervision to the FISA court. The Obama administration continued to operate the program under FISA rules. But in 2009, it was revealed that the government had been involved in 'overcollection' of domestic communications in excess of FISA.

When Edward Snowden, a former employee of the CIA released classified documents, the can of worms about government data collection was opened wide. Obama, not only was following prior Bush policies but his administration had also extended them. It was revealed that the government had collected millions of phone records, conducted internet surveillance in the name of national security. In fact the government had been snooping not only on its own citizens but also on heads of states.

In a changing world under constant threat from terrorism, governments have been collecting data and snooping not only on their own citizens but also on heads of state. To address the revelations the President said:

> *"It's important to recognize that you can't have a hundred percent security and also then have a hundred percent privacy and zero inconvenience,"*[16]

Obama had promised more transparency as a presidential candidate but the irony of the above statement is that as President he finds himself in the difficult position of placing security ahead of his rhetoric. Citizens today do not have the same liberties that were written in the Constitution, many new executive orders have been put into effect, limiting citizens' right to privacy. Meta data collected, which are just numbers, have seemingly not been used to snoop on private citizens. However, we should also be vigilant, to prevent the use of data collected. Our Government task is to protect us, citizens, and should also be accountable for safeguarding secrets in the national interest.

The New Emperor

On December 16, 1773 the political protest known as the 'Boston Tea Party' took place and was the precursor to the American Revolution. The Thirteen American Colonies broke from the British Empire and formed an independent nation, which *defacto* got rid of King George III as ruler and monarch of the new United States. Presidents in the past have used executive powers to change legislation to implement their own visions and agendas. Obama, unlike others before him has succeeded to push the envelope. During his tenure more executive orders have been passed than many presidents before him, in doing so fulfilling his ambitions to transform America.

The founding fathers ensured in the Constitution that a clear separation existed between the three branches of government: The Executive, The Legislative and the Judicial. The Constitution was designed that each branch be equal. This assured that tyrannical and dictatorial powers be kept at bay. The Legislative branch made up of the House of Representatives and the Senate have the power to 'make the law'. President Obama has gone way beyond his executive powers and in fact re-written and change many laws passed by Congress.

Executive Orders

Nowhere in the law does it give the President the right to change the terms of the law. An Executive order that tells how the law should be enforced is consistent, but if the Executive order frustrates the law by in fact re-writing it, the order goes around the constitution. All the provisions of a piece of legislation work together but every change made by a President will deconstruct the law, and therefore the law, is no longer the same law that was originally passed. The President has used these powers to change laws on overtime pay, Affordable Care Act (39 times), not enforcing some immigration law, minimum sentencing requirement, state defense of marriage laws, and more.

In those cases the separation of powers does not exist. Presidents do not write laws. This is a lawless President doing the job of Congress. These actions threaten the delicate orbit of the separation of government. In many circumstances the President has gone beyond his executive powers to re-write or change the laws passed by Congress and his desire to 'use his pen and phone' to change the law has created a concern among even his supporters.

Jonathan Turley a liberal and professor of Law at George Washington University in a testimony before Congress said:

> *"The danger is quite severe. The problem with what the president is doing is that he's not simply posing a danger to the constitutional system. He's becoming the very danger the Constitution was designed to avoid. That is the concentration of power in every single branch."*[17]

Given Obama's dictatorial approach to policy making, it makes one wonder about his academic days as a professor of 'constitutional law'. More importantly, what was he teaching his students; respect or disregard for the U.S constitution?

The President often believes that his opponents are bigots and therefore he believes that he has the duty to make changes to the laws as he sees fit to fulfill his ideological agenda. The problem is that the Federal courts have avoided looking at his abuse of power. The media has been silent and the silence of the people has been deafening. The Democrats are passive and are endangering democracy. Under the Constitution, the three branches are equal but if one takes more power the result may be tyranny.

Nuclear Option

Supported by the Senate majority Leader Reid of Nevada, this administration has blocked or prevented many motions to come to the floor for a vote. To make sure that his appointments are approved, the Democrats passed the 'nuclear option' a parliamentary procedure that allows the Senate to decide any issue by majority vote. Therefore instead of requiring 60 votes for a filibuster or 67 votes for amending a senate rule, now only a simple majority of 51 is required. In 2013 the Nuclear Option eliminating filibuster for Presidential Nomination was passed 52/48, thus eliminating 225 years of precedence. This action comes from the same people who during the Bush presidency complained about the use of a 'nuclear option' the following are some of the comment made:

April 13 2005. Sen. Obama blocking Bush environmental appointees to get lead paint environmental policy:

> *"I sense the talk of nuclear option is more about power than about fairness. I believe some of my colleagues propose this rule's change because they can get away with it, rather than because they know that it is good for democracy."*

May 18, 2005. Sen. Reid:

> *"The filibuster is far from a procedural gimmick it's part of the fabric of this institution we call the Senate."*

May 23, 2005 Sen. Biden said:

> *"This nuclear option is ultimately an example of the arrogance of power*

While the action of the Democrat majority senate may help them in the short term, they may rue the day they passed the nuclear option, because they will not be in power for ever. If the Democrats believe that there will be no future repercussions, they are delusional.

In view of these dictatorial actions by the President, Charles Krauthammer the famed syndicated columnist puts it best:

> *"A Senate with no rules. A president without boundaries. One day, when a few bottled-up judicial nominees and a malfunctioning health-care Web site are barely a memory, we will still be dealing with the toxic residue of this outbreak of authoritative lawlessness."*[18]

This administration has been able to address controversial issues by obfuscating, denying and then lying about its failed policies. When it could no longer defend its actions in the face of undeniable facts, it resorted to the race card. After a previous day's cantankerous House Judiciary Committee hearing, AG Holder addressed Al Sharpton's National Action Network. While he did not refer to race in his comments, the choice of venue and audience shows the intent, when he said:

> *"… I am pleased to note that the last five years have been defined by significant strides and lasting reforms, even in the face, even in the face, of unprecedented, unwarranted ugly adversity. And if you don't believe that, you look at the way … forget about me … forget about me, you look at the way the Attorney General of the United States was treated yesterday by a House committee. Had nothing to do with me what Attorney General has ever had to deal with that kind of treatment? What President has ever had to deal with that kind of treatment?"*[19]

One can understand AG Holder's frustration in the face of his own inefficiency, ineptitude and partisanship in dealing or not dealing with matters of judicial importance. However, his comments ignored history. He conveniently forgot the impeachments of Presidents Andrew Johnson and Bill Clinton, the articles of impeachment against President Richard Nixon, convictions and jail sentences against U.S. AG John Mitchell and AG Richard Kleindienst.

Last address as President

During his tenure Obama has made several speeches, which the left embraced as a show of leadership. However this president continuously made promises and reversed them when it came time for action. With statements like "ISIS is not Islamic," or "We will not get dragged into another ground war in Iraq", he has greater ambiguity in his so-called strategy to "degrade, and ultimately destroy, [ISIS] through a comprehensive and sustained counter-terrorism strategy," when Secretary Kerry says 'we are not at war with ISIS." It is no wonder that his 'lead from behind foreign policy' has not worked and that America's staunchest allies do not follow him willingly.

It may be time to remedy this view of Obama as a great orator and instead show him as an arrogant, disengaged, stubborn and ideological President. The following is a hypothetical, satirical and cynical draft for a January 2017 speech by departing President Obama. It attempts to sum up his presidency which started with so much hope but ended in so much chaos and waste.

> *"As I leave office I would like to talk about my promises and the accomplishments of my Administration:*
>
> *I promised that I would change the way that Washington works and with the help of Senator Reid and Speaker Pelosi I was able to provide a 'bipartisan' leadership without having to consult the Republican opposition on any new legislation.*
>
> *Climate change has wreaked havoc with our way of life and I promised to lower the seas and saved coastal cities. I succeeded in keeping California dry, they had a three year drought. Sec. of State Kerry was finally able to find the WMD – Climate Change. I also promoted alternative sources of energy by funding enterprises that supported my initiatives with large sums of taxpayers' money. Solyndra and others were unfortunately unable to produce any significant results or provide a boost to the economy.*

I wanted to be known as a 'green president' instead I turned yellow by endangering the country's security by refusing to approve the Keystone pipeline for political reasons prior to the 2014 mid-term elections

The African American community, so deprived in previous generations, can thank me for the rise in youth unemployment. Most citizens in their twenties and early thirties can now boast longer holidays as they could not find any jobs for years.

As I extended my open hand to Iran and others I was able to promote the Arab Spring which produced more turmoil in the Middle East and was able to sow more seeds of nefarious terrorism weeds in that part of the world. To use the words of my Vice President 'Iraq was my greatest achievement'. I stopped the wars as promised. Removed all the troops and as a result Northern Iraq, including Mosul and Tikrit at one time fell into the hands of the worse of the Islamists terrorists ISIS, or ISIL as like to call them.

My relationship with Russia improved when my Secretary of State Hillary Clinton presented, a reset button to her counterpart Sergei Lavrov. It was a master coup in diplomacy that provided a 'Staples Easy button' to Russia which enabled Vladimir Putin to object and oppose any proposal I made on Iran, Syria, Ukraine and other hot spots in the world. For quite some time, I even ignored Russia's missile test which broke the 1987 treaty that ended the Cold War.

I want to make it perfectly clear, that you can no longer keep your doctor if you like it and that you have to pay higher premiums for health insurance, and services you don't need. I will bail out insurance companies who in the past have refused care to some 15 million citizens who were not covered, and now some 20 million may not be covered.

> *To those who have criticized my administration, I apologize for missing the mark. I said that "we had 5 days to transform America", but it took me eight years to make the change. I promised to unite the country and I am sorry that I leave America more divided than when I came in. American exceptionalism is no more, but I certainly am exceptional.*
>
> *I cannot leave without thanking the sycophantic mass media, who during my entire presidency have supported me blindly without scrutinizing or criticizing my policies. Your lack of scrutiny was the catalyst for my success.*
>
> *As I depart for greener pastures to make money on the speaking circuit I can really say that change has arrived and that the State of the Union is anything but strong.*
>
> *Après moi le deluge. I hope somebody else can clean up after me."*

William James Durant said:

> *"A great civilization is not conquered from without, until it is destroyed from within."*

Yes we could, and I was able to do it all."

CHAPTER 15

MITT MCIVER OR RIC ROMNEY?

The quirky title of this chapter is a play on the names of two conservatives who ran for office. Mitt Romney ran against Barack Obama in the 2012 U.S. presidential elections for the highest office in the world. Ric McIver ran in the 2010 Mayoralty race in Calgary, one of the most conservative cities in Canada. The parallels are uncanny, with both men losing to progressives, and the consequences are being felt by all parties. We shall explore the reasons for their losses, as an example for future conservative candidates.

Mitt Romney

After an unsuccessful run at the Republican nomination in the 2008 presidential election, Mitt Romney positioned himself has the front-runner for the 2012 Republican presidential nomination. But even after more than stellar careers both as a business man and a politician, he remained unknown to the general public. Given the dismal first term of the Obama presidency, the race to the White House was there for Romney to win, so why is he not President of the United States?

First let us examine Mitt Romney's background as man, businessman and politician. A Mormon Bishop of his ward, Romney is a man of strong religious conviction and is greatly influenced by his father, George Romney who ran against Nixon in 1968.

He attended Stanford University in 1965-66, during the anti-Vietnam war protests, but he joined a counter protest group. As a Mormon Missionary he served a thirty-month stay in France. He showed his leadership by becoming co-president of a mission of 175. During his stay he developed a strong affection for the people and became fluent in French. Upon his return to the United Sates, he attended Bingham Young University and earned a Bachelor of Arts degree in English, While he was in France, Mitt missed the tumultuous Vietnam protests. Upon his return, despite his father George serving as Secretary of Housing and Urban Development in the Nixon cabinet, Mitt Romney became disillusioned, referring to the war as being misguided. Taking leave from his studies he went to work on his mother's unsuccessful 1970 campaign as U.S. Senator for Michigan.

Mitt Romney continued his academic career by joining the four year program coordinated by the Harvard Law School and Harvard Business School and completed both degrees in flying colours. As Hugh Hewitt wrote:

> *"He graduated in 1975 cum laude from the law school, in the top third of that class, and was named a Baker Scholar for graduating in the top five percent of his business school class."*[1]

After graduation Mitt was sought after by many Fortune 500 corporations. His goal to become a future executive, led him to believe that he had to acquire a number of skills, resulting in his choice to join the Boston Consulting Group as a management consultant. In 1977 he joined Bain & Company where he became the vice-president of the consulting company which gave him the opportunity to work with some of America's largest corporations. In 1986, he left Bain & Company, and in a deal with Bill Bain, which protected him from professional or financial risk, Romney co-founded the private equity investment firm Bain Capital.

As President and CEO of Bain Capital, Mitt Romney focused the company's activities on venture capital investments, which helped start Staples Inc. Later he switched the company's activities to leveraged buyouts. This decision made both the company and himself a lot of money, but also became a source of attacks during the 2012 presidential campaigns.

Leveraged buyouts involve the purchase of companies with money borrowed from banks and using the assets of the newly bought company as collateral. Once the companies had improved in value they would be sold. Very often, the process to increase profits and bottom line of the purchased company required layoffs. The goals and objectives of the company, after all, was return on investment rather than job creation. Two of the most lucrative deals were in TRW and Yellow Pages of Italy. Reportedly, the investment of $51.3 million in the Italian Yellow Pages returned approximately $1.17 billion. Deals like this enabled Bain to raise its share of profits to 30%, this compared to the 20% industry average. Given that the deals involved investment by the company's partners, it is reported that Romney's wealth grew to $250 million or more.

Despite his success in business Mitt Romney aspired to be involved in politics. Just like his father who was chairman and President of American Motors Corporation and who left to become the 43rd Governor of Michigan, Mitt decided to run for office. His first foray into politics was to run for the U.S. Senate, against Edward M. Kennedy. First he had to win the GOP nomination. However, not being part of the establishment and having supported Democrat Paul Tsongas in the past, his run was more arduous. But with the help of his family and his father's former contacts, he defeated John Lakian for the GOP nomination.

The race between Romney and Kennedy was now on. Kennedy had been the Senator since 1962, but his behavior and the shadow of Chappaquiddick was still looming large. The odds were in Romney's favour. His strategy was to be all things to everyone. While he pushed for tough on crime policies, requiring welfare recipients to work and creating more private-sector jobs, he courted the Log Cabin Republicans, a gay rights group. He also changed his position on abortion rights. While being personally opposed to abortion, he endorsed the use of the abortion drug RU-486, and attended fundraiser for Planned Parenthood. He went on to oppose the "Contract with America" a Gingrich initiative in Washington, he supported raising the minimum wage tied to inflation, and two gun-control measures , the Brady Law and the five-day waiting period on gun sales. Both these initiatives were opposed by the National Rifle Association. In effect his position during the campaign was becoming more liberal.

His faith became the next hurdle as the Kennedy campaign inferred that the Church of Jesus Christ and Latter Day – Saints excluded blacks and women from leadership roles. As polled showed Kennedy pulling ahead the campaigns agreed on two debates. During the first debate Romney defended his faith and his business record quite well. Then he faulted miserably on healthcare and support for women in the workplace, but most of all let it slip that he was an independent during the Reagan-Bush era.

Helped by local unions and appealing to largely black and poor Roxbury, Kennedy branded Romney as a suburbanite who did not understand city life. On Election Day, Kennedy won by a clear 58 to 41% majority. That was Romney first political defeat.

After his loss to Kennedy, Romney went back to Bain. The late nineties were extremely lucrative for Bain and of course for Romney. The 2002 Olympic Games in Utah were fast approaching. The organizing committee mired in an influence-peddling scandal, were badly in need of a new leader. After many deliberations and an executive search on February 11, 1999, Romney was formally introduced as Chief Executive of the Salt Lake Organizing Committee.

Not without criticisms about his ties with the Mormon church, Romney brought with him a sense of high ethical standards. He reform and established a new budget for the games with an emphasis on austerity and removal of extravagant lunches and dinners. He also used his business connections to bring back corporate sponsors who had been skeptical due to the corruption scandals. As a result of the 9/11 attack, he also focussed on the games' security. He acquired additional federal funding as the games were declared to be a national special security event. Up to this point Romney had been known for his business acumen. In producing one of the best Olympic Games, with a $100 million surplus, there is no doubt that his leadership skills in the public sector had been solidified.

Bolstered by his Olympic success, and despite his bruising defeat at the hands of Kennedy, Mitt Romney decided to go back to politics. He ran for Governor of Massachusetts, and was elected in November 2002. The State was in dire financial straits, by the time that Romney left office in 2006, he had balanced the budget over three consecutive years, resolved the $2 billion shortfall he had inherited, and created a surplus of $1.2 billion. He also implemented the nation's first universal health care program. Although vastly different from Obama's Affordable Care Act, this decision will later haunt him during his presidential bid in 2012.

Following his success in Massachusetts, in 2005 he announced that he would not be seeking a second term. To no one surprise, Romney made a bid for the White House and sought the GOP nomination in 2008. The strategy was to seek the support of the right, and while McCain and Giuliani to split the votes of the moderate members of the GOP. In Iowa, where Romney spent $10 million in advertising, he was challenged on the right by Governor Huckabee. Once again his Mormon faith and his past support for abortion rights became an issue in this evangelical stronghold. Huckabee, once ignored by his campaign, became a thorn in his bid to win Iowa and proceed to New Hampshire without any wounds. But he did not count on Giuliani pulling back his resources in New Hampshire, which gave the moderate vote to McCain. As history would have it Romney lost both Iowa to Huckabee and New Hampshire to McCain respectively. The once hopeful campaign of winning the nomination fizzled, as he failed in South Carolina. On Super Tuesday McCain won Arizona, California, Connecticut, Delaware, Illinois, Missouri, New Jersey, New York, and Oklahoma. Two days later. Romney announced the suspension of his campaign and ultimately endorsed Mc Cain as the GOP nominee.

As they say, the rest is history. McCain failed to galvanize the American public. In effort to gain the women vote he asked Governor Sarah Palin of Alaska to be his running mate. Due to the rapid economic deterioration, for some reason he suspended his campaign to go back to Washington. Sarah Palin, a firebrand of the right, who had pushed Mc Cain ahead in the polls, although moderately, then proceeded to do badly in an interview with Kathy Couric. The McCain campaign failed largely because fatigued by two wars and the Bush unpopularity Americans wanted a change. McCain did not provide that change. The people were hypnotized by the one term Senator Obama who made promises about 'hope and change'. An American public ready to embrace anything voted in droves in one of America's highest voter turnout. Eventually the result was the historic election of the first African American president, as Barack Obama garnered 53% of the votes and 365 electoral votes.

Armed with a majority in both the House and the Senate, Obama proceeded to manage the country in a virtual totalitarian manner. First he got the Affordable Care Act passed with no Republican support. On the economy he advanced a purely Keynesian approach and increased the national debt to heights not previously seen. Social programs were gradually increased or designed to garner further support from the left. With the economy continuing on a downward path, what was not possible in 2008 became plausible in 2012. Mitt Romney once again threw his hat into the race for President in 2012.

In the 2010 mid-term elections, The Tea Party had gathered strength and helped return the House to the Republicans. With a continuing economic downward spiral, and stubborn unemployment rates, this was an environment ripe for an expert with strong business acumen to take the reins of the country.

Obama's popularity continued to waiver. Acknowledging that in 2008 he had failed to get across who he really was, this time Romney was determined to get his message across with his Three Pillars for America as described in his book '*No Apology*':

1. A Strong Economy
2. A Strong Military
3. A Free and Strong People

Karl Rove, former President Bush political strategist, advised Romney to run against Obama from the outset. Ronald Scott recalls:

> *"He should avoid mixing it up (for now) with other primary candidates. Romney was encouraged to emphasize his competency and experience and to steer way wide of anything remotely connected to social policy and religion ... except to stick religiously to the talking points, no matter how tedious and tiresome the routine becomes, day after day, week after week, month after month."*[2]

No matter what strategy Romney chose, there were two issues that always dogged him. One was the inevitable question about his Mormon faith, and the other his variable stance on several issues which inevitably branded him as a 'flip-flopper'.

Romney's signature achievement as governor was the Massachusetts health care plan. But in the heat of the campaign when Santorum called the plan a blueprint for Obamacare, Romney said 'what works in one state is not going to work somewhere else.'

At first he endorsed, in general terms, embryonic stem cell research, he told the *New York Times* that he would 'criminalize' the work because it breached 'ethical boundaries'.

Romney had supported McCain and Bush's approach to immigration, but later vehemently opposed the McCain/Kennedy immigration Bill, stating that he did not believe in rounding up 11 million people and forcing them out of the country at gun point.

He said he wanted to stop illegal immigration and impose workplace verification of immigration status but would oppose any amnesty for those now in this country without valid documents.

In 1994 and 2004 he was on the side of 'choice' on the abortion issue but later he claimed to have been on the side of 'preserving the sanctity of life'.

Romney did not oppose The Troubled Asset Relief Program (TARP) when Bush passed it in 2008, nor was he against it in 2009 when Obama expanded it. But in 2009, he questioned the program and that bailing out banks was alarming, and there were good reasons for people to question it. Yet in 2010, he defended TARP as the "right thing for the country." He also told Fox's O'Reilly that Obama was right to try and push a stimulus plan yet in his book *No Apology*, he declared that Obama's government was the first one to declare war on free enterprise.

Over the course of his many campaigns Romney displayed a tendency to contradict himself on many issues. We expect politicians to change their views but in Romney's case it has been so frequent that it is perhaps the reason which, in 2007, prompted Steve Deace, the radio host of *Deace in the Afternoon* to opine:

> *"Given the nature of his ever-evolving positions on absolutely every issue ... Governor Romney either ranks first or second behind John Edwards 'on my most despicable liar running for president power ratings'. No Republican in my mind is phonier than Governor Romney."*[3]

Harsh words, but perhaps the Governor may have been responsible for attracting such ire. The most harmful attacks on Mitt Romney came from fellow conservatives, who question his true colors and conservatism. In the run to the GOP nominations for the 2102 presidential race, he was attack for his wealth by non-other than Newt Gingrich the former House Speaker.

In the debate, held at the University of North Florida and aired on CNN, which was the 19th for the Republicans. Gingrich launched some of his harshest attacks on Romney, a definite sign of the pressure he was feeling, and he said:

> *"[Romney] has an investment in Goldman Sachs, which is, today, foreclosing on Floridians. Maybe he should tell us how much money he's made off of how many households that have been foreclosed by his investments."*[4]

Not satisfied, he continued to say:

> *"We discovered, to our shock, Governor Romney owns shares of both Fannie Mae and Freddie Mac. Governor Romney made $1 million off of selling some of that."*[5]

Wolf Blitzer the Debate moderator, asked Gingrich if he was satisfied that Romney had been transparent enough about releasing his tax returns, Gingrich the lecturer reprimanded Blitzer and characterized the question as 'nonsense'. To which Blitzer reminded the speaker that he had said of Romney:

> *"He lives in a world of Swiss bank and Cayman Island bank accounts."*[6]

Romney's wealth came under constant scrutiny by the left. When 'right thinking' conservatives who believe in capitalism and support the free market attack a Republican colleague's wealth, it is virtual heresy. Who was Gingrich trying to appeal to? Ultimately his comments provided more fodder to Obama's team. Romney did not help, when he was caught on video berating the entitlement culture he said:

> *"There are 47% of the people who will vote for the president no matter what. There are 47% who are with him, who are dependent upon government, who believe that they are victims, who believe that government has a responsibility to care for them, who believe that they are entitled to health care, to food, to housing, to you name it."*[7]

He was right, to some extent. The fact is that 46.4% (2011) of Americans do not pay Federal income taxes, but pay other taxes. In retrospect, Obama has increased the dependency culture in America. However for a wealthy man to make such comments is tantamount to pouring gasoline on a fire pit. Americans, in general do not dislike rich people. In a survey Gallup asked a sampling of Americans whether they thought the United States benefited from having a class of rich people. 63% answered 'yes'. The left will always use wealth as a wedge between the rich and the poor as they use race and similar strategies to gain votes. It is time for Republicans to stop using the same argument to make political hay among themselves.

As the race got tighter, Romney was given the opportunity to make more inroads as the debates loomed. The first debate was a clear knock out for Romney. He aggressively attacked the President's and the Democrats policies on the economy, healthcare and taxes. The President seemed to be tired and sometimes lethargic. The leftist media was aghast and despondent at their candidate's performance. As reported Chris Mathews of MSNBC went on a rant as reported by Real Politics:

> *"Where was Obama tonight? He should watch – well, not just Hardball, Rachel, he should watch you, he should watch the Reverend Al [Sharpton], he should watch Lawrence. He would learn something about this debate. There's a hot debate going on in this country. You know where it's been held? Here on this network is where we're having the debate," Matthews said.*
>
> *"We have our knives out," Matthews said, admitting his network is trying their best to defend Obama and his policies. "We go after the people and the facts. What was he doing tonight? He went in there disarmed."*[8]

The second debate saw a more aggressive Romney. He went on the attack right from the start, but Obama was better prepared to play to his base and give his supporters every reason to come out and vote. When Benghazi came up the President responded to a question from one of the citizens on stage who asked: "Who was it that denied enhanced security and why?"

Romney was presented with an unbelievable opportunity when the administration fumbled the Benghazi attack, claiming that the assault was the result of a video and not a planned terrorist attack. The President said:

> *"The day after the attack, Governor, I stood in the Rose Garden, and I told the American people and the world that we are going to find out exactly what happened, that this was an act of terror."*[9]

Romney went on the attack and said that the President had taken 14 days before he called the attack an 'act of terror'. In an unprecedented media bias move by moderator Candy Crowley, she interjected herself into the debate and defended the President when she said: **'He [Obama] did in fact, sir.'**[10] At this moment, instead of attacking, Romney lost the momentum and the debate. Hours after the debate, Crowley recanted her statement and acknowledged that Mitt Romney was **right** to criticise Barack Obama for his response to the attack on the U.S. consulate in Benghazi. The tables had already turned in favor of Obama. The President had avoided another disaster and reassured his supporters – winner Obama.

The third debate may have been the turning point, held two weeks before the elections; it was perhaps the last opportunity for Romney to turn the tables. Romney attacked the President on foreign policy, citing Libya and the Middle East. But uncharacteristically, he did not bring Benghazi up again and lost a huge opportunity to score some badly needed points. His five points lead in the polls fizzled.

Another wrench was thrown into Romney's campaign as hurricane Sandy approached; he cancelled a rally in Virginia Beach. Both candidates suspended their campaigns for a little while; but the President continued his duty and made appearances in areas affected by the hurricane. To add to Romney's faltering poll numbers, New Jersey Gov. Chris Christie repeatedly praised the President for his help during the storm.

During most of the campaign, Romney had to defend himself on many fronts. His faith, the 47% comment, his wealth and political positions came under scrutiny. Not only was he attacked by his Democrat opponents but he was not spared by his conservative colleagues. The fiercest attacks came from the right who were reticent to consider him one of theirs. He had to proclaim himself a 'severely conservative' candidate to qualify.

Paul Ryan is a very competent member of the House, a budget and finance policy wonk who is highly regarded in the GOP. Romney's choice of Ryan as his Vice President running mate did not give him any bounce in the polls. During the debates, Romney lost the opportunity to showcase his credentials as a successful businessman who could repair the current economic situation, which would have given him the upper hand, but he failed to do so. As a complement to his financial and economic experience, Romney should have chosen somebody like Senator Marco Rubio or Governor Susana Martinez of New Mexico. Either of these two for Vice President could have brought more Hispanics votes to the Romney camp.

Among all the problems Romney ran into during his bid for the White House, a crucial one was the lack of a social media strategy. While the President was making full use of the social media for his fundraising as well as communicating his policies, Romney's campaign failed to understand and use the new technology; which prompted Robert Draper of the *New York Times* Magazine to write:

> *"Romney's senior strategist, Stuart Stevens, may well be remembered by historians, as one House Republican senior staff member put it to me, "as the last guy to run a presidential campaign who never tweeted." ("It was raised many times with him," a senior Romney official told me, "and he was very categorical about not wanting to and not thinking it was worth it)."*[11]

There ends what could have been a different turn of events and change in history. As a result Obama won a second term in the White House, and the United States continues to move to the left.

Ric McIver

Despite the fact that what we are going to relate takes place at a local authority level instead of the high level of the highest office in the world, this is a similar political twist, which saw another historical result.

Richard (Ric) McIver is a conservative politician in the province of Alberta, Canada. He first came on the political scene in 1998, in a losing bid when he ran against the late Alderman Sue Higgins in Ward 12. In 2000 he sought the position of Alderman in a bye election for Calgary's Ward 13. He ran a competitive campaign, which included the construction of the elusive South Calgary Ring Road, but lost to Diane Colley-Urquhart. In 2001, he sought the nomination to represent the Progressive Conservative in the Alberta constituency of Calgary Shaw, and he lost to Cindy Ady who went to serve as a member of the legislative Assembly until 2012 when she decided to retire.

Never one to give up, Ric continued to be a municipal watchdog and participated and helped on a number of community initiatives. When fiscal conservative Alderman Sue Higgins retired, Ric threw his hat into the race to represent Ward 12. He won the election in 2001, he was acclaimed in 2004 and in 2007 he was re-elected with a 91% majority, he represented Ward 12 until he ran for Mayor in 2010.

As a businessman Ric is a staunch fiscal conservative. On Council he always argued for fiscal restraint and accountability. Ric has an appreciation of the realities of running a successful enterprise and understood how government regulations and red tape affect its success and, in particular, whether and when growth, investment and hiring can take place. Ric made the drive for fiscal conservatism, accountability and legislative transparency the hallmarks of his time spent at City Hall. His strong opposition to ever increasing taxes put him at odds with then tax and spend Mayor Bronconnier. McIver hasn't shied away from speaking his mind in the years since he became an Alderman, and his stance on small government and low taxes made him arguably council's most loved and loathed alderman. A principled conservative, Ric sticks to his beliefs and what you see is what you get. Outspoken on issues, he used to own a hybrid Ford Escape SUV, and yet he was critical of Andrew Weaver 2008 talk about climate change, accusing the renowned climatologist of campaigning "to take some Calgarians' jobs away". He practices what he preaches; fiscal restraint is reflected in where he lives, a modest 1,200 square foot house in the established Calgary community of Willow Park.

On a Council made up of fourteen Aldermen and one Mayor, Ric often was on the opposite side of many votes. On tight 8/7 votes, he seemed to have been on the losing side more often than not. Although he put many excellent proposals forward, his motions did not garner enough votes to pass, as the 8 liberals on Council voted against the initiatives. For the nine years and three terms on Council, his opposition to taxes and policies which he believed would place an undue burden on taxpayers, earned him the name of 'Dr. No'.

When embattled Liberal Mayor Bronconnier, who had served for nine years, decided that he would not seek re-election in 2010, Ric declared that he was running for Mayor. McIver gathered a campaign dream team that included some of the people who helped Stephen Harper land the country's top job. Sam Armstrong and Devin Iversen, are experts at identifying target voters, understanding what makes them tick and getting the vote out on election day. They were helped informally by Tom Flanagan, Mr. Harper's former chief of staff. The plan was to make sure that the conservative base would support McIver and thus in one of the most conservative cities in the country, guarantee a win for Ric.

McIver's platform was rock solid. Given the past six years of fiscal blunders and lack of accountability at City Hall, he advocated more transparency and accountability at City Hall, better budget management and cost control. Based on sound conservative principles the more important points of his campaign included:

- Revamp the budget process to maximize efficiency to keep taxes manageable and make Calgary more competitive.

- Make growth benefit instead of costing Calgarians and without harming the environment and their quality of life
- Promote a quality of life that embraces art and culture without the burden of higher taxes
- Manage and reduce the debt level of the City and its partners
- Stop hiding the true nature of all fees and charges, and eliminate 'hidden taxation wherever possible
- Create and maintain more accountability and improve municipal electoral rules
- Establish a register of interest in land within city limits for all members of Council and senior staff
- Implement the use of a 'Hansard' for all Council meetings
- Improve the use of LRT and provide an extension to the SE of Calgary

With no incumbent running, several former Aldermen and other fringe candidates entered the race. But the most damaging entrance into the race was Barb Higgins, the local CTV News anchor. A cabal of well-known conservative operatives, including Rod Love, once Ralph Klein's right hand man, Don Lovett one time Higgins campaign manager, Thompson MacDonald, who possibly switched his allegiance from Alderman Bob Hawkesworth to Higgins, Pollster Janet Brown and Hal Walker, encouraged Higgins to enter the race. In their opinion, they didn't approve the landscape as none of the candidates appealed to them. They didn't think anybody was strong enough to take on Ric McIver. So the establishment conservatives backed Higgins, a political neophyte, with absolutely no experience in local politics. In effect somebody with whom they might garner future favors to control the civic agenda; in essence their own political puppet.

With fourteen candidates the contest was overcrowded. Higgins had moved into a strong second place in the polls, but things were about to change. Closer to the election date, cracks began to appear in Higgins campaign. The most damaging was her appearance on *Breakfast*

Television with Mike McCort. Since Higgins had not attended any of the debates, McCort seized the moment and asked Higgins for her decision to run for Mayor. Higgins replied that she had been encouraged by the community. To which McCort followed by suggesting that she had been drafted and could be seen as "*a marionette dancing on somebody else's strings.*" At this point Higgins got very angry and replied:

> *"An election is about people asking you to step forward. People cast their ballot. That's what an election is. So by people emailing and calling me,* ***who have no political interest whatsoever*** *that is the electorate. That's what we're doing on Monday.* ***These were not people with political interests.*** *These were people who were in the community that I had touched base with over many, many years. So, you know, it's an interesting comment you make, but I'll just tell you there's no truth to it."*[12]

In fact as reported by Trevor Scott Howell of *FFWD Weekly*:

> *"MacDonald worked at CFCN for 25 years in several roles, including vice-president, news and public affairs, before becoming Ralph Klein's media advisor. He's also a former chairman of the board of directors for Enmax, sits on the board of advisors of land and real estate behemoth Walton International Group, is a director on Preston Manning's right-wing think tank the Manning Centre and a strong supporter of retiring Calgary Mayor Dave Bronconnier."*[13]

It is reported Higgins stormed after the show, and in a display of temper she berated members of the volunteer group ArtsVote Calgary. The whole point of the 'political interest' question was to clarify the rumours of who were the people in the shadows pulling the strings of Higgins campaign. All the people who were previously mentioned as her supporters may have had a vested interest. Many of these people wanted to get a foot in City Hall or stay close to the City's Electric Utility – Enmax.

There had been rumours of extravagant expenses by senior executives of Enmax. Subsequently after the elections it was revealed that the CEO had allegedly benefitted from luxury trips to Monaco, and held company 'marketing parties' at his home featuring Tom Cochrane and Tragically Hip frontman Gord Downie, events perhaps attended by Barb Higgins. For years McIver had been one of the harshest critics of the Enmax's management. It is alleged that during the campaign, McIver's team received a phone call from a very prominent ex-politician, who warned them not to attack Enmax, because he had heard that some people were prepared to spend a lot of money to campaign against him.

In a poll on September 2010, with two months to the election McIver had 43% support from decided voters. Barb Higgins received 28% with Naheed Nenshi polling a distant third with 85%. With the recent Higgins outburst, McIver success was looking promising. But while all of the attention was on the front runners Nenshi, who had unsuccessfully ran for Council in 2004, was quietly plotting a masterful strategy.

The Harvard graduate and lecturer at Mount Royal University, took a page from the very successful 2008 Obama campaign. He made full use of the social media and gathered a very strong following among young voters. Although the candidates platform were not that much different, Nenshi focussed all of his energy and attacked McIver for having been part of the Council which had created a mess; he campaigned for 'change' at City Hall, and painted McIver as an insider, this tactic resonated with the young voters who are clueless about civic affairs and politics..

McIver's *Dream Team,* was entrenched in historical misguiding's that ignored the power of social media and the untapped power of the youth vote. They refused to post responses on the internet to explain why he had said **'No'** to several Council decisions. Nenshi painted him as a participant of the 'status quo'. When asked by the media of his plans to deal with a dysfunctional administration, McIver refused to say that he may reorganize the organization or even fire some members of staff. This decision cost him the endorsement of the right-leaning local newspaper *The Calgary Sun*, who instead endorsed Nenshi for Mayor. This may have been the last blow to McIver's bid to become Mayor. In politics, one should never get angry, but should at least get even. Similar to Romney, McIver never got angry, nor did he get even.

On Election Day, there was still hope that McIver could win, but as the polls closed and the numbers came in, it became quite apparent that the Higgins' candidacy had been a dagger into the heart of McIver's bid, splitting the conservative vote, just like Ross Perot was to George H. W. Bush in 1992. The final results were:

Candidate	Votes	%
Naheed Nenshi	140,263	39.6
Ric McIver	112,386	31.7
Barb Higgins	81,359	25.8

While it was a surprise to many, the media just built the win as historic, which it was; Naheed Nenshi had become the first muslim Mayor elected in the third largest Canadian city. A city portrayed as one of the most conservative in the land. While the whole country was ecstatic, one Conservative MP was not feeling particularly congratulatory the day after the vote. Rob Anders, the Conservative MP for Calgary West, who can spot a Liberal light years away and who has known Mr. Nenshi since high school and calls Nenshi the "Obama of Alberta, told the *Globe and Mail*:

> *"I think what Calgarians are going to find is they will be very surprised at just how Liberal their new mayor is,"*[14]

This statement will turn out to be prophetic.

Nenshi, became one of the most talked about politician around the world; attending such events as The World Economic Forum in Davos. He campaigned on a 'fiscal conservative' platform, and just like Obama's promises they turned up to be lies. His first tenure as Mayor saw anything but change. Calgary moved further to the left as he ran a Council which implemented some of the most 'social engineering policies', as well as imposing the highest tax increases in Calgary's history – 32% in 2012, all the time blaming everybody but himself, for any policy failures.

Supported by innocuous polls he remained popular, however nobody knows to what extent, because the questions are designed to skew the results. In 2013, he ran for re-election and won a second term. But this time there was no other credible candidates and no endorsement from The *Calgary Sun*, who once bitten were twice shy. His 77% majority is dubious at best considering that the voter turnout was only 33%, therefore in reality 75% of Calgarians did not vote for him.

As for McIver, he subsequently ran for the Alberta Progressive Conservative and won a seat in Calgary and became Minister of Transportation in the Redford government. As Minister he finally concluded an agreement with the Tsuu T'ina Nation to build the remainder of the Calgary Ring Road, one of the primary reasons for his entry into politics in 2000. In 2014, he is seeking the Leadership of the PC party of Alberta.

The moral of the story, in both Mitt Romney's and Ric McIver's cases, is that conservatives should be very careful what they do during electoral campaigns. Their actions against their own candidates can, and usually does, inflict very costly defeats. Too many so-called pundits and power brokers seeking a seat at the table interfere in the selection process. The number of candidates also makes it difficult to have meaningful debates. With over four candidates the debates become a cacophony. Conservatives must choose their representatives carefully, and once selected support them fully. Elections have consequences and a divided conservative vote does result in the election of a Liberal

CHAPTER 16

THE SOCIALISM TRENDS

Europe has been in decline for the past two decades. Socialist policies which have created an entitlement society have put most members of the European Union under a severe economic test. Southern European countries including Greece, Portugal, Spain and Italy have suffered the most with little or slow economic recovery. Across the Atlantic with Obama's second term, the shift to the left is undeniable. In Canada, the majority Conservative government continues to be under constant attack from the left, after some cataclysmic blunders. As the economic recovery stalls, where this trend leads us is yet to be known, but it nevertheless demands that we look closely at the cause and effect of such a shift.

In 2008, when Obama was elected as the first black president of the United States, it was not so much his ethnic background that made him so popular. When he toured Europe and gave speeches, he seemed to have mesmerized his audiences. They all believed in some way that this guy was the 'second coming'. Of course not in a religious sense, but he was the man who would bring social justice and most importantly would be the one to bring socialism to a new height. In America his promise of 'hope and change' gave the far-left the hope that at last America would move in a direction that even the Kennedys, Bill Clinton and Lyndon Johnson were unable to achieve.

As Americans embraced for his eloquence, they fail to analyze his policies and affiliations. In the United States there seems to be this idea that the Democratic President Barack Obama can do no wrong. Although, after a first term he was still an unknown quantity to the vast majority, his candidacy has been backed by the far left wing of the party and is now the de facto Democratic reformer, which no Kennedy or Clinton has been able to achieve. Despite Obama's past affiliations to screaming left wing supporters like Pastors Wright and Pfleger, the President is still the darling of the establishment, and strongly backed directly or indirectly by Moveon.org, Bill Ayers and George Soros. The continued presidency of Obama, although in the last stages of his second term, should be troubling to Canadians. He is a strong supporter of socialist policies which include increased taxes, the redistribution of wealth and government involvement in perhaps every aspect of American life. A democrat president backed by a democratic majority in Congress and the Senate has already changed the economic face of the country. Let us not forget the Jimmy Carter days when we experienced, double digit inflation and interest rates, as well as conflicts in Iran and Angola.

As a major economic partner, a change in economic policies by the U.S. has a direct impact on Canada's prosperity. A proposed change of NAFTA by Obama and strongly supported by the NDP could certainly curtail the economic advantage that Canada has experienced in the last decades. The trend for this shift to the left has been unwittingly supported by an increasingly liberal media.

The continuous use of language in the media to spin the left wing rhetoric is rampant. In most news today we see the use of selective words to report on issues. For example 'investing' has replaced 'spending'. 'Social housing' is now 'affordable housing'. The environment is increasingly being used to put in place socialist policies which will affect every aspect of our lives. A carbon tax is a start to redistribute wealth, while others are considering taxing windfall profits. Under the cover of environmentalism we are constantly being told that the only way to save the planet is through policies which prefer the 'stick' instead of the 'carrot'. The 'neocoms' have jumped on this band wagon to propose nationalisation of the energy industry, prevent further oil exploration and the use of coal while discarding the use of nuclear energy. Alternatively they embrace the use of biofuels which are reducing the ability to feed people in countries of the third world. Presumably, they are the same people who will advocate that foreign aid should be increased to alleviate the problem of high food costs in these countries.

Beware of the new trend towards socialism. As Vaclav Klauss, president of the Czech Republic, who has lived most of his life under communism, stated: 'climate alarmism may be the next Stalinism'. Are we to accept creeping socialism without a proper debate?

With the Presidency of Obama and very few true conservative governments left in the industrialised world, and a world recession, which does not seem to be ready to go away anytime soon, the chosen remedy to date has been to revive Keynesian economic concepts. The problem is that we are looking at the cure instead of looking at the disease, because it is easier to do so when you have an ideology based on large government and countless regulations. While there may be some other peripheral issues, the main causes for the economic downturn were the housing policies in the United States and the lack of oversight in the private sector, more importantly in the banking sector.

Let us start with the housing debacle. Successive governments in the U.S. have supported policies to make the ownership of a house a priority. Despite the Savings and Loans problems of the past, it seemed that no one learned anything. They forgot that '*having a home is a right, but owning a house is a privilege*'. The policy of allowing Fannie May and Freddie Mac to guarantee loans, for people who could not really afford a mortgage, and when banks were asked to provide loans below prime it was the beginning of the end. With a booming economy, it seemed that everybody forgot about simple economic concepts. In short, with higher demand for houses, values went up. Under mark to market valuation banks' lending increased. To cover risks banks started to hedge their bets by creating derivatives sold to other banks around the world.

When the housing market and the banking system collapsed, many governments focussed their efforts into injecting large amounts of money into the economy. While this strategy may be a tactic to stimulate the economy, what is alarming is that there were no rules to differentiate between winners and losers for bailouts. The numbers used are in the 'trillions', supported by government debt. The unspoken result of this entire stimulus is that governments have taken control of many industries in what can be defined as 'back-door nationalization'. In Canada, the often labelled 'intransigent' Prime Minister Harper presented a budget creating a deficit of approximately $40 billion dollars. For a man who is so 'uncompromising', Mr. Harper went against all of his economic principles as expressed in his Master's thesis. With this new found weakness in his armour, every industry and government came begging for money. While he stimulated the economy with large expenditures, there did not seem to be many strings attached to the new government largess. Infrastructure spending could have been granted with specific 'caveats'; that the money be used for specific projects and be delivered through P3s, which would have helped both public and private sectors. The auto industry received money without a firm guarantee that labor costs will be reined in, and the industry restructured. Some say that this policy could saddle future generations with debt repayments. Obama said "2009 is a year to make a clear break from the troubled past and set a new course for our nation." What is not being said is that the 'socialists' around the world have or will use this debacle as an excuse to set a course for government intervention by means of an economic stimulus.

It is said that we can judge somebody by the company he keeps. During the last two presidential elections in the U.S. there was little scrutiny of candidate Obama's qualification and associations. Now that he is in power we can clearly see that the United States is rapidly losing its lead as a free market economy. An examination of recent legislation demonstrates a clear shift to the left. Of course this new direction has been helped by a world recession and has given the left the opportunity to blame everything on capitalism.

We should examine the rise of the 'neocoms' led by Obama. Very few people know that Obama was an adviser to **ACORN** the organization under scrutiny for using government grants to promote many dubious entities and social expenditures His association current or previous with people who have either been appointed by his administration, has never been clearly examined by the media, with the exception of a few people on the right. Let us look at some of them: **Rev. Jeremiah Wright** once a pastor to Barack Obama made anti-Semite remarks and 'has blamed America and whites for starting the AIDS virus to kill off blacks' among other comments. On the economy, in an interview with PBS, he said:

> *"People don't realize that to be rich you've got to keep somebody poor"*[1]

The Service Employees International Union (**S.E.I.U),** with some 2.1 million members in over 100 occupations in the United States, is a labor union associated with the President and pushing for 'card check' a means to expand union membership in the U.S. Other affiliations and connections include: **Van Jones a** self-proclaimed green advocate associated with a Marxist group, **Anita Dunn** former White House Communications Director an admirer of Chairman Mao Zedong, **Hilda Solis** U.S. Secretary of Labor whose agenda is to enact 90 new rules and regulations to give more power to unions, **Bill Ayers** a former member of the radical Weather Underground organization that claimed responsibility for a dozen bombings in the seventies. There are other associations either directly or indirectly connected to the Obama Whitehouse that should be scrutinized so as to provide a better understanding of the agenda and direction that the resident may choose during his tenure as president.

To his credit Obama is in good company, he is charismatic like John F. Kennedy, articulate like Martin Luther King, but too much has been made of his so-called 'rock star' status. This was clearly demonstrated by his Nobel Peace Prize. The European left loves Obama, because he will bring the United States to the same socialist level of Europe, thus making the U.S., less competitive. Josef Joffe, the editor of *Die Zeit,* the highbrow German weekly, has a different opinion as expressed to David Remnick of *The New Yorker*, he believes that in Obama "There is certainly consistency and coherence in his attempt to retract from the troubles of the world, to get the U.S. out of harm's way, in order to do 'a little nation-building at home,' as he has so often put it. If you want to be harsh about it, he wants to turn the U.S. into a very large medium power, into an XXL France or Germany."

It is ironic that a first year President involved in a war would be given a peace prize. Is it because on Nov 21, 2007 then Sen Obama, in a display of ideological arrogance, naiveté or political correctness said: "I truly believe the day I am inaugurated not only does the country looks at itself differently, but the world looks at America differently. If I am reaching out to the Muslim world, they understand that I have lived in a Muslim country and I may be a Christian, but I also understand their point of view. I think that the world will have confidence that I am listening, to that. That will ultimately make us safer."

Given the recent recipients, Al Gore, Jimmy Carter and Yasser Arafat, it shows that there no longer is anything noble about the Nobel Peace Prize anymore. This prize was given to 'force' his hands into implementing many socialist reforms that Europe had been hoping for years, so has to regain some sense of their lost colonial power. Obama handed it to them by agreeing to seek enforcement of laws and financial regulations through international bodies, which includes a dysfunctional U.N. In fact he has now joined Chamberlain as an appeaser. As the U.S. economy falters and debt rises to levels never previously seen, America will become more indebted to an ever rising China, endangering its security and foreign policy.

With Obamacare in place it may well be that health care in the United States will fall in quality and reach the same level of inefficiency of single payer systems. Through the failed Copenhagen accord taxes will rise and with the new idea of sending money to third world countries to help them combat climate change we shall see the long awaited socialist dogma of wealth transfer take place. The Canadian connection should not be ignored as Trudeau advocated a North/South transfer of wealth.

Furthermore Maurice Strong, now a resident of Beijing, was instrumental in the Rio and Kyoto negotiations which are now consolidated as the Copenhagen agreement. From Global Warming to Climate Change, we end up with Climate Reparations.

We should not be surprised at all. Had we paid attention to Obama's eloquent diatribe when he said: "We have five days to fundamentally transform America." As an historic president he will do just that and at the same time change the world economy that may or may not recover for years. When Obama was first elected, I was puzzled by a report that hundreds of students at the University of Calgary cried while watching the Obama inauguration. I could not understand the connection between Canadian students and Obama the so-called 'anointed one'. In retrospect, now I believe that these students were being prophetic as it seems that they were crying because they perhaps understood that they would be saddled with the highest government debt levels, and that their financial future would be in jeopardy for a generation as a result of his policies.

When Obama came into power the U.S. debt was around $12 trillion, today it is quickly approaching $18 trillion. We can blame some of this on the Bush administration. There were two wars and a number of bad policies which acerbated the situation. But to continue to blame former President Bush after six years as President, Obama's excuses for the failure of Bush's policies are redundant.

Unemployment in early 2014 is still at a high of 7.6%, and more people have stopped looking for jobs, otherwise the true rate would be closer to 13%. The Keynesian policies of the Obama administration are very quickly creating an American society very similar to some south European countries.

More citizens in the United States are now dependent on government programs. The food stamp program in summer of 2013 now accounts for 47.7 million people, and costs $81 billion. There is also startling statistics comparing the first decade of the 21st century to the 1950s.

Fox News the *O'Reilly Factor* produced the following comparisons:

Unemployment rate: 1950s – 4.5% (average),2013 – 7.6%
High School Dropout Rate: 1950s – 2.7%, 2011 – 7%
Babies were born out-of-wedlock: 1950s – 5%, 2010 – 41%

For all of his talk of 'hope and change', Obama can show very little true progress. His massive expenditures have not created jobs but instead have increased the debt to a never seen before level. Yet despite these failures he persists, with the help of the Senate majority and a minority in Congress to push for more spending and more government interference in the economy. His crowning legacy, the grandiose reform of the health care system, has yet to reform anything. In reality, it is gradually falling apart as more and more Americans are learning about its ramifications and impact on their pockets and freedom of choice.

Emboldened by the election of one of the most socialist of all American Presidents, some European countries have taken the view that following his example may be the right way to solve their problems. France moved further to the left by electing François Hollande, who quickly proceeded to make some changes to France's tax laws. He put forward a 75% tax on the ultra-wealthy. The plan was designed to tax incomes over €1million ($1.3m), but it would have only affected a small number of taxpayers, bringing in approximately €300million ($390m) in revenue, insignificant if compared to France's roughly €85billion ($111b) deficit. In effect, another socialist wealth transfer plan that does not do anything in economic terms. But the plan backfired when the country's highest court threw the plan out as being unconstitutional. Hollande revised the plan and unfortunately the court approved this new tax in December 2013. As reported by Bloomberg:

> *"French President Francois Hollande received approval from the country's constitutional court to proceed with his plan to tax salaries above 1 million euros at 75 percent for this year and next.*
>
> *Under Hollande's proposal, companies will have to pay a 50 percent duty on wages above 1 million euros ($1.4 million).*

> *In combination with other taxes and social charges, the rate will amount to 75 percent of salaries above the threshold, the court wrote in a decision published today.*
>
> *"The companies that pay out remuneration above 1 million euros will, as expected, be called upon for an effort of solidarity on remuneration paid in 2013 and 2014," the Economy Ministry said in an e-mailed statement."*[2]

These policies only resulted in the alienation of France's wealthiest citizens who, as they can, may decide to leave the country.

In Canada, the late Jack Layton of the NDP successfully guided his party to take over the position of Her Majesty's loyal opposition away from the Liberals. What we must remember is that The NDP is a leftist party, with strong socialist ideology, although well-disguised. Layton's success was largely due to his ability to persuade the Quebec voters on the left that he was supportive of redistributing the wealth as much if not better than the province's main representative party the separatist party The Bloc Québécois.

On the local level, the city of Calgary situated in the most conservative of all provinces decided to elect a liberal. Then after a three year term marred by the worst tax increases in years, 30% over three years, he was re-elected in 2013 with some of his staunchest left-wing supporters. Although there were some definite shift in some constituencies, Calgary the home of the conservative Prime Minister of Canada, and the home of the Province of Alberta Progressive Conservative Premier still elected a liberal. In Council he is backed by some of the worse leftist ever elected to Calgary's Council.

Socialism, with Obama has made a full comeback. The successes of leftist politicians and parties, is no doubt due to the groundswell adulation of Obama by the left. Fortunately, it seems that the collapse of certain European economies may have awakened people up to the demise of socialism, but will that be enough?

The United Nations

To add to the growth of socialism, we must consider the role of the United Nations, Established on October 24, 1945 to promote international co-operation, it replaced the ineffective League of Nations to prevent the advent of a World War. Created with the best intentions this organization has become a nest of socialism. When it was founded there were 51 member states, and following the widespread de-colonization in the 1960's, it now has grown to 193 members. The six principal organs of the organization have been filled by representatives from mostly socialist member states. Over the years the U.N. policies has morphed into a series of mandates and dictates encompassing climate change, education and health. With so many members most of the decisions are made by committees which may have genuine concerns for the issues, but too often end up making decisions based on ideology and even sometimes bribery.

Actions are subject to veto by members of the Security Council. With a divided membership made up of China and Russia, too often real important decisions come to a stalemate and nothing really gets done. Wars continue in many parts of the world and more conflicts arise. Terrorism is on the rise and it seems that the world cannot come to grips on how to get rid of it. In effect the organization has become a place where very little is achieved, and it consumes an enormous amount of capital, mostly funded by Western countries. The U.N's main goals seem to be to diminish Western values, promote a social agenda and create a one-world government.

More importantly the increase in membership due to the creation of many new nations after World War II has brought about appointments to several committees which may not be in the greatest interest of the world, but rather to allocate membership to please its members.

Over the years we have seen some strange appointments. Many nations, who are ruled by dictators who have no regard for human rights, have been placed in decision making position on issues which they do not espouse. Appointments of countries like Syria, Libya who have not practice freedom of expression in their own countries, have been some of the greatest farcical and ludicrous ones.

Canada has a long history of working with the U.N. Many of our sons have died in wars supported by the U.N. Over the years our governments, notwithstanding their political stripes have helped to make the world better. Either it was Lester Pearson who headed the Canadian delegation to the U.N from 1946 to 1956, and was elected to the presidency of the Seventh Session of the General Assembly in 1952-1953, or Brian Mulroney's strong support for the abolition of apartheid in South Africa. But today Canada cannot secure a seat on important U.N committees. Canada became the first wealthy nation to be probed by a U.N rapporteur for its food supply chains and government policies regarding the right to food. At the same time the chronic starvation of people in African and other third world countries continues.

The problem with the UN today is that many of the votes are acquired under the veil of bribery. Funds and economic gains are being transferred or positions on certain committees being exchanged through dubious agreements. The U.N is fast becoming an instrument for the redistribution of wealth through treaties which most of us do not understand. Large loans or grants are being given to third world countries. On the face of it, for the betterment of citizens in these countries, however in many cases much of the money have not be allocated properly or worse disappeared, or embezzled. The U.N has fast become a place for politicians from small countries to stall progress on human rights as they plunder their own countries' treasury and allow their population to starve.

U.N. sanctions are becoming a joke. Sanctions are believed to change the behaviour of regimes, but they do not work. Sanctions usually affect working class citizens, while the governments and leaders continue their lavish lifestyles. By the same token, the Liberal left believes that the U.N. should have greater powers in the world and become a one world government. In some quarters they even consider that the former Secretary Koffi Annan could be installed as the secular Pope. Let us not forget that during his tenure we have seen atrocities grow in many countries, genocide committed and the inability for the world to deal with terrorism.

Increasingly, President Obama's failed leadership frequently differs to the United Nations on many important decisions, and he seems to be prepared to relinquish some of the United States autonomy. For those who have been paranoid about a world government and the growth of socialism, it seems that their fears are coming true. The U.N. is fast becoming that organization. – Alas with no accountability.

The Second Wave

With the election of a progressive Mayor in New York, it seems that Canada's 2015 and the United States Presidential elections in 2016 will see major players from the left being touted as the second wave of progressivism in North America. The electorate must be very careful when choosing a leader. The past has shown us that the lack of scrutiny by the media produced Obama, who despite the constant support from his leftist supporters, has not been able to make any progress on the economy, foreign affairs and most of all on race relations.

Canada has always been a 'progressive' country as illustrated by a recent survey about 'inspirational' Canadians which showed nine liberals and only one conservative in the Top 10 list. This list will surely be used as propaganda for the next election.

Justin Trudeau

The Canadian 2015 election will decide whether the Conservatives stay in power or if the Liberals can make a comeback under their new hope Justin Trudeau. This is for the electorate to decide. Once again a politician with absolutely no track record is being thrusted upon the electorate because of his likeability.

The media ignores the ideology of Justin Trudeau. But we must be vigilant and examine the prospects of a Trudeau led Liberal Party. Trudeau may be inexperienced but he will be guided by many astute Liberals who have served his father and are chomping at the bit to recreate what they lost. Problem is the same old divisive policies may resurface.

Even with his youth, good looks and name pedigree, Justin Trudeau has very little to show for. Just like Obama who came into the Presidency, he has absolutely no executive credentials. His policies are so vague and inconsistent that the only people who think that he can make a difference are the Facebook followers and Twitter devotees. His appeal to the youth of this country will be just as great as it is for Obama. With promises to include them in his future policies, as well as communicating with them on Twitter will resonate and create a formidable opposition to the Conservative Party if ignored.

Watch out for his support of the middle class, the perennial target for politicians' support and who yet, always bear the brunt of policies which tax them to the hilt. As a former teacher, he will tout education as one of his platform's most important issues, but will continue to support the current education system of heavy union involvement and which in recent past has been less than stellar.

His record in Parliament has been eclipsed by Thomas Mulcair, the leader of the Opposition NDP, and that does not say very much for credible politics. His parliamentary attendance is dismal, and accounted for only two days per week during the 2013 fall session of Parliament. He prefers to hold public meetings and fundraisers. What we should look at are some of Trudeau's very interesting remarks in an out of Parliament. His public appearances have not produced much in terms of substance, but rather have identified his lack of leadership maturity and proclivity for social media rhetoric, including a 250 dollar-a-head cocktail party for ladies only to get to know 'the future prime minister'. He has acknowledged smoking pot and has endorsed the legalization of marijuana.

Trudeau's campaign strategy is quite wise. His team is banking on changing demographics, young pot smoking voters, and his glamour boy image.

It seems that Trudeau, the crown prince of the Liberal Party, will say anything to gain publicity. In Calgary, a place once decimated by his father's NEP policy, he said that he would like to see more trade with China, but he opposes the Northern Gateway pipeline, because the aboriginal communities oppose it, and that it creates environmental risks.

To cater to the Quebec crowd, while believing that Bill 101 – Quebec's French language law is fine, he rejects any notion of constitutional 'accommodations' for Quebec. Yet, in an interview with CTV he remarked: "Quebecers are better that the rest of Canada. Because you know, we're Quebecers or whatever"

We should be reminded that the 'acorn does not fall very far from the tree':

> *"Under the War measures Act, the federal government can use all the powers that it deems useful – and it alone is judge – to achieve its goals. The government is not required to obtain either an opinion or authorization from anybody. In other words, war measures entitled the government in the twentieth century to say exactly what Louis XIV said centuries earlier,* "L'Etat, c'est moi."[3]
>
> *After Justin Trudeau's first Liberal convention under his leadership, Andrew Coyne proclaimed:*
>
> *"This isn't just his party. He is the party, and with good reason. He owes them nothing; they owe him everything* ...Le parti, c'est lui."[4]

His declarations and statements on foreign policy mirror those of his father who was fond of Chairman Mao Zedong. Fidel Castro, Julius Nyerere of Tanzania, and had a penchant for Soviet leaders – while desperately distancing himself from Ronald Reagan, Margaret Thatcher and Richard Nixon. During his 'ladies night' fundraiser Justin Trudeau said:

> *"There's a level of admiration I actually have for China. Their basic dictatorship is actually allowing them to turn their economy around on a dime."*[5]

We should also take note of the comments he made that belittled the very serious crisis in the Ukraine. His insensitivity and childish remark about a possible invasion by Russia, shows a complete lack of maturity and understanding of foreign affairs.

While he has not released any significant economic policies, we can assume that he will follow many of his father's failed socialist policies which damaged the country's economy by removing the incentive to work and creating personal and regional stagnation.

We cannot ignore the cadre of advisors that he has around him. At his first Liberal Convention, as leader, he had in attendance the Former economic adviser to Obama, Lawrence Summers, Ryan Adam, a senior organizer for Obama's 2012 re-election campaign, Jennifer O'Malley Dillon, former deputy campaign manager for Obama in 2012, digital director for Obama in 2012, Teddy Goff and he also had Chima Nkemdirim, Mayor Nenshi's chief of staff on board.

With many of his father's confidants on his advisory team it is unlikely that he will depart very much from the other international socialists' wealth redistribution mantra, In fact, in a recent op-ed Justin Trudeau has already claimed:

> *"In the past 30 years, the Canadian economy has more than doubled in size. But unlike times before, virtually all of the benefit of that growth has accrued to a small number of wealthy Canadians."*

Canadians should be careful not to pay too much heed to the media frenzy and hype created by social media. He may have the arrogance of his father, but lacks in academic background and intellect of his father. We should demand more in depth analysis of his policies and promises. Just like Obama, Trudeau will appeal to the social media followers, most of them Hollywood types, who as it turns out are just as empty as their candidate – more twits than tweets! The result may be another likeable, yet vacuous politician.

With the mainstream media ready to unleash its support for a Liberal return to power under Trudeau, Canadians should ask themselves the following question: Is Canada ready for a second Trudeau government?

Hillary Rodham Clinton

At the start of 2014, the wife of Bill Clinton, the 42nd President of the United States and former Secretary of State Hillary Rodham Clinton (HRC) has not yet declared her intentions about a possible run at the 2016 presidential election. With titles like First Lady, Senator and Secretary of State and most of all being a progressive woman, one can be sure that the Democratic National Committee establishment is chomping at the bit for her entrance into the fray.

Hillary Clinton has the gravitas and a resume to make her a DNC favorite, but for America it is best to examine her record on issues before crowning her first as the Democratic Party nominee and then as President of the United States. Over the years she has been involved in many issues that demand a more in depth scrutiny.

Unknown to most people HRC started her political career as a Republican. In fact she was the President of Wellesley College Young Republicans. Later she changed her political allegiance while writing a thesis on Saul Alinsky, who she described as:

> *"Alinsky was a colourful and controversial figure who managed to offend almost everyone during his long career. His prescription for social change required grassroots organizing that taught people to help themselves by confronting government and corporations to obtain the resources and power to improve their lives"*[6]

In the early days of her political involvement, Hillary Clinton was chair of the New World Foundation which funded many New Left interest groups and in the 1960s were associated with liberal, Marxist, radical student groups. She was a board member of Wal-Mart and pushed for environmental practices, while remaining silent on the company's anti-labor union policies.

Hillary Clinton, rightly or wrongly, has been the subject of several investigations by the United States Office of the Independent Counsel. Starting with the Whitewater controversy which alleged that Mrs. Clinton had been in conflict of interest as a lawyer with the Rose Law firm representing the bank, and being investors in the Whitewater development Corporation whose losses were financed by their friends the McDougals who operated the Madison Guaranty. When her billing records were subpoenaed by counsel, they were impossible to be found, but later surfaced in the First Lady's White House book room. After years of investigation, in 2000 a final report was released stating that there was insufficient evidence that the Clintons had been involved in criminal wrongdoing.

As First Lady, she was implicated in 'Travelgate', whereby she was alleged to have replaced White House travel office employees by friends from Arkansas. Independent Counsel concluded that she had made 'factually false' statements, but that there was insufficient evidence to warrant prosecution.

In 1993, her husband the President appointed her to head the Task Force on National Health Care Reform (Hillarycare). Despite Democrat control of both The House and the Senate, her proposal did not get the necessary votes and was abandoned in September 1994. Given the troubles of Obamacare, we should not forget that Hillary Clinton once said that she was a supporter of a 'single payer' system, which could be even worse for Americans.

In typical rich liberal fashion, notwithstanding the hundreds of thousands of dollars in book deals and speaking engagements that she and her husband Bill have amassed, Hillary Clinton claimed, on her latest book tour, that they were poor. With reportedly a $100 million fortune, it is hard to believe that they qualify as 'poor' citizens. Once again a typical liberal disconnect with reality and income inequality.

When the presidential term of her husband Bill was over, she decided to run for the U.S. Senate in New York, and won the 2000 election. In her first term she served on several Senate committees. She fought for the redevelopment of the World Trade Center site after the 9/11 attack. She supported both the 2001 military action in Afghanistan, and the 2002 Iraq War Resolution. She won re-election for a second term in 2006. During that term in March 2007 she opposed the Iraq War troop surge, and voted for the $700 billion bailout during the 2007–2008 financial crises, while all along preparing for a possible candidacy for the U.S. Presidential campaign of 2008.

In 2007, the polls showed Hillary Clinton leading a bevy of Democratic candidates, including Senator Barack Obama. At first she was seen as the *de facto* favourite to represent the DNC. Hoping to clinch nomination by Super Tuesday, she spent a lot of money to secure the nomination, but ran out of cash as the race tightened while Obama surged in the polls. Damaged by a number of statements made either by herself or husband Bill, branding Obama as a racially limited candidate, she saw her support dwindle. By June 2008, after the final primaries Obama had garnered enough delegates to secure his position as presumptive nominee for the DNC. Clinton ended her campaign and endorsed Obama in a passionate speech at the Democratic 2008 convention.

When Obama became the 44th President of The United States, he invited Clinton to become his Secretary of State. At first, she refused but later accepted and became the first former First Lady to serve in the United States Cabinet.

During her husband's presidency, Hillary Clinton became the most travelled First lady in history. As Secretary of State she continued to log many miles around the world. But was it Obama's design to keep her away from Washington? One will never know.

Her term as Secretary can be characterized as nothing less than mediocre. With the exception of her sitting down in the Situation Room while Osama bin Laden was being captured, there have been no spectacular agreements or diplomatic solutions reached to major problems under her leadership. In fact the world has seen the dwindling of American influence. Resetting the 'button' with Russia has in fact reduced American respect in the old iron curtain countries. China has grown in might and flexing its military muscles in South East Asia. Both China and Russia continuously oppose any American initiative to prevent Iran's nuclear ambition.

While supporting the 2011 intervention in Libya, which resulted in overthrow of Gaddafi, we must be reminded of the Arab Spring protest which has thrown the whole of the middle-east in turmoil. The fall of Hosni Mubarak in Egypt gave rise to the Muslim Brotherhood, resulting in further violent conflicts in the country. In Syria, Bashir al-Assad, who was once touted by HRC as 'somebody we can work with' decided to kill thousands of his own citizens to solidify his dictatorship.

Her worse days as Secretary came on September 11, 2012, when the U.S. diplomatic mission in Benghazi, Libya was attacked. After days of denial by the administration that the attack was an act of terrorism, and stating that the attack was a reaction to some obscure video, it took her months before testifying in Congress about the attack.

After treatment for a blood clot suffered as a result of a concussion she appeared in front of a Congressional Committee investigating the attack. In a statement that may come back to haunt her next bid for the presidency, she said: "Was it because of a protest or was it because of guys out for a walk one night decides they go kill some Americans? What difference at this point does it make?"

For somebody aspiring to be President of the United States, it is ironic that the death of an Ambassador and three other Americans should not be considered as a significant difference. Moreover in a published book "*DUTY*" by former Secretary of Defense Robert Gates, he recounts a conversation between President Obama and Sec. Clinton in those terms:

> *"Hillary told the President that her opposition to the (2007) surge in Iraq has been political because she was facing him in the Iowa primary ... the president conceded vaguely that opposition to the Iraq surge had been political. To hear the two of them making these admissions and in front of me, was surprising as it was dismaying."*

While we should not be surprised that a politician of any colour or ideology would make 'political decisions', we should be very wary of politicians, who aspire to the highest offices, to put their political ambitions first and foremost before their country. In 2016, these statements alone should give the electorate food for thought.

In 2015 and 2016 Canada and the U.S respectively will hold elections which may significantly change the political landscape. Shall we see the fall of liberalism and socialism, only time will tell.

CHAPTER 17

STAYING ALIVE

Going forward there is at least two schools of thoughts on how conservatives will perform in the future. Right and left political pundits have their own agendas, and opinions. Based on the previous chapters, I will summarize what I believe could happen and how true conservatism can survive and provide the required leadership for a better future.

In their book the *Big Shift*, Bricker and Ibbitson put forward that many factors have changed in Canada to allow the Conservatives to run the country

They wrote:

> *"The decline of the Liberal Party is, for us, particularly fascinating, not because we wish it ill ... But the party and the elites who guided Canada simply failed to recognize what was happening to what they had created. In essence Canada changed and the Liberals didn't."*[1]

The other point of view is from Liberal stalwart Warren Kinsella, who wrote in the *Calgary Sun* that 'The left is making a comeback.' His premise is that in the past two years there has been a conservative ascendancy due to better funding, corporate support and the state of the economy. He even, perhaps sarcastically, mentions the impact of a rightist media

– as if such a thing existed. True the media has Fox News and the Sun News Network, but to say that they drive the political discourse is far from reality.

Kinsella believes that with Justin Trudeau and Tom Mulcair, Canada's left is now competitive. He also mentions the new Pope Francis, who in his view is the most influential progressive leader, as a revolutionary who challenges the Roman Catholic Church orthodoxy. Kinsella concluded and opined:

> *"The ideological pendulum – which had been careening off to the right – is now swinging to the left ... Post-recession jitters have faded. Stimulus spending worked. Austerity measures are increasingly unpopular. Voters are just plain sick of conservative policies and politicians."*[2]

Looking at these two different views, one cannot but ask which one is correct? Through the course of this book I have contrasted left and right policies in both the United States and Canada. Contrary to Kinsella's opinion I do not believe that the left ideology had disappeared. In Canada the skillful management of the country by Harper has certainly placed the left in a hiatus, but around the world the situation has been far more different.

On the other side of the 49th parallel, Republicans could see a resurgence, but should be careful not to overdo it, by feeling to confident and choose the wrong candidates. Obama's 2008 election and re-election in 2012 proved that the left ideology never faded away. In fact, as discussed earlier, his presidency has given hope to many liberal thinking politicians who will use his strategy of government interference to promote their liberal/socialist agenda. Promising free stuff and get re-elected is a mantra of the left as they always believe that governments know best. Canada has been the exception, rather than the rule. Europe, to the exception of the Conservative/Liberal coalition of the U.K and Germany, is generally dominated by leftist governments.

There are those on the left who never liked the policies of austerity who will continue to push for their tax and spend agenda. Ignoring that it was bad Keynesian, housing policies and lax banking regulations that caused the recession, they will try once again to buy votes with empty promises. As the world economy crumbled the European socialist/liberal model of economic management has showed itself to be badly flawed. Portugal. Ireland, Greece and Spain (PIGS) proved to be the worst of these economic policies of entitlement. These countries had to be bailed out of there virtual bankruptcies. The call for austerity was answered by riots and citizens refused to give up the huge benefits provided under leftist labour laws.

President Obama's policies, when properly analyzed, demonstrate that they were ideologically rooted in socialist beliefs. His revamped of the American Healthcare has been nothing but a disaster, and the worst is yet to come when real costs kick in. His economic record is perhaps the worst since the Great Depression. Stealthily siding with protesters like 'Occupy Wall Street' and the environmental groups he has argued about economic disparity and the destruction of the environment. Using these arguments he proceeded to increase taxes and the national debt, while embarking on 'crony capitalism' to gain corporate support for his campaigns. Imposing his leftist ideology through executive orders he has bypassed Congress on numerous occasions. Many of his dictatorial actions should be a wake-up call for Americans who value freedom. In retrospect history may well show that the man, who came in as a change agent for hope, has only succeeded in further dividing America along race and economic lines. Obama is the poster child for the cliché: 'Beware of leftist politicians promising the moon.'

The left has succeeded to use wedge issues such as income inequality, abortion, the war on women and gay rights to increasingly corner conservatives into a state of timidity and silence. For fear of being branded as bigots, racists and uncaring, conservatives have had to accept many leftist policies while ignoring their own values and principles. Helped by the media, who in recent past have lost all sense of fairness and impartial reporting, the news on most networks on both sides of the border has become propaganda.

The promise of free social services and programs has created a world of entitlement. Governments no longer spend peoples' money they now 'invest' in the future. In reality they are catering to special interest groups to gain votes and guarantee their next election. Obama perfected the art of decision making on ideological grounds rather than for the good of the country. The Keystone XL pipeline is a perfect example of his delaying tactics to cater to the environmental movement to try and prevent any more Democrat's losses in the mid-term elections of 2014. He further unconstitutionally altered the original provisions of the Affordable Care Act no less than 39 times to shore up his leftist base.

In these moments of failed socialist policies and dogma, I am always reminded of what a former student from the old Soviet Union told me; she said "Socialism is like bad toilet paper; it always fails when you most need it – then you are in deep s**t."

The conservative movement embodies a number of views and does not come from any dogma and has no creed. While there may be a diversity of interpretations. Russell Kirk a Distinguished Scholar at The Heritage Foundation summarized what he believed to be the following ten articles of belief that reflect the emphases of conservatives in America[3]:

- First, the conservative believes that there exists an enduring moral order.
- Second, the conservative adheres to custom, convention, and continuity
- Third, conservatives believe in what may be called the principle of prescription.
- Fourth, conservatives are guided by their principle of prudence.
- Fifth, conservatives pay attention to the principle of variety.
- Sixth, conservatives are chastened by their principle of imperfectability.
- Seventh, conservatives are persuaded that freedom and property are closely linked.

- Eighth, conservatives uphold voluntary community, quite as they oppose involuntary collectivism.
- Ninth, the conservative perceives the need for prudent restraints upon power and upon human passions.
- Tenth, the thinking conservative understands that permanence and change must be recognized and reconciled in a vigorous society.

While the above list seems to be lengthy, conservatives over the years have used these principles either in totality or in combination with each other to formulate policies. History has three great leaders to thank for their contribution to the world. Each in his own way has paved the road to true conservatism; Winston Churchill, Ronald Reagan and Margaret Thatcher. There are many lessons, good and bad, to be learned from these leaders, and it would be very wise for Conservatives and Republicans to examined them and ensure that they can survive the next Liberal onslaught.

To do so conservatives around the world should adopt three basic principles of conservatism, which I believe embraces Kirk's principles and provides a basis for immediate conservative policies.

Three Principles

Reagan's 11th Commandment

Earlier, we discussed the demise of two conservative candidates – Romney and McIver. Their failures may be attributed to the lack of support from within their own conservative ranks.

During the 2012 GOP primaries for the Presidential race, the hostility between some of the candidates (Santorum and Gingrich) was so apparent that it destroyed Romney from within the party. In Calgary, a bastion of conservatism, McIver lost to a Liberal because of the lack of support from the self-appointed conservative establishment. Attacks or lack of support by conservatives went beyond the Reagan 11th Commandment:

> *"Thou shalt not speak ill of any fellow Republican."*[4]

In Canada, the fracture within the conservative movement is still apparent despite the Conservative Party's success at the federal and at some provincial levels. There are still some resentment left from some Reform members and some Progressive Conservatives, as a result of the Mulroney/Manning feud.

In contrast to the Left, too often Canadian conservative politicians shy away from overtly supporting each other. It seems that there exists a tacit reluctance among conservatives to collaborate with politicians in other levels of government. Wouldn't it be better to have conservatives elected to Federal, Provincial, and Local governments? So why not openly support conservative candidates at all levels. It is done in other countries, why not in Canada?

The demise of Allison Redford who was pushed out as Premier of Alberta stems from a number of complex issues. In 2011, she won the leadership race under a strange preferential vote system. After the first choice selections were tallied, no candidate had a majority. A three-way race for the party's leadership was cut to two candidates, and the third-place finisher was dropped and the second choices of his supporters were allocated among the remaining two candidates. Many believe that the system was flawed right from the start because; many non-conservatives bought memberships and supported Redford.

In 2014, Ric McIver ran for the leadership of the Alberta PC party. At the onset, it was fascinating to see that he received no support from any member of the current PC caucus. As the only true fiscal conservative out of the three candidates, his loss to former federal cabinet minister Jim Prentice, a 'Red Tory', is further proof that McIver is the right man for the job – but perhaps for the wrong party. Fiscal conservatives have left the party and it shows that true conservatives no longer govern in Alberta. The Progressives have truly taken over and Alberta will never be the same again. This is why it is important to identify true conservative candidates prior to any elections. Having a big tent does not mean that one should encourage 'Pinkos' or 'Rhinos'. The left, as exemplified by Trudeau, are very selective, why should conservatives be different?

This pattern of conservatives shooting each other may alas continue. As we approach a federal election in 2015, the knives are out, as former Prime Ministers Brian Mulroney and Joe Clark enter the fray once again. Having failed to deliver promises they now become advisers on issues pertaining to the perennial First Nations problems and foreign affairs. Mr. Mulroney's advice regarding relations with the United States is a bit disingenuous. He must recognize that he was fortunate to have a Republican in the White House during his tenure, while Mr. Harper has to deal with a far-left ideologue Democrat. Both Mulroney and Clark also lament the disappearance of the word 'progressive' from the party's name. Times have changed, their advice is welcomed but they should live in the present rather than try to rewrite history. If they are true conservatives they should support the conservative government not foment dissention to protect or revive their progressive agenda.

The Tea Party in the U.S. had a significant role in the capture of the House in 2010. Their resolve to oppose the establishment of the GOP has caused a fissure in the party. It is imperative that the GOP finds a way to reconcile its differences prior to the 2016 Presidential elections in order to select a conservative candidate who can defeat the presumptive Democrat candidate Hillary Clinton or any other leftist coming to the fore.

Conservatives should watch and learn how Democrats continuously circle the wagon and support a failed President Obama, on all of his policies no matter what.

Smaller government less taxes

It is not the role of government to provide services. Its role is to facilitate the provision of services.

The conservatives' mantra should be no debt caused by undue budget deficits. The only debt that a nation should carry is for future infrastructure, and even then it could be minimized by private sector involvement. Since infrastructure will be used by future generations, it is the right choice to share the repayment of debt incurred for these investments with future users. True fiscal conservatives should never indulge in expanding the debt caused by deficits.

True conservatism is about providing a 'hand up' not giving a 'hand out'. Social issues are not about gay rights, abortion and other leftist wedge issues. They are about education, health care, aging population and immigration. We should always provide programs that help the disadvantaged, but always with a means test and sunset clauses. Conservatives too often ignore these real issues at their peril. As a result they leave the door open for the Left to institute programs with no end in sight. Once established these programs are difficult to reverse and thus perpetuate a culture of entitlement.

Canada will have a budget surplus by 2015, thanks to the great work done by former Finance Minister Jim Flaherty. He understood that in a global recession a revival of the economy depended on a stimulus. He also understood that as soon as the economy recovers it will be time to rein in unnecessary expenditures, and reduce taxes.

The continued increase in the size of governments, ergo the size of the public sector workforce is a real millstone around the necks of taxpayers. The cost of benefits and pension plans of public workers will cause a major problem for governments at all levels.

As the Harper government seeks to make changes to labour laws, he should take notice of the consequences of Obama's coziness with the Unions. Any increase in Union influence will affect trans-border unions and trade in the future. In Canada there is an increase in union membership while there is a decline in the U.S.

In past years there has been a movement towards the right-to-work (RTW) in the United States. Wisconsin saw a very acrimonious battle between Unions and the State Government, and a recall of the Governor by Unions was soundly defeated at the ballot box.

On December 11, 2012 Michigan became the 24th State to pass a right-to-work legislation. What is significant is that Michigan is the bastion of the union movement, the birth place of the Auto Workers Union, one of the most powerful unions, which also has a foothold in Canada.

Statistics show that unemployment is lower in most of the states that have adopted RTW policy. Union membership is dwindling in the United States where the huge settlements made through collective agreements in the public sector are the main cause of bankruptcies at the local and state levels. Governments can no longer sustain the costs of promised pensions in a changing economy. Detroit should serve as a perfect example for the need to control and curtail public sector labour costs.

Harper's Conservatives should follow the United States in the sea change in laws governing unions. At the very least we should amend the Rand Formula to give workers the right to choose where their dues are being spent, or as in some cases designate where the money collected should go (e.g. to charities of their choice). The right-to-work, without joining a union should be encased into the Canadian Charter; alternatively those who want to join a union can do so freely.

Unions have a role to play in the private sector, but no longer in the public sector, where as a result of their size they have become too powerful and less conciliatory. Unions are not only adept at increasing compensation for its members, but too often Unions have used their considerable financial resources to fund political campaigns, and increasingly dues are being used to influence political outcomes. Canada is unique in allowing mandatory collection of union dues, and permitting the funds to be used for political activities. Unions existence has become too expensive and they deter any chance of making changes required to make the public sector more efficient. They are perhaps the greatest cause of low productivity in Canada. It is time for Canadian taxpayers to demand that their money is better spent on services and not on Unions.

By the same token, conservative governments should clearly define what role they should play in the economy. Too often governments stoke the flame of leftist's rhetoric of corporate favouritism. It is time for governments to reduce and finally stop corporate subsidies. This is a burden on public sector finances, and taxpayers. If conservatives truly believe in the power of the free market, they should let the free market decide the fate of corporations. No corporation is too big to fail.

Rules and regulations are stifling economic growth. Small businesses are being hampered by increasing rules and administrative red tape caused by increased government interference in the economy. Obama has been a steadfast supporter of government expansion without any regard for the economic costs. For example, his recent EPA regulations which purport to reduce carbon emissions by 30 % by 2030 will by kill an estimated 224,000 per year in coal mining, power plant and railroad jobs by 2035, and impose $50 billion in annual costs, and will significantly increase electricity rates. Conservation which is a mark of conservatism should be promoted and embraced. The use of free market principles has a better chance to help the environment than punitive laws and vicarious taxation.

Canada's Federal and provincial rules are no less onerous. Governments constantly create rules to control every aspect of citizens' lives. Each of these regulations created by a 'nanny state' mentality, in most cases, increases the size of the bureaucracy and hence taxes.

A true conservative government should promote open trade. The proposed Canada/EU trade deal and other agreements should be signed as soon as possible. At the same time Harper should push provinces to open their borders to trade between each other. It is preposterous that in the 21st century there still exist protectionist rules and regulations that prevent free trade within the same country. Furthermore Canada should start discussions about an 'open sky' policy as a way to increase competition and lower air travel costs within the country.

The time is now for conservatives everywhere to curtail the increase in rules and regulations that stifles economic growth.

Strong Security

Since September 11, 2001 the world is a more dangerous place. The Western world is under constant threat from Islamist terrorists. We cannot have a more secure world unless we take drastic measures to eradicate the threat.

The Left's idea of talks and negotiations with the enemy is not only ludicrous but darned right utopian. Today's enemy is not a country, but a well-organized group of fanatical thugs with whom it is not only difficult to reason with, but also difficult to reach; since most of them live in caves or hide in bushes. They do not have any diplomatic representation. Whether Islamic terrorism is motivated by Western policy or justified by Quranic teachings, we would be ill advised to make any distinction between the diverse terrorists groups. Today's terrorist may well be a civilian without a uniform. In effect we are dealing with a totally new type of enemy. Al-Qaeda, Hamas, Hezbollah, ISIS, ISIL, Khorasan, etc., are just different names, but all have the same intentions – They are hell bent on the establishment of an Islamic Caliphate sworn to destroy Israel and the West. Too often these terrorists are funded by states like Iran, Qatar and Saudi Arabia.

Furthermore, despite Obama's claim that this war is not about Islamic beliefs, there is a more nefarious issue that is not being discussed. The problem is that while this war is predominantly against the West, there also is an internal war between two sectarian factions of Islam, namely Shia against Sunni. Any deal made with Iran, a major sponsor of terrorism is indirect support for Hamas and Hezbollah. Iran, a mainly Shia regime, is supporting a war against ISIS only because they want to get rid of a threat by a Sunni terrorist group. In fact Iran would like nothing more than to become a nuclear power in total control of the Middle East, including supremacy over a Sunni Saudi Arabia. Obama's timid approach to the problems of the region may provide Iran with just what they want.

The approach to security by Liberals and conservatives are too often miles apart. In view of the recent threats by Islamists terrorists and Putin's will to annex Ukraine, we see how reluctantly a liberal ideologue President Obama acknowledged the threats. He continuously 'leads from behind' and takes no decisive actions. By contrast Prime Minister David Cameron of the U.K made what can be called a 'Churchillian speech' on August 22, 2014. He clearly articulated the fact that ISIS was a threat to Britain, as well as the Western world, and that his government was prepared to address the crisis with drastic measures to protect his country. Prime Minister Stephen Harper of Canada made it quite clear that the Russian invasion of Ukraine was a world problem that should be taken more seriously, and contributed forces to NATO to try and halt the Russian invasion. Obama like Nero dithers and plays golf while the world is falling apart. A liberal approach to conflicts is no way to safeguard the world. The increasing American 'superpowerlessness' under Obama has become a catalyst for enemies of the free world to threatened us all.

The killing of two soldiers, Cpl. Nathan Cirillo and Warrant Officer Patrice Vincent, in Canada and a hatchet attack on one police officer, Kenneth Healey, in New York by so-called 'lone wolves' on October 19th and 20th, 2014 showed us that the enemy has changed its tactics. The terrorists are at our door steps. We must not panic and react with harsh measures and laws, but we must all be vigilant. The idea that these lone terrorists are suffering from mental ill health should be fully examined and understood, however we must recognize that they may all be psychopaths on the rampage aided and abetted by religious fanaticism propagated through social media by the same old enemy. Political correctness must not be the starting point in any discussions on this very serious and ultimately dangerous international security problem. We must stop using mealy, passive language, labels and epithets when discussing Islamic terrorism and its roots. Closing our eyes and attributing attacks to mental health conditions and self-radicalization, will not make terrorism go away.

While war is not advocated it is sometimes necessary. Citizens who have joined terrorist groups should no longer have the protection of their governments. While there is a discussion about Obama's right to kill American citizens by drones, it is one area where he has made the right decision. Americans on foreign soil who have become terrorists should be treated as any other enemy of the state. Canadians who have joined terrorists' organizations should have their citizenship revoked as soon as they have been identified. As governments pass new laws to deal with threats, why bother to restrict radicalized citizens from joining the terrorists abroad. Monitor their activities and once they have left the country for the battle field, they should never be allowed into the country again. Human Rights advocates will surely cringe at these suggestions, but what should come first – terrorists' rights or the country's security?

Security means a strong military presence. In the past, Canada has silently relied on the United States for its security. Supremacy and control of the Arctic is going to be the next possible dispute. In view of today's changing threats and Obama's continued military budget cuts, it is wise for Harper to increase Canada's military budget. We must spend wisely to defend ourselves.

But the responsibility for security also comes with the obligation for our Veterans. Both the United States and Canada have been derelict in their handling of their veterans returning from the wars of the past twelve years. The U.S. Veterans' Scandal and Veterans Affairs Minister Julian Fantino's handling of Canadian veterans are examples of governments sending young men and women to battle and forgetting them upon their return. These men and women fought for our freedom and deserve better, whether it be from a Liberal or Conservative government; anything else would be a dereliction of duty. In the past the military and conservatives have been a good fit. Conservatives who ignore the plight of veterans do so at their own peril.

As a result of the Syrian and now the Iraqi conflicts, there is talk of western countries accepting thousands of refugees. While it is a humanitarian act to look after refugees, the West would be well advised to examine the situation very carefully. Despite the calls by the U.N. that countries must open their doors, we cannot ignore the fact that some of these refugees may be radicalized later, or even form part of 'sleeper cells' which may be used to attack us from within.

While Pope Francis called the conflict 'World War III', President Obama and his administration have great difficulty to use the words 'war', and

'Islamic State' preferring to use 'counter terrorism' and 'war on humanity' to explain their strategy. The continued ambiguity from the Administration did not help to garner support from allies. More importantly, given the dismal performance of Obama and Justin Trudeau's comments on foreign policy Canada and the world cannot afford a Liberal approach to domestic and international security.

The Long-term View

Too often conservatives have taken a beating because of the divisions that have crept in due to the increased focus on social rather than fiscal conservatism. In recent years the 'progressives' have diluted the true conservative principles of less government, less taxes, entrepreneurship, property rights and law and order. So how do conservatives gain the upper hand and keep it?

First and foremost, conservatives should stick to economic freedom and equality of opportunity. Focus on the pockets of the citizens and allow them the freedom to make decisions for themselves.

Recent economic results clearly show that conservative policies based on free-market concepts, have not only worked but have provided shelter for its citizens. In Canada, provinces with conservative or right-leaning governments have fared better than those led by progressive governments. Alberta, Saskatchewan, British Columbia and Newfoundland have produced economic growth compared to Quebec and Ontario, which have accumulated enormous debt caused by deficits and social programs. In the U.S, it is undeniable that low tax states like Florida, Texas, Ohio and Wisconsin all under Republican governments are doing better than New York, and California which are run by Democrats.

Second, in making policies conservatives should compromise on process, but never compromise on principles. Andrew Coyne is always rambling and making allegations that Harper is a dictator; he should look no further than south of the border to see an 'emperor' at work. However, he rarely comments on Obama's failings. The Canadian parliamentary system provides for the ruling government to make policies and implement them. The United States Constitution on the other hand provides for all three branches to work together, not the President alone by dictate.

When the opposition and most of all the media demands that policies are watered down, conservatives should make a strong case for their position, and stick to their principles.

A move by conservatives to the centre is always a move to the left since the left never moves to the centre. Bipartisanship and compromise are words used by the left only when they are in a minority. Trudeau never compromised on the National Energy Program. His son Justin does not compromise on members of his party being 'pro-life'. Obama and his Democrats never compromised on Obamacare. The Senate majority leader Democrat Harry Reid never compromises on any issue, and does not allow many bills to come to the floor for fear of being defeated by some members of his own party.

Third, conservatives should educate the public, and freedom of information should be extended to balanced, fair and unbiased reporting. Conservatives should communicate their agenda better and challenge their opponents. They should no longer play possum to the media. Perhaps then better informed Canadians may no longer be predisposed to lean and vote left. To achieve this goal, in the U.S, conservatives have the Leadership Institute. In Canada Preston Manning through his foundation, has taken the initiative to educate the electorate. The Foundation states:

> *"Our goal is to generate and communicate fresh ideas in policy areas where Canada's political participants are perceived to be inadequately equipped."*[5]

Canadians are ill-informed by a left leaning media. Too often the news as reported has a liberal bias. In a world dominated by technology, social media has taken the role of news propagation; today fewer young people read or watch the news. This growing situation clearly validates what Albert Einstein said: *"I fear the day that technology will surpass our human interaction. The world will have a generation of idiots.*" Unfortunately, it seems that this day has arrived.

Conservatives must debunk the use of certain words used by the left. In today's political environment, 'progressive' has nothing to do with 'moving forward'. Instead the left uses it to promote government expansion, the nanny state and wealth redistribution. Similarly the word 'community' is used to promote everything which too often is supported by a minority instead of the majority. Community, like 'it takes a village', is a move towards collective thinking and the removal of individual ideas. The left promotes the community as the end and be all and moves closer to socialism and then communism. As demonstrated by these two examples, education of the electorate should become a priority for conservatives.

The goals of the Manning Foundation are not only noble, but also very perceptive. However, what type of education should the Foundation provide? During the 2013 Calgary Municipal elections, the Foundation started a program to fulfill its goals of educating candidates. Preston Manning was immediately accused of political interference and manipulation to elect conservatives to Council. On the new *QR77* show with former Liberal MLA Dave Taylor, the host immediately stated that: "Manning and his minions" were being disingenuous and planning to take over council. So what? – Presumably only liberals are allowed to plot and plan to control Council!

The problem is that the Foundation defended itself very poorly. Too many members of the establishment (some of the same people who scuttled McIver's bid for mayor of Calgary) wanted to distance themselves from the original strategy to get involved and to acknowledge that the ultimate goal was to elect a majority of conservative candidates to Council. Many candidates who wanted and needed help dis-associated themselves from the Foundation. As a result many of them were ill-prepared. The only reference to the left's involvement was done by The Concerned Calgarians Coalition, who identified CivicCamp as a leftist organization involved in the organizations of forums and support for leftist candidates including the Mayor.

To educate people in the art of campaigning, the use of social media, conducting polls and door knocking is very worthy. But what the Foundation should have done is teach candidates how to be more media savvy, especially during attacks on conservative principles. The courses should have included city budgeting, planning, accountability and transparency issues so that candidates could have had better prepared platforms to counteract any leftist campaigns.

Future training by the Foundation should be about, the benefits of the free-market, basic macro-economic concepts, conservation, public sector finance and conservative values and principles based on economic liberty. Failure to do so will allow the left to fill this enormous gap in Canadian political education.

Ed Broadbent, the former leader of the NDP, has formed his own Institute with the following goals:

> *"The Broadbent Institute is an independent, non-partisan organization championing progressive change through the promotion of democracy, equality, and sustainability and the training of a new generation of leaders."*[6]

Already the programs of the Institute are addressing the left's agenda. It already has a strong plan to be involved in communities to push for a progressive agenda, which includes the left's perennial mantra about income inequality, a new deal for the young people, and models for social change. In partnership with 270 Strategies the Institute is incorporating the strategies from the successful Obama campaigns.

The Canadian education system is full of left leaning educators. Our schools and colleges do not provide any courses on civic responsibilities; as a result there seems to be a growing lethargy among the younger electorate. There is something quite right with strong former political leaders to get involved in training future leaders. However, the approach to do so differs greatly. The left is not shy to use a very aggressive approach and tactics to indoctrinate the youth. In contrast conservatives are not pro-active, and too often they allow the media to put them on the defensive. Preston Manning has considerable influence on the political right; he should be using his Foundation and his guidance to educate future conservative leaders. The right cannot sit back and wait, because Ed Broadbent will use his influence to educate the left, and as his web site says: 'Protect Canada from Harper's Dangerous Agenda', which translates into: 'Let's Create a Socialist Canada'.

Over the years conservative governments have created economic growth and wealth. Too often they have caved in and followed the demands of the left. Sometimes they mishandled situations which have made them unpopular. To create a better world I believe in giving a 'hand up' instead of providing 'hand me downs' through social programs. The free-market does not have all the answers, but it provides a better platform for success than heavy handed government interference as we have seen in recent past. A 'nanny state' does not bode well for the future as we have seen Europe experience. The culture of entitlement permeates the new generation, and the costs of supporting social programs continue to increase.

In Ontario with the promise of further spending and continued increasing debt, the voters brought back a spent Liberal Party to power in 2014. Liberal scandals notwithstanding, it was the PC leader's inability to articulate his vision of fiscal conservatism that was at the root of the defeat. More importantly, it seemed that the electorate had no stomach for austerity. They were presented with clear choices. The Liberals promised to increase spending, raise taxes and borrow more. While the Conservatives said they would cut spending, cut taxes and borrow less. And in every case the electorate chose the Liberals' promises.

Conservatives must inform, educate and persuade the public about the consequences of Liberal entitlement philosophies and 'nanny state' governments. More importantly conservatives should be reminded of Napoleon's statement: "*Never interrupt your enemy when he is making a mistake*". Too often conservatives attack an already badly wounded opponent, instead of promoting and moving their own agendas.

Despite the untimely defeat of the Ontario PCs in the 2014 provincial elections, after some six years of gradual move to the left, a few electoral results bode well for conservatives. After his election as leader of the Alberta PCs, Jim Prentice called four bye-elections and won them all. Perhaps it is a revival of the conservatives in the province. With the Wildrose failing miserably, it is perhaps time to start talking about a merger and reconciliation among true conservatives in Alberta, just like Harper did at the national level.

Luckily for Toronto, the 'Ford Nation' shenanigans came to an abrupt halt and John Tory, former leader of the Ontario Progressive conservatives was elected Mayor with a large majority of the right on Council, despite the fact that Toronto is usually viewed as a liberal constituency. In Australia, and the EU Parliament elections have resulted in a strong move to the right, unfortunately in some cases – the far-right. Whereas a well – managed campaign based on low taxes, repayment of the national debt and strong conservative values shall see the return of a Harper government in Canada.

Mid-term elections frequently result in setbacks, especially in second terms. In 2012, Obama called the take – over of the House of Representatives by the Republicans a 'shellacking', but for two years he pursued his imperialistic ways and moved the country closer to chaos. Make no mistake the 2014 elections was a referendum of his policies. Americans finally came to their senses and elected a majority Republican Senate, and maintained the majority in The House. Republicans must not be too smug about these results, as a win does not guarantee a Republican Presidential victory in 2016. With the support of the electorate Republicans no longer have the luxury of being the party of 'no'. Conservative values and policies must be implemented immediately including: tax reform, amendments to Obamacare, approval of the Keystone Pipeline, immigration reform, and most importantly they must remove the regulations that stifle economic growth. With these changes in place they will have a better chance to curtail the negative activities of 'Emperor Obama'.

The presidential race in 2016 could bring back a Republican President, provided their choice of candidate is stellar. The game plan to avoid previous blunders should be, a strong candidate coupled with the knowledge that a divided party will only hinder conservatives success. Going forward, "Unity is Strength" should perhaps be the party motto for all Conservatives in the future, regardless of what type of conservative label they carry. The implementation of conservative values is what is at stake.

A failed Obama presidency opens the doors for conservatives around the world to bring back the golden age of conservatism. Political comebacks could be in the offing – Nicolas Sarkozy in France, perhaps even Mitt Romney in the United States. In Canada one of the important campaigning messages is to expose Justin Trudeau. Primarily his immaturity, lack of executive experience, his close relationship with Obama stalwarts and most important of all, we must expose his looming socialist agenda.

Conservative values are about freedoms – the freedom to choose, the freedom of speech, the freedom of association and most of all economic freedom. True social values are about education, healthcare, respect for seniors and the rule of law.

Conservatives should leave their egos at the door and avoid being trapped by social wedge issues set up by politically correct liberal zealots of convenience. I am optimistic about the future of conservatism, but cautious about candidates who will compromise conservative principles to gain and stay in power.

ENDNOTES

Chapter 1 – What's in a Name

1. Andrew Heywood, *Political Ideologies*, an Introduction, p 3
2. Andrew Heywood, *Political Ideologies*, an Introduction., p59
3. F. Wigforss, quoted in Tilton, op, cit., p52
4. Roger Eatwell and Anthony Wright. *Contemporary Political Ideologies* p 100
5. Yaron Brook and Don Watkins *Free Market Revolution: How Ayn Rand's ideas can end big government.* P185
6. http://abcnews.go.com/Politics/video?id=3406937 viewed and transcribed May 20, 2013
7. Ronald E. Merrill. *Ayn Rand Explained; from Tyranny to Tea Party.* P176
8. Roger. Eatwell and Anthony. Wright., *Contemporary Political Ideologies* p 53

Chapter 2 – Great Conservative Leaders

1. Famous Quotations and Stories. The Churchill Centre and Museum. Winston Churchill.org accessed May 04, 2013
2. Philip White. *Our Supreme Task, How Winston Churchill's Iron Curtain Speech defined the Cold War Alliance* Public Affairs New York 2012. p199.
3. Shelley Summer, *John F. Kennedy: His Life and Legacy*. New York HarperCollins 2004. p 17
4. Mikhail Gorbachev. *The River of Time and the Imperative of Action* may 6, 1992 http://www.nationalchurchillmuseum.org/the-river-of-time-and-the-imperative.html. Accessed May05, 2013
5. Lou Cannon, 'Reagan A Healing Hand on the GOP' *Washington Post,* August21, 1976 A1
6. *A Time for Choosing: The Speeches of Ronald Reagan*1961-1982(Chicago:Regnery Gateway1983) 189
7. Britain Awake. Margaret Thatcher Foundation. Jan 19, 1976 Speech Retrieved 21 April 2013
8. Paul Wilenius. Enemies within: Thatcher and the unions. news.bbc.co.uk/2/hi/uk_news/politics/3067563.stm Accessed April 24, 2013
9. *Margaret Thatcher. The Downing Street Years*. Harper Collins 1993, p382
10. Richard Aldous. *Reagan and Thatcher , The Difficult Relationship*, W.W. Norton & Company Inc. 2012 p82
11. *Margaret Thatcher. The Downing Street Years*. Harper Collins 1993, p173
12. *Margaret Thatcher. The Downing Street Years*. Harper Collins 1993, p 235
13. Gorbachev policy has ended the Cold War, Thatcher says. The *New York Times.* Associated Press. 18 November 1988. Accessed 30, April 2013.
14. John Nott. *Here Today, Gone Tomorrow. Recollections of an Errant Politician* (2003) p.183

Chapter 3 – Great Canadian Conservative Leaders

1. http://www.theglobeandmail.com/news/national/brian-mulroney-tells-the-globe-about-his-his-fight-against-apartheid-and-his-unique-friendship-with-nelson-mandela/article15876622/
2. http://www2.macleans.ca/2013/01/17/listening-to-brian-mulroney-on-trade-tactics-and-more/
3. http://www.theglobeandmail.com/report-on-business/economy/after-25-years-free-trade-deal-with-us-has-helped-canada-grow-up/article4576313/?page=all
4. http://www.theglobeandmail.com/report-on-business/economy/after-25-years-free-trade-deal-with-us-has-helped-canada-grow-up/article4576313/?page=all
5. Stephen Harper. Separation, Alberta-Style: It is time to seek a new relationship with Canada. *National Post*. Fri Dec 8 2000
6. Bob Plamondon. *Blue Thunder . The truth about conservatives from MacDonald to Harper*. Toronto. Key Porter Books 2009. P 397
7. Bob Plamondon. *Blue Thunder: The truth about conservatives from MacDonald to Harper*. Toronto. Key Porter Books 2009. P 405
8. Bob Plamondon. *Blue Thunder: The truth about conservatives from MacDonald to Harper*. Toronto. Key Porter Books 2009. P 413

Chapter 4 – The Canadian Divides

1. Ramsay Cook. *Canada and the French Canadian Question*. Macmillan, Toronto 1966. p14
2. Hugh Bingham Myers. *The Quebec Revolution*. Montreal. Harvest House 1964, p 51
3. Guy Bouthillier. EdouardCloutier. *Trudeau's Darkest Hour. War measures Act in Time of Peace,* October 1970. Montreal Baraka Books 2010, p15
4. Link Byfield. Identity Crisis and the Rise of Quebec. Edmonton. CanMedia Inc. 2009, p130
5. Graeme Hamilton.. Creole not welcomed in PQ's Quebec. *National Post*. Dec.20, 2013. A2
6. Statutes of Great Britain (1930), 20–21 George V, chapter 26.
7. R.S.C. 1985, c. I-5 [Indian Act]. Web: http://laws-lois.justice.gc.ca/eng/acts/I-5/ "A First Nations – Federal Crown Political Accord on the Recognition and Implementation of First Nation Governments" (PDF). Assembly of First Nations and Government of Canada. Retrieved 2013-12-29
8. Ravina Bains and Mark Milke. More Money won't solve aboriginal's woes. *The Calgary Herald*. Jan. 11, 2014. A13.

Chapter 5 – Race – America's Great Divide

1. Transcript from Civil Rights Act (1964). Retrieved January, 14 2014
2. http://www.nytimes.com/2014/02/13/opinion/blow-thomas-speaks-blindly-about-race.html?hpw&rref=opinion&_r=0
3. http://www.indexmundi.com/united_states/demographics_profile.html.

Accessed January 16, 2014

4. http://www.realclearpolitics.com/video/2013/06/19/msnbc_panelist_salamisha_tillet_pro-life_legislation_a_crucial_way_of_reproducing_whiteness.html. Accessed June 19.2013
5. http://redalertpolitics.com/2012/08/15/new-black-panthers-threaten-violence-at-the-republiklan-national-convention/ Retrieved February 06, 2014
6. http://www.youtube.com/watch?v=03876wG1pmY. Transcribe February 06, 2014
7. http://hotair.com/archives/2013/08/09/harry-reid-i-sure-hope-republicans-are-opposed-to-obama-because-of-his-policies-and-not-his-race/ Retrieved February 09, 2014
8. http://www.nydailynews.com/entertainment/gossip/oprah-winfrey-president-obama-disrespected-black-article-1.1518299#ixzz2swEJUWNv
9. http://www.huffingtonpost.com/2013/11/15/oprah-racists-die_n_4280460.html
10. David Remnick. Going the Distance. http://www.newyorker.com/reporting/2014/01/27/140127fa_fact_remnick?currentPage=all
11. http://www.smh.com.au/world/nelson-mandela-quotes-12-of-his-most-famous-statements-20131206-hv4nl.html#ixzz2rSLimIxe .
12. The University of Delaware Office of Residence Life Diversity Facilitation Training document. Page 3
13. http://www.americanthinker.com/2012/07/morgan_freeman_on_obama.html#ixzz2YrCRYiNh Retrieved 12/07/2013

Chapter 6 – The Carbon War

1. United Nations. 1987. “Report of the World Commission on Environment and Development.” General Assembly Resolution 42/187, 11 December 1987. Retrieved 17/06/2013
2. Judi McLeod. Obama’s involvement in Chicago Climate Exchange–the rest of the story. March 25, 2009. http://canadafreepress.com/index.php/article/9629. Accessed June 18,2013
3. Ilan Brat and Christopher Bjork . Spain Said to Be Poised to Cut Renewable Subsidies June 6, 2013 http://online.wsj.com/article/SB10001424127887323844804578528992849528304.html. Accessed June 18,2013
4. Margaret Wente. McGuinty’s legacy is a green nightmare. The *Globe and Mail.* Feb. 02,2013 http://www.theglobeandmail.com/commentary/mcguintys-legacy-is-a-green-nightmare/article8131320/ Accessed June 18, 2013
5. Robert Mendick and Edward Malnick. True cost of Britain’s wind farm industry revealed. The Telegraph, June 15, 2103 http://www.telegraph.co.uk/earth/energy/windpower/10122850/True-cost-of-Britains-wind-farm-industry-revealed.html. Accessed June 18, 2013
6. Ashley Southall. House Passes Solyndra Act Aimed at Obama. The *New York Times* Sept. 14, 2102. http://thecaucus.blogs.nytimes.com/2012/09/14/house-passes-solyndra-act-aimed-at-obama/?ref=solyndra . Accessed June 18, 2013

7. Hunter Stuart. Washington State Rep. Ed Orcutt Says Bike Riders Pollute The Environment, Should Be Taxed http://www.huffingtonpost.com/2013/03/04/ed-orcutt-bike-riders-pollute-environment-washington_n_2805658.html Accessed 12/07/2013
8. Patrick Moore. *Confessions of a Greenpeace Dropout: The Making of a Sensible Environmentalis*t. Beatty Street Publishing Inc. 2010. p 6.
9. Peter Wood http://www.insidehighered.com/views/2008/04/28/wood#ixzz2Wh5pqoyG. Accessed 19/06/13
10. Alexander (Sandy) Miller. Environmental Racism in Canada? http://www.cehe.ca/ER. Accessed 19/06/2013
11. Steven F. Hayward. Ronald Reagan and the Environment. *inFocus Quarterly*. Fall 2009. http://www.jewishpolicycenter.org/1409/ronald-reagan-environment. Accessed 24/06/2013
12. Jerin Mathew. Germany's Angela Merkel Thwarts Move to Cut Vehicle Carbon Emissions http://www.ibtimes.co.uk/articles/484600/20130629/angela-merkel-eu-carbon-emissions-david-cameron.htm. Retrieved 30/06/2013
13. John Roberts. Critics accuse Keystone foe of hypocrisy over oil investment historyhttp://www.foxnews.com/politics/2013/06/27/critics-accuse-keystone-foe-hypocrisy-over-oil-investment-history/?intcmp=obnetwork – ixzz2Xjv4iy5k
14. Patrick Moore. *Confessions of a Greenpeace Dropout: The Making of a Sensible Environmentalist*. Beatty Street Publishing Inc. 2010. p 256.
15. Vivian Krause: U.S. greens shut down Canadian oil. http://opinion.financialpost.com/2012/11/28/vivian-krause-u-s-greens-shut-down-canadian-oil/ Retrieved 01/07/2013
16. Dieter Helm. *The Carbon Crunch. We're Getting Climate Change Wrong – and How to Fix It*. New Haven and London: Yale University Press. P 242
17. Canadian Biodiversity Strategy; Canada's Response to the Convention on Biological Diversity. Minister of Supply and Services Canada,1995. P 3

Chapter 7 – Heathcare

1. Luke, Mitchell. Understanding Obamacare. http://harpers.org/archive/2009/12/understanding-obamacare/ retrieved 06/07.2013
2. Canada's Health care system. http://www.hc-sc.gc.ca/hcs-sss/medi-assur/index-eng.php retrieved 30/07/2013 2013
3. Health Care System. Archived – Recommendations in brief. http://www.hc-sc.gc.ca/hcs-sss/com/fed/romanow/recomm-eng.php retrieved 30/07/2013
4. 4. Stuart N. Soroka. Canadian Perceptions of the Health Care System. 2007. ISBN 0-9739726-8-8
5. Terry Boychuk. After Medicare Regionalization and Canadan Health Care Reform – Making Medicare. University of Toronto Press 2012. P117
6. Jeffrey Simpson. *Chronic Condition. Why Canadian health-Care System needs to Dragged into the 21st Century*. Allen Lane 2012. P 370

7. CNN, Tips for getting insurance when you have a pre-existing condition, May 14 2009, http://edition.cnn.com/2009/HEALTH/05/14/preexisting.condition.insurance/index.html
8. Huckabee Fox News April 2013, 14
9. Stephen Duckett and Adrian, Peetoom. *Canadian Medicare. We Need It and We Can Keep I*t. McGill –Queen's University Press 2013 . P 40
10. Stephen Duckett and Adrian Peetoom. *Canadian Medicare. We Need It and We Can Keep I*t. McGill –Queen's University Press 2013 . P 91

Chapter 8 – Education

1. http://www.dailymail.co.uk/news/article-2562178/College-textbook-Social-Work-Social-Welfare-fire-suggesting-Reagan-sexist.html#ixzz2tnqk6bxr
2. The Principles for Fair Student Assessment Practices for Education in Canada 1993.p 10(4)
3. Cara Smusiak. Why Schools Need to Scrap the No-Zero Policy http://www.canadianfamily.ca/parents/why-schools-need-to-scrap-the-no-zero-policy/ Accessed January 28, 2014
4. Amy Chua. *Battle Hymn of the Tiger Mother*. Ny The Penguin Press 2011. P51
5. http://calgary.ctvnews.ca/canadian-skeleton-athletes-bring-sait-designed-sleds-to-sochi-1.1661522#ixzz2sIQSuW9k. Retrieved February 04, 2104
6. Nick Logan. http://globalnews.ca/news/1070386/parents-across-canada-fight-for-return-to-traditional-math-lessons/. Accessed January 31, 2014
7. Emily Mertz. http://globalnews.ca/news/1113635/math-petition-presented-to-alberta-education-officials/ Accessed January 31, 2014
8. Jen Gerson. Unions shield bad teachers, N.S report says. *National Post* Mar. 19, 2014
9. Gore climate film's nine 'errors' http://news.bbc.co.uk/2/hi/7037671.stm , Accessed Feb. 04 2014
10. http://www.oecd.org/pisa/pisaproducts/pisainfocus/PISA-in-Focus-N36-%28eng%29-FINAL.pdf
11. https://albertaviews.ab.ca/2013/11/06/private-schools/
12. http://www.corestandards.org/resources/frequently-asked-questions Retrieved February 03, 2014
13. http://michellemalkin.com/2014/02/21/why-parents-are-paranoid-about-common-core/ Accessed April 09, 2014
14. Jason Clemens , Frazier, Fathers. Technology Might Revolutionize Education. https://www.fraserinstitute.org/publicationdisplay.aspx?id=20305&terms=Education Retrieved Feb. 03. 2014
15. Rodney A. Clifton. Obtaining Better Teachers for Canadian Public Schools. http://www.fraserinstitute.org/uploadedFiles/fraser-ca/Content/research-news/research/publications/obtaining-better-teachers-for-canadian-public-schools.pdf . Accessed February 1, 2014
16. Jen Gerson. Educational staff spending unwarranted, report finds. *National Post.* Mar 14, 2014. P A6

17. Michelle Rhee. Radical, Fighting to Put Students First.NY Harper Collins Publishers 2013. p277

Chapter 9 – Building a Nation

1. Daniel Francis. *Selling Canada. Three propaganda campaigns that shaped a nation*. Vancouver. Stanton Atkins & Dosil Publishers.2011. p 7
2. Charles M. Campbell. *Betrayal & Deceit. The Politics of Canadian Immigration.* BC . Jasmine Books. 2000. P 1.
3. John English. *Just Watch Me: The Life of Pierre Elliot Trudeau* 1968-2000. Toronto. Alfred A. Knopf. 2009. p 146
4. Ezra Levant. This is War. *Calgary Sun* .Sunday May 26, 2013 Comment 16
5. http://www.immigrationwatchcanada.org/2013/07/12/support-suzukis-immigration-statement/ Retrieved April 10.2014
6. Charles M. Beach et al. *Canadian Immigration Policy for the 21st Century*. p34
7. Jeffrey, G. Reitz. Canadian Immigration Policy for the 21st Century. P474
8. Michael Sleigh & Marcel Latouche. *The Mobility of Professionals – A new perspective*. Halifax Conference. The ACCA 2003.
9. Terence Corcoran. Working it Out. The Golden Age of Foreign Labour. *National Post*. May 1, 2013
10. http://en.wikipedia.org/wiki/DREAM_Act#2012 . Accessed April 07, 2014
11. Congressional Budget Office Cost Estimate S.3992 Development, Relief, and Education for Alien Minors Act of 201 Accessed April 07, 2014

Chapter 10 – The Media, Hollywood and The Liberal Elite

1. David Taras. *Power & Betrayal in the Canadian Media*. Broadview Press ltd. 2001. P 19
2. David Taras. *Power & Betrayal in the Canadian Media*. Broadview Press ltd. 2001 P172
3. Christine Dobby. Al Jazeera wants checks on Arabic version lifted. *National Post* Feb 04, 2014. p
4. Howard Kurtz, *Media Circus: The Trouble with America's Newspapers*. NY Times Books 1994, p 13
5. http://gatesofvienna.net/2013/05/sweden-is-more-dangerous-than-mogadishu/ Accessed June 02,2013
6. 6. http://www.huffingtonpost.com/2008/02/13/chris-matthews-i-felt-thi_n_86449.html. Retrieved feb.04 2014
7. http://fullcomment.nationalpost.com/2014/01/19/michael-den-tandt-neil-young-and-his-fellow-oil-sands-critics-have-yet-to 2013-propose-a-single-credible-alternative/ Accessed Jan.21
8. 8. Ezra Levant: Does Young practice what he preaches? The *Calgary Sun* January 26. 2014. P 16.
9. http://www.cbc.ca/news/canada/edmonton/desmond-tutu-calls-oilsands-filth-urges-cooperation-on-environment-1.2660804

Chapter 11 – Morality, Norms, Values and Politics

1. *Roe v. Wade,* 410 US, 113, 160 , 93 S Ct. 705 , 730 (1973)
2. http://www.plannedparenthood.org/about-us/newsroom/press-releases/planned-parenthood-statement-gosnell-verdict-41303.htm . Accessed May 28,2013
3. http://www.lifesitenews.com/news/10-surprising-quotes-from-abortionists/
4. 4. Ari Melber: MSNBC Panel Suggests Racist Motivation by Pro-lifers, Goal of 'Reproducing Whiteness'http://newsbusters.org/blogs/brad-wilmouth/2013/06/17/msnbc-panel-suggests-racist-motivation-pro-lifers-goal-reproducing-wh#ixzz2WgZGYDQP Accessed June 19,2013
5. Jonathan Kay. Capitalist forced Law into Limbo. *National Post* May 30, 2013. A1
6. "*The Legal Brief*" "Don't Ask, Don't Tell, Don't Pursue, Don't Harass: Reference (a): Personnel Manual, COMDTINST M1000.6, Ch. 12.E"." (PDF). United States Coast Guard Ninth District Legal Office. May 2010. Retrieved May 28, 2013
7. http://abcnews.go.com/Politics/obamas-evolution-gay-marriage/story?id=19150614#.UaUgx5yS-cU. Accessed May 28,2013
8. Barbara Kay. What would the bonobos do? *National Post* May 29, 2013. A10
9. Stacy Meichtry Pope says 'Gay Lobby' Is at Work in Vatican. *The Wall Street Journal* (U.S. ed.) June 12, 2013
10. Hillary Clinton. *It Takes a Village and other lessons Children Teach Us.* Simon & Schuster 1996. p49
11. Abortion rights: Significant moments in Canadian History http://www.cbc.ca/news/canada/story/2009/01/13/f-abortion-timeline.html. Accessed June 04, 2013
12. Janine Brodie. *Choice and No Choice in the House. In The Politics of Abortion,* ed. Janine Brodie, Jane Jenson, and Shelley Gavigan. Toronto: Oxford University Press 1992
13. Stephen Harper. Speech to the House of Commons 16 February, 2005 . http;//www2.parl.gc.ca/housechamberbusiness/ChamberHome.aspx
14. James Farney. *Social Conservatives and Party Politics in Canada and the United States.* University of Toronto Press 2012. P129
15. Hillary Clinton. *It Takes a Village and other lessons Children Teach Us.* Simon & Schuster 1996. p313
16. Eva Ferguson. Premier urges candidates' to be careful'. *Calgary Herald* .June 18. 2014
17. Chris Selley. Chris Selley: Ron Paul gives Canadian conservatives a refreshing look at an ideologue. *National Post* 13/03/09.

Chapter 12 – Say No More …

1. *Charter of Rights and Freedom* section (2) 'fundamental freedoms'
2. "Bill of Rights Transcript". Archives.gov. Retrieved March 10, 2014
3. Cox Archibald (1986). "First Amendment". *Encyclopedia of the American Constitution.*

4. Ezra Levant. *Shakedown. How Our Government Is Undermining Democracy in the Name of Human Rights*. Toronto. McClelland & Stewart Ltd. 2009. P42
5. http://www.nationalpost.com/news/canada/story.html?id=303895 . Retrieved Mar 11. 2014
6. Chris Selley. Rights tribunal says immigrant who failed exam three times was discriminated against. *National Post* Feb. 18, 2014
7. Joseph Brean (March 22, 2008). "Scrutinizing the human rights machine". *National Post*. Archived from the original on 2008-04-03.
8. John Carpay. MRU is getting a costly lesson in free speech. *Calgary Herald*. Mar. 22, 2014
9. John Carpay. Protecting unpopular views is critical to a free society. *The Province*. Opinion. July 4, 2013
10. Steven Chase. Ann Coulter speech in Ottawa cancelled. *Globe and Mail*. Mar 23. 2010
11. http://pointdebasculecanada.ca/images/data/pdf/nypd_report-radicalization_in_the_west.pdf p67
12. http://www.forbes.com/sites/margiewarrell/2014/03/14/instead-of-banbossy-how-about-embracebossy/
13. http://www.telegraph.co.uk/women/womens-life/10695191/Cherish-that-bossy-streak-sweetheart-youll-need-it.html. Retrieved Mar. 17, 2014
14. 14. Episode 86. HBO's *Real Time with The Bill Maher*. HBO October 20, 2006.
15. 15. Chloe Atkins. Transparency in Politics has gone too far. *Calgary Herald*. Mar.29. 2014. A13
16. 16. Mark Steyn. *America Alone. The End of the World as We Know It*. Regnery Publishing. Inc. 2006 .p 201
17. 17. http://www.gq.com/entertainment/television/201401/duck-dynasty-phil-robertson?currentPage=2
18. 18. http://www.foxnews.com/entertainment/2013/12/18/phil-robertson-suspended-after-comments-about-homosexuality/ Retrieved Mar. 18. 2014.
19. http://www.latimes.com/entertainment/tv/showtracker/la-et-st-duck-dynasty-phil-robertson-20131228,0,7784571.story#axzz2wLCatZ5Q Retrieved Mar 18, 2014
20. Paul Handley. Cameron affirms partnership with Church. *Church Times*. April 16,2014
21. https://blog.mozilla.org/blog/2014/04/03/brendan-eich-steps-down-as-mozilla-ceo/
22. http://www.brainyquote.com/quotes/quotes/v/voltaire109645.html#sjG4hmOhwpxizdBm.99

Chapter 13 – Harper's Canada

1. Andrew Coyne. Politics explains Flaherty's divided legacy. *National Post* Mar 20. 2014
2. http://fullcomment.nationalpost.com/2014/01/07/matt-gurney-yet-another-part-of-the-canadian-firearms-system-that-doesnt-work/

3. http://www.pm.gc.ca/eng/node/22000
4. http://www.pm.gc.ca/eng/news/2007/07/09/prime-minister-stephen-harper-announces-new-arctic-offshore-patrol-ships#sthash.LzqTZi2l.dpuf
5. The Commonwealth. What is it for? *The Economist* November 16th-22nd 2013. P 18
6. Andrew Coyne. Harper puts principles on the line. *National Post* . October, 19, 2013
7. http://www.ottawacitizen.com/news/Public+database+child+offenders+part+pedophile+crackdown/9554509/story.html
8. http://www.cbc.ca/news/canada/prime-minister-stephen-harper-s-statement-of-apology-1.734250
9. http://news.gc.ca/web/article-en.do?nid=814399
10. http://news.nationalpost.com/2014/03/02/mike-duffy-vowed-to-bring-down-high-ranking-tories-if-expense-scandal-led-to-charges/
11. http://www.ottawacitizen.com/newsConservative+downsizing+public+service+bark+worse+than+bite+report/9270677/story.html

Chapter 14 – The State of the Union

1. http://www.mrc.org/biasalerts/harry-reid-insists-obamacare-horror-stories-are-lies-big-three-nets-ignore Retrieved April 24, 2014
2. "Muslim Nations React to Obama Inaugural Speech". *Voice of America*. 22 January 2009. Retrieved 25 April 2014.
3. http://www.americanthinker.com/blog/2014/04/ben_rhodes_at_center_of_plan_to_whitewash_white_house_on_benghazi.html
4. Rob Bluey. http://blog.heritage.org/2014/05/01/sean-hannity-believes-smoking-gun-benghazi-video/
5. http://www.bloomberg.com/news/2011-03-27/u-s-won-t-intervene-in-syria-unrest-clinton-says-on-cbs.html
6. http://blogs.wsj.com/washwire/2013/09/04/flashback-red-line-in-syria-what-obama-said-in-2012-remarks/
7. Michelle Arrouas. Almost all of Syria's chemical weapons have now been removed. Time.com. April 24, 2014.
8. Dylan Stableford. Kerry on Iran Deal: 'It's not based on Trust'. Yahoo News. November 24, 2013
9. http://pjmedia.com/tatler/2013/11/24/menendez-to-administration-an-iran-sanctions-bill-is-still-coming-from-congress/
10. Jake Tapper. http://abcnews.go.com/blogs/politics/2012/03/president-obama-asks-medvedev-for-space-on-missile-defense-after-my-election-i-have-more-flexibility/
11. Mitt Romney. *No Apology*. NY, St. Martin Press. 2010. P 63
12. Yann Le Guernigou. Sarkozy tells Obama Netanyahu is a "liar". Reuters.com. November 08, 2011.
13. Paul Waldman. Kerry "apartheid" controversy shows limits on debate over Israel. *Washington Post*. April 29,2014

14. Justin, Wingerter. http://stlouis.cbslocal.com/2013/05/17/mccaskill-calls-for-firing-of-all-involved-in-irs-targeting-scandal/
15. Abraham Brown. http://www.forbes.com/sites/abrambrown/2013/05/10/irs-to-tea-party-were-sorry-we-targeted-your-taxes/
16. http://www.huffingtonpost.com/2013/06/07/obama-national-security_n_3401808.html
17. http://www.realclearpolitics.com/video/2013/12/04/turley_obamas_become_the_very_danger_the_constitution_was_designed_to_avoid.html
18. http://tellmenow.com/2014/04/charles-krauthammer-brilliantly-sums-up-all-of-obamas-power-grabs/
19. Thomas Lifson. Pathetic Holder plays the race card before Al Sharpton's group. http://www.americanthinker.com/blog/2014/04/

Chapter 15 – Mitt McIver or Ric Romney

1. Hugh Hewitt. *A Mormon in the White House*. Trilennium Productions Inc.2007 p 46
2. Ronald B. Scott. *Mitt Romney. An Inside Look at the Man and His Politics*. Lyons Press.2012. p 190
3. Steve Deace. *Deace in the Afternoon Show*. Podcast 2007.
4. http://news.nationalpost.com/2012/01/27/newt-gingrich-hammered-in-last-florida-debate-as-mitt-romney-shows-rare-steel/
5. http://www.washingtonpost.com/politics/mitt-romney-and-newt-gingrich-square-off-in-republican-debate/2012/01/26/gIQA2KzBUQ_story.html
6. http://www.washingtonpost.com/politics/mitt-romney-and-newt-gingrich-square-off-in-republican-debate/2012/01/26/gIQA2KzBUQ_story.html
7. http://www.usatoday.com/story/news/politics/2012/10/05/romney-47-percent-i-was-wrong/1614703/
8. http://www.realclearpolitics.com/video/2012/10/03/chris_matthews_freaks_out_at_obama_after_debate_romney_was_winning.html
9. http://www.dailymail.co.uk/news/article-2218841/Presidential-Debate-2012-Outrage-moderator-Candy-Crowley-sides-Obama.html#ixzz2z4Hrbzaz
10. http://www.dailymail.co.uk/news/article-2218841/Presidential-Debate-2012-Outrage-moderator-Candy-Crowley-sides-Obama.html#ixzz2z4FQzKrN
11. http://www.nytimes.com/2013/02/17/magazine/can-the-republicans-be-saved-from-obsolescence.html?ref=magazine&_r=0. Retrieved April 17, 2014
12. http://www.ffwdweekly.com/calgary-blogs/the-howler/2010/10/14/higgins-says-supporters-have-no-political-interest-except-for-the-ones-that-do-541/
13. Trevor Scott Howell. Higgins says supporters "have no political interest"-except for the ones that do. *FFWD* Oct. 14.2010
14. http://www.theglobeandmail.com/news/politics/well-connected-ric-mciver-had-a-lock-on-victory-or-so-it-seemed/article4329542/

Chapter 16 – Socialism Trends

1. PBS,org interview: *Religion & Ethics*. Episode 1051. August 17. 2007.
2. Rudy Ruitenberg. Approval for 75% Millionaire Tax. http://www.bloomberg.com/news/2013-12-29/france-s-hollande-gets-court-approval-for-75-millionaire-tax.html
3. Guy Bouthillier, Edouard Cloutier. *Trudeau's Darkest Hour* . Montreal Baraka Books 2010. P 14
4. http://fullcomment.nationalpost.com/2014/02/23/andrew-coyne-justin-trudeau-in-total-control-after-liberal-convention/
5. http://www.cbc.ca/news/canada/toronto/justin-trudeau-s-foolish-china-remarks-spark-anger-1.2421351
6. *Hillary Rodham Clinton. Living History*. NY. Simon & Schuster 2003. P 38

Chapter 17 – Staying Alive

1. Darrell Bricker and John Ibbitson. *The Big Shift*. HarperCollins Publishers.Ltd. 2013 p 279
2. Warren Kinsella. The left is Making a Comeback. *Calgary Sun*. March 16. 2014. P 19
3. 3. Russell Kirk. Ten Conservative Principles. http://www.kirkcenter.org/index.php/detail/ten-conservative-principles/
4. Williams Brian (17 October 2007). "the 11th commandment". *NBC Nightly News*. Retrieved June 09 2014.
5. http://www.manningfoundation.org/
6. http://www.broadbentinstitute.ca/

Bibliography

Adams. I. (1993) *Political Ideology Today*. Manchester University Press

Alinsky, Saul. *Rules for Radicals* New York: Vintage 1989

Ashbee, Edward. *The Bush Administration, Sex and the Moral Agenda*. Manchester: Manchester University Press 2007

Balz, Dan. *Collision 2012. Obama vs. Romney and the Future of Elections in America.* NY. Penguin Group.2013

Barrett, S. *Environment and Statecraft: The Strategy of Environmental Treaty-making.* Oxford: Oxford University Press 2005

Barrett, S. *Why Cooperate? The Incentive to Supply Global Public Goods*. New York: Oxford University Press 2007

Barry, N.P. *The New Right* (London, Groom Helm. 1987)

Beach, Charles. Green, Alan. Reitz, Jeffrey. *Canadian Immigration Policy for the 21st Century*,. Queen's University Press. 2003

Bellamy, R. *Liberalism and Pluralism*, Rutledge, London, 1999

Berman, Sheri. *The Social Democratic Moment: Ideas and Politics in the Making of Interwar Europe*. Cambridge: Harvard University Press 1998

Betts, Kate. *Everyday Icon*. New York: Clarkson Porter, 2011

Brook, Yaron, and Watkins, Don. *Free Market Revolution; How Ayn Rand's ideas can end big government*. New York: Palgrave MacMillan 2012

Buckley, William F. Jr. *Let Us Talk of Many Things; The Collected Speeches* New York: Basic Books, 2008

Burns, Jennifer. *Goddess of the Market: Ayn Rand and the American Right* . New York: Oxford University Press 2009

Bush, George and Scowcroft, Brent. *A World Transformed* New York: Knopf 1998

Campbell. Charles. M. *Betrayal & Deceit. The Politics of Canadian Immigration.* Jasmine Books West Vancouver 2000

Chernow, Ron. *The House of Morgan* New York: Grove Press 2010

Chernow Ron. *Titan* New York: Vintage Books 1998

Chua, Amy. Rubenfeld, Jed. *The Triple Package.How three unlikely traits explain the rise and fall of cultural groups in America*. NY. The Penguin Press 2014

Coates. Ken. S, Morrison, Bill. *Campus Confidential*. Toronto. James Lorimer & Company Ltd. 2013

Cook, Ramsay. *Canada and the French-Canadian Question* MacMillan of Canada/ Toronto 1966

Corsi, Jerome R. T*he Obama Nation* New York: Pocket Star, 2008

D"Souza, Dinesh. *Ronald Reagan: How an Ordinary Man Became an Extraordinary Leader* New York: Free Press, 1997

D'Alessandro. David.F. Brand *Warfare: 10 Rules for Building the Killer Brand*. New York: McGraw-Hill 2001

Dalrymple, Theodore. *Life at the Bottom: The Worldview that Makes Underclass* Chicago: Ivan R. Dee.2001

de Tocqville, A. *Democracy in America,* ed. J.P. Mayer and M. Lerner,Fontana, London, 1968

Department of Canadian Heritage (Parks Canada) *Implementing the Canadian Biodiversity Strategy.* Government of Canada 1997

Duckett,Stephen. *Where to from Here. Keeping Medicare Sustainable.* Kingston:School of Policy Studies, Queen's University.2012

Farney. James. *Social Conservatives and Party Politics in Canada and the United States.* Toronto: University of Toronto Press 2012

Friedman, David. *The Machinery of Freedom: Guide to a Radical Capitalism.* Second Edition, La Salle: Open Court 1989a

Galbraith, J.K., *The Contented Society,* Sinclair-Stevenson, London, 1992

Galbraith, J.K., *The New Industrial State,* Signet, New York, 1968

Gamble. A. *The Free Economy and The Strong State* (London, Macmillan, 1988)

Gibbins, Roger. *Conflict and Unity. An Introduction to Canadian Political Life.* Nelson Canada 1990

Goyle, Diane. *The Economics of Enough.* Princeton, NJ: Princeton University Press 2011

Gray.J. *Limited Government: A positive Agenda*, IEA, London 1989

Greenspan, Alan. *The Age of Turbulence.* New York: Penguin 2008

Hall, J.A. *Liberalism: Politics, Ideology and the Market* (London:Paladin, 1988)

Hanley, D. (ed), *Christian Democracy in Europe*, Pinter, London , 1994

Hannaford, Peter. *The Reagans: A Political Portrait*, New York Coward-McCann 1983

Hardy, J.T., *Climate Change: Causes, Effects and Solutions.* Chichester: J. Wiley 2003

Harrington, M., Socialism, Past and Future (London Pluto Press, 1993)

Hartmann, Thom. *Threshold:The Crisis of Western Culture.* New York: Viking 2009.

Hayek, F.A., T*he Road to Serfdom*, Routledge, London 1944

Helm, Dieter. *The Carbon Crunch: We're Getting Climate Change Wrong-and How to Fix I*t. Yale University Press 2012

Herf, J., *Reactionary Modernism*, Cambridge University Press, Cambridge 1984

Hill, Austin. and Rae, Scott. *The Virtues of Capitalism: A Moral Case for the Free Markets*, Chicago: Northfield Publishing 2010

Honderich,Ted. *Conservatism*, Penguin, Hamondsworth, 1992

Hsieh, Tony. *Delivering Happiness* New York: Business Plus 2010

Hucbert, Jacob, H. *Libertarianism Today*, Santa Barbara : Praeger 2010

IPCC, *Aviation and the Global Atmosphere: A Special Report of IPCC Working Groups I and III.* 1999

Jacobs, Ron. *Obamaland.* Honolulu: Trade 2008

Jenkins, Phillip. *Decade of Nightmares: The End of the Sixties and the Making of*

Eighties, America New York 2006

Kissinger, Henry. *Diplomacy.* New York: Simon & Schuster, 1994

Klein, Edward. *The Amateur: Barack Obama in the White House*, Washington: Regnery Publishing.Inc. 2012

Kranish, Michael and Helman, Scott. *The Real Romney*. NY. Harper Collins. 2012

Kristol, Irving., *Neo-Conservatism: The Autobiography of an Idea*. New York :Free Press 1995

Kristol Irving. *Two Cheers for Capitalism*. New York: Signet 1979

Kurtz, Stanley. *Radical-in-Chief*. New York: Threshold 2010

Laing. Richard. *Implementing Ecological management – At the Landscape or Bioregional Level: A Practitioners Guide*. IPS Ltd. 2004

Lane, D. *The Rise and Fall of State Socialism* ,(Oxford Polity Press, 1997)

Laski, H. *Democracy in Crisis,* Allen and Unwin, London, 1933

Lawson,N. *An Appeal to Reason: A Good Look at Global Warming*, London: Duckworth 2005

Locke, John. *Two Treaties of Government*. Cambridge: Cambridge University Press. 1967.

Mackay, D.J.C. *Sustainable Energy-Without the Hot Air*. Cambridge: UIT, 2008

MacMillan, H. *The Middle Way*, MacMillan, London, 1938

Malkin, Michelle. *Culture of Corruption*. Washington.D.C.: Regnery 2009

Mann, James. The Rebellion of Ronald Reagan. New York: Viking, 2009

Marchildon, Gregory. (ed) *Making Medicare*, New Perspective on the History of *Medicare in Canada*. University of Toronto Press 2012

Maritain. J. *True Humanism*, Centenary Press, London 1938

Meili, Ryan. *A Healthy Society. How a Focus on Health can Revive Canadian Democracy*. Purich Publishing Limited 2012

Mencken, Henry L. *The Philosophy of Friedrich Nietzche*. Torrance. Noontide. 1982

Miller, Kenton, R. *Balancing the Scales. Guidelines for increasing Biodiversity's Chances Through Bioregional Management*. World Resources Institute. Washington D.C. 1996

Morton. F.L. *Morgentaler v Borowski: Abortion, the Charter, and the Courts*, Toronto: McClelland and Stewart 1992

Myers, Hugh. Bingham. *The Quebec Revolution*. Montreal, Harvest House 1964

Narveson, Jan. *The Libertarian Idea*, Philadelphia : Temple University Press 1988

Nash, G.H. *The Conservative Intellectual Movement in America since 1945*; Basic Books, New York, 1976

Newman, S. *Liberalism at Wit's End*, Cornell University Press, Ithaca, NY, 1984

Nisbet, R. *Conservatism*, Longman, Harlow, 1986

Nozick, R. *Anarchy, State and Utopia*. Oxford: Blackwell, New York: Basic, 1974

Oakeshott, M. *Rationalism in Politics*, Liberty Press, Indianapolis 1991

O'Gorman. F, *British Conservatism*, Longman, Harlow, 1986

Olasky, Marvin. *The Tragedy of American Compassion*, Washington D.C.: Regnery 1992

O'Sullivan, N. *Conservatism*, Dent. London, 1976

Perry, Ralph Barton. *General Theory of Value*. Cambridge: Harvard University Press. 1926

Plamondon, Bob. *Full Circle: Death and Resurection in Canadian Conservative Politics*. Toronto: Key Porter 2006

Posner, R.A. *Catastrophe: Risk and Response*. New York: Oxford University Press, 2004

Quinton, A. *The Politics of Imperfection*, Faber and Faber, London, 1978

Ramsay, M. *What's wrong with Liberalism? A Radical Critique of Liberal Political Philosophy*, London: Leicester University press, 1997

Rand, Ayn. *Capitalism: The Unknown Ideal*, New York Signet, 1967

Ravitch, Diane. *Reign of Error*, New York. Alfred A. Knopf 2013

Raz, Joseph. *Ethics in the Public Domain*, Clarendon Press, Oxford 1994

Raz, Joseph. *The Morality of Freedom*, Clarendon press, Oxford 1986

Rhee, Michelle. *Radical*. NY, HarperCollins Publishers 2013

Robinson, Eugene. *Disintegration*. New York: Doubleday, 2010

Ropke, W. *A Humane Economy*, Regnery, Chicago 1971

Rousseau, J.J., *The Social Contract and Discourse*, ed. G.D.H. Cole. London: Dent (Glencoe,Ill,: Free Press, 1969)

Saletan, William., *Bearing Right: How Conservatives Won the Abortion War*. Berkley: University of California Press 2003

Sandel, M. (ed), *Liberalism and its Critics*, Blackwell, Oxford , 1986

Sassoon, D. *One Hundred Years of Socialism* (London:Fontana. 1997)

Schweizer, Peter. *Reagan's War: The Epic Story of his Forty-Year Struggle and Final Triumph Over Communism*. New York Anchor Books 2002

Scruton. R. *The Meaning of Conservatism*, 2nd edn. (Basingstoke, Macmillan 1984)

Shirley, Craig. *Rendezvous with Destiny*. Wilmington ISI Books 2009

Simon J.L., *The Ultimate Resource*, Oxford: Martin Robertson, 1981

Simpson, Jeffrey. *Chronic Condition. Why Canada's health – care system needsto dragged into the 21st century*. Toronto Allen Lane 2012

Smith, Adam. *The Theory of Moral Sentiments*. Indianapolis: Liberty Classics 1976

Smith, Adam. *The Wealth of Nations*. New York Bantam. 2003

Sowell, Thomas. *Basic Economics: A Common Sense Guide to the Economy* 2nd ed. New York: Basic Books2004

Spengler, O. *The Decline of the West*, Allen and Unwin, London 1961

Srivastava, Jitendra, Smith. J.H. Nigel, Forno. A. Douglas. *Biodiversity and Agricultural Intensification*. The World Bank . Washington D.C. 1996

Stern, Nicholas. The Economics of Climate Change: *The Stern Review* HM Treasury

Cambridge University Press. January 2007

Tannsjo,T. *Conservatism for Our Time*, Routledge, London, 1991

Taras, David and Waddell, Christopher. *How Canadians Communicate IV*. Media and Politics ed. AU Press Athabasca University 2012

Tuccille, Jerome. *It Usually Begins with Ayn Rand*. New York. Stein and Day 1972

Victor, D.G. *The Collapse of the Kyoto Protocol and the Struggle to Slow Global Warming*,. Princeton: Princeton University Press. 2004

Vigurie, Richard. A., *The New Right: We're Ready to Lead*, VA: Viguerie Company 1980

Waldman, Lorne & Swaisland, Jacqueline. *Inadmissible to Canada: The Legal Barriers to Canadian Immigration*. Lexis Nexis. 2012

Walker, Jeff. *The Ayn Rand Cult*. Open Court 1999

Walker, Lee H. *Rediscovering Black Conservatism*. Chicago:Heartland, 2009

Walton, Gary.M. and Rockoff Hugh., *History of the American Economy*, 9th ed., Toronto: Thomson Learning 2002

Willets, D. *Modern Conservatism*, Penguin, Harmondsworth, 1992

Wolffe, Richard. *Renegade: The Making of a President*, New York: Random House 2009

Woodward, Bob. *Shadow: Five Presidents and the Legacy of Watergate*, New York: Simon & Schuster, 1999

Woodward, Bob. *Obama's Wars*. New York: Simon & Schuster 2010

Wright, A. *Socialism: Theories and Practices*, Oxford and New York: Oxford University Press, 1987

Yergin, D. *The Prize: The Epic Quest for Oil, Money and Power*. New York: Free Press 1991

ACKNOWLEDGEMENTS

Writing this book had been on my mind for quite some time. Although I had some ideas about the road I wanted to take, it would have been impossible to finish it without the help and support of a few people who quite unselfishly provided me with an insight on different issues discussed in the book.

I must thank Tristan Emmanuel of Freedom Press for taking the risk to publish my book; Steve Chapman for his help in creating my e-manuscript, and editor Lisa Kates whose diligence and punctilious attention took my raw material and brought it to a different level.

Along the way I also needed some dedicated helpers. Among those, I would like to thank the Honourable Minister of Citizenship and Immigration, Jason Kenney, who despite his heavy schedule took the time to meet with me and share his views on the very important topic of immigration. It would have been very hard to write about rights issues without the expert views of one of the best contemporary defenders of free speech. John Carpay of the Justice Centre for Constitutional Freedoms. He generously spent his time to review the 'Say no More' chapter dealing with the right to speak and the right not to be offended. Not being a scientist or an expert in Meteorology, I had to seek the expertise of someone who works in the field of conservation. My neighbour, Richard Laing, who disagreed with a few of my views on the subject of climate change, nevertheless chose to share his thoughts on the subject matter to provide a better analysis for my views on the Carbon War.

My thanks also go to Troy Wason, Calgary VP of the Progressive Conservative Association of Alberta for his expertise on Canadian politics and his insights on Canadian political ideologies. I must also acknowledge the contribution of Bev De Santis who had been a campaign manager for several of Ric McIver's campaigns for her thoughts on the man and his drive to serve his constituents. Last but not least my thanks go to John Pollock for his great cover design.

The writing of "Conservatives: Dead or Alive?" was a long road that needed a lot of help from some friends, and my sincere thanks go to all of them.

ABOUT THE AUTHOR

Marcel Latouche, consultant, author and trainer is the President and CEO of MLG Associates, Management Consultants & Trainers, who specialize in harnessing the power of change through Leadership, Economic and Marketing strategies. Commonly known as 'The Master Change Agent', he is a Fellow of the Association of Chartered Certified Accountants (UK) and holds an MBA from Manchester Business School. He draws from his experience of over 40 years as a financial manager in both the public and private sectors. His experience spans the Banking, Publishing, Local Government and consulting industries. Until his recent retirement, he was a lecturer of Economics and Public Sector Finance at SAIT Polytechnic and has lectured at Mount Royal University and Columbia College in Calgary.

Marcel has written opinion columns on political matters for the *Calgary Sun, The Calgary Herald* and the *Financial Post*. He is a frequent contributor on Radio Canada and local TV channels. He has published two books, namely *Take Back City Hall,* and *Leadershift: Collaboration in the 21st century.*

A strong believer in volunteerism, Marcel has served on the boards and committees of many organizations including Tennis Alberta, Tennis Canada, the Calgary Chamber of Commerce, the Canadian Association of Professional Speakers, the Association of Chartered Certified Accountants (International), and the Southern Alberta Institute of Technology's BA Management Advisory Committee. He received the Alberta Achievement Award in 1990, and is an inductee in the Tennis Alberta Hall of Fame.

Contact : mlgassociates@shaw.ca

CPSIA information can be obtained at www.ICGtesting.com
Printed in the USA
LVOW07s1428281114

415907LV00003B/20/P

9 781927 684146